Photoshop® Elements 2

TOP 100

Simplified®

Tips & Tricks

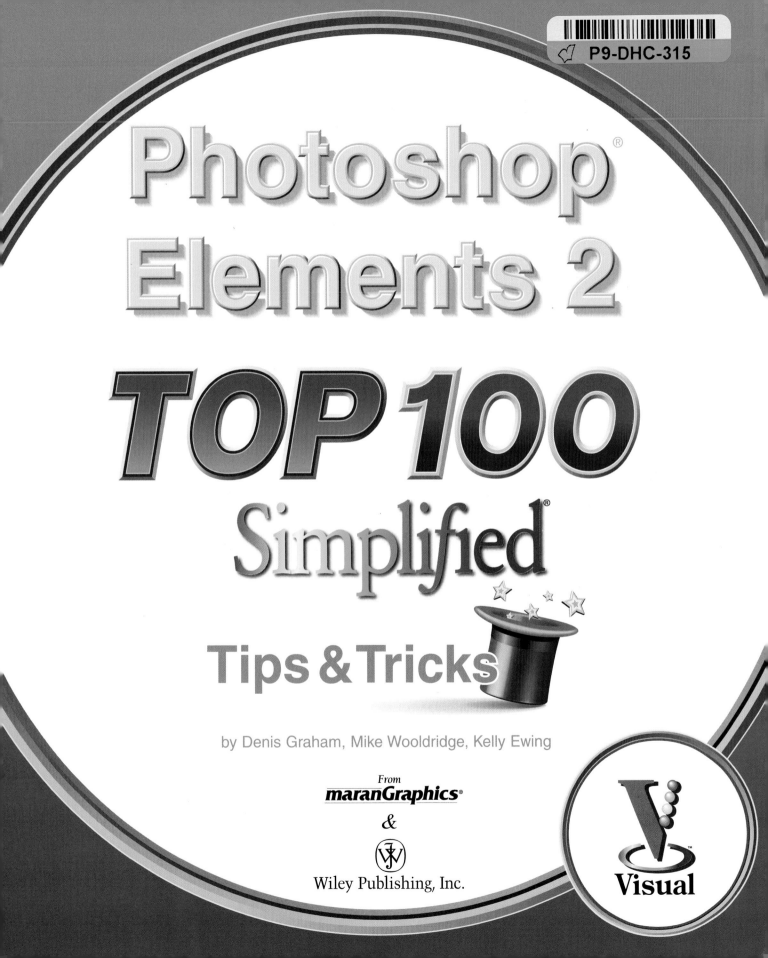

by Denis Graham, Mike Wooldridge, Kelly Ewing

From
maranGraphics®

&

Wiley Publishing, Inc.

Visual

Photoshop® Elements 2: Top 100 Simplified® Tips & Tricks

Published by
Wiley Publishing, Inc.
111 River Street
Hoboken, NJ 07030

Published simultaneously in Canada
Copyright © 2003 by Wiley Publishing, Inc.,
Indianapolis, Indiana
Certain designs, text, and illustrations Copyright ©
1992-2003 maranGraphics, Inc., used with
maranGraphics permission.

maranGraphics, Inc.
5755 Coopers Avenue
Mississauga, Ontario, Canada
L4Z1R9

Library of Congress Control Number: 2003110024
ISBN: 0-7645-4353-9
Manufactured in the United States of America
10 9 8 7 6 5 4 3 2 1

1K/QV/QY/QT/IN

Trademark Acknowledgements

Important Numbers

For U.S. corporate orders, please call maranGraphics at
800-469-6616 or fax 905-890-9434.

For general information on our other products and
services or to obtain technical support please contact
our Customer Care Department within the U.S. at
800-762-2974, outside the U.S. at 317-572-3993 or
fax 317-572-4002.

Permissions

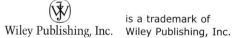

Wiley Publishing, Inc.   is a trademark of
Wiley Publishing, Inc.

U.S. Corporate Sales	U.S. Trade Sales
Contact maranGraphics at (800) 469-6616 or fax (905) 890-9434.	Contact Wiley at (800) 762-2974 or fax (317) 572-4002.

CREDITS

Project Editor:
Jade L. Williams

Acquisitions Editor:
Jody Lefevere

Product Development Manager:
Lindsay Sandman

Copy Editor:
Jill Mazurczyk

Technical Editor:
Dennis Short

Editorial Manager:
Rev Mengle

Permissions Editor:
Laura Moss

Manufacturing:
Allan Conley, Linda Cook,
Paul Gilchrist, Jennifer Guynn

Production Coordinator:
Maridee Ennis

Book Design:
maranGraphics, Inc.

Layout:
LeAndra Hosier, Kristin McMullan,
Kathie S. Schnorr

Screen Artist:
Jill A. Proll

Illustrators:
Ronda David-Burroughs,
David E. Gregory

Proofreader:
Sossity Smith

Quality Control:
Laura Albert, Robert Springer

Indexer:
Joan Griffitts

Special Help:
Adobe Systems, Inc.

Vice President and Executive Group Publisher:
Richard Swadley

Vice President and Publisher:
Barry Pruett

Composition Director:
Debbie Stailey

ABOUT THE AUTHORS

Denis Graham is a Human Resources Generalist by profession and Freelance Graphics Designer by passion and hobby. He is a self confessed Photoshop junkie who lives in Norman, Oklahoma with his wife, three kids, three cats, a parakeet, hermit crab, and a hamster named Chubby. Denis has done computer graphics since the TRS-80 computer, and has worked as a Technical Editor on 10 different Photoshop, Elements, and Illustrator books.

Mike Wooldridge is a writer in the San Francisco Bay Area. He is the author of several other VISUAL books, including *Teach Yourself Visually Photoshop Elements 2*.

Kelly Ewing is a writer and editor who lives in the wonderful community of Fishers, Indiana, with her husband Mark, her daughter Katie, her son Carter, and furry friend Cheyenne. She is the author of *Candle & Soap Making For Dummies*.

maranGraphics is a family-run business
located near Toronto, Canada.

At **maranGraphics**, we believe in producing great computer books—one book at a time.

Each maranGraphics book uses the award-winning communication process that we have been developing over the last 28 years. Using this process, we organize screen shots and text in a way that makes it easy for you to learn new concepts and tasks.

We spend hours deciding the best way to perform each task, so you don't have to! Our clear, easy-to-follow screen shots and instructions walk you through each task from beginning to end.

We want to thank you for purchasing what we feel are the best computer books money can buy. We hope you enjoy using this book as much as we enjoyed creating it!

Sincerely,

The Maran Family

Please visit us on the Web at:
www.maran.com

HOW TO USE THIS BOOK

Photoshop Elements 2: Top 100 Simplified Tips & Tricks
includes the 100 most interesting and useful tasks you can perform in Photoshop Elements 2. This book reveals cool secrets and timesaving tricks guaranteed to make you more productive in Photoshop Elements 2.

Who is this book for?

Are you a visual learner who already knows the basics of Photoshop Elements 2, but would like to take your Photoshop Elements experience to the next level? Then this is the book for you.

Conventions In This Book

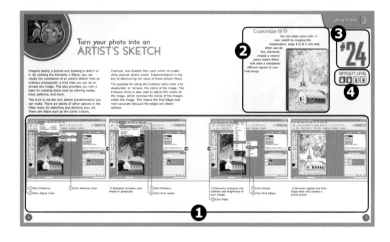

① **Steps**

This book walks you through each task using a step-by-step approach. Lines and "lassos" connect the screen shots to the step-by-step instructions to show you exactly how to perform each task.

② **Tips**

Fun and practical tips answer questions you have always wondered about. Plus, learn to do things in Photoshop Elements 2 that you never thought were possible!

③ **Task Numbers**

The task numbers, ranging from 1 to 100, indicate which self-contained lesson you are currently working on.

④ **Difficulty Levels**

For quick reference, symbols mark the difficulty level of each task.

 Demonstrates a new spin on a common task

Introduces a new skill or a new task

Combines multiple skills requiring in-depth knowledge

Requires extensive skill and may involve other technologies

TABLE OF CONTENTS

1 Working with Layers

2 Working with Selections and Masks

3 Using Filters

4 Work with Effects and Styles

TABLE OF **CONTENTS**

7 Working with Color

8 Preparing Images for Printing and the Web

⑩ Working with Other Elements Tools

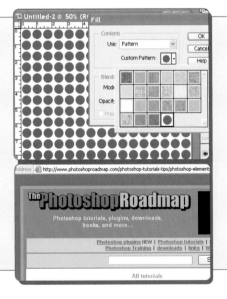

CHAPTER 1

Working with Layers

You can create, design, edit, and manipulate images and graphic art in a much more powerful way than before with layers in Photoshop Elements. Previously, any image adjustments you made to a photo or image were permanent — there was no undoing the changes made to the images pixels. With the introduction of layers, you can create floating canvasses that overlap each other, very similar to a cartoonist design. Cartoons have overlapping layers of images, starting with a background and then separate layers for the characters, props, and sundry items placed upon it. Layers are like transparent pieces of paper with single items drawn upon them.

In Elements, you can open an image with layers and adjust all of the objects on one layer without affecting the other layers directly or permanently. You can move, apply special effects, colorize, erase, and distort whatever is upon the individual layer without permanently affecting any other layers. This is an enormous contribution to creating art and editing photos.

This chapter discusses some of the tricks in using layers to their fullest advantage. You can learn how to add special effects, use layers to change other layers, and even make one layer semitransparent so another shows through. There are so many advantages to layers when it comes to graphic arts, and Photoshop Elements really delivers.

TOP 100

ADD LAYERS

You can combine a great number of different objects and items in one image, while retaining the ability to affect each one separately. You can do this with layers. *Layers* are described as invisible sheets of paper that overlay one another. You can place objects on these layers and they will overlap and combine with the others to create a total image. Each layer is independent of the other layers, but you can merge them together, causing one to affect the appearance of another. You can even link two or more layers together so they move and transform in scale together but are still separate.

You can add layers easily. Adding layers is a common function when you need a new object or text line while working on a project. Placement and naming of layers are important. Layers on top cover layers that are below them. You can place your layer in relation to the other layers to properly place your object. Giving the layers descriptive names keeps them organized.

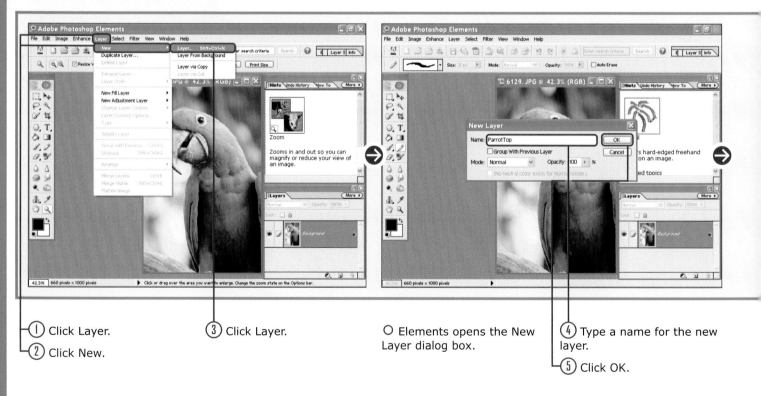

① Click Layer.

② Click New.

③ Click Layer.

○ Elements opens the New Layer dialog box.

④ Type a name for the new layer.

⑤ Click OK.

Did You Know? ✳

You can hide a layer if it is distracting you while you work with another layer. In the Layers palette, click the layer you want to hide and then click the Eye icon (👁) next to it. The layer disappears. Click the box where the Eye icon was to turn the layer visible again.

Did You Know? ✳

You cannot change the Background layer. The Background layer is the bottommost layer, and it is protected against adjustments. You can see a Lock icon on the Background layer, denoting its locked status. There is a Lock icon in the Layers palette that locks any selected layer as well, preventing accidental changes to your layers. To lock a layer, select your layer and then click the Lock icon. You can click it again to unlock the layer.

DIFFICULTY LEVEL

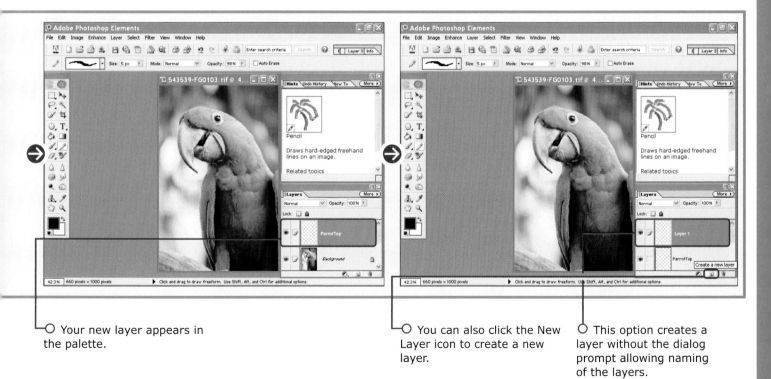

○ Your new layer appears in the palette.

○ You can also click the New Layer icon to create a new layer.

○ This option creates a layer without the dialog prompt allowing naming of the layers.

5

Achieve transparency effects with the
OPACITY SETTING

You can achieve an almost surreal look in your photos by adjusting the opacity of layers within your image. When you adjust the opacity of a layer, you are simply making it more see-through, allowing pixels beneath the layer objects to become visible based on the opacity settings you apply. This semitransparency effect has some very useful results. You can apply it to text to create a more subtle impact of the words you choose, you can make an image semitransparent to show a second

image below it, and you can give shapes and layer objects an almost spectral visibility for backgrounds or image overlays.

You can change your opacity settings at any time. You can also use opacity for working on layers below an object, while still being able to detect the boundaries of the object. This has great use with images that have many layers that overlap objects.

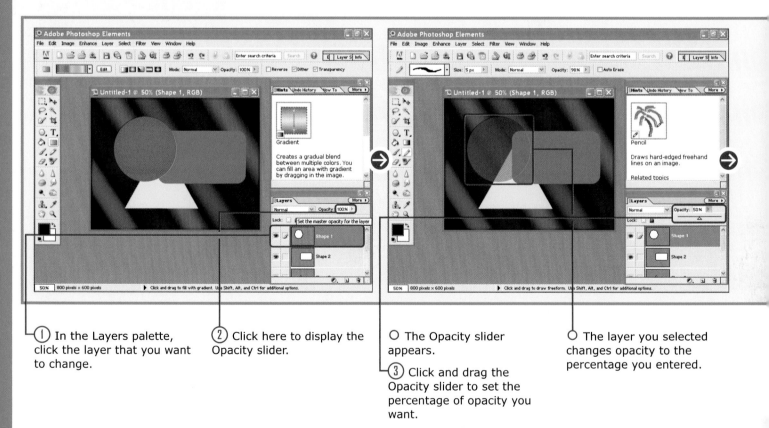

① In the Layers palette, click the layer that you want to change.

② Click here to display the Opacity slider.

○ The Opacity slider appears.

③ Click and drag the Opacity slider to set the percentage of opacity you want.

○ The layer you selected changes opacity to the percentage you entered.

Did You Know? ※

You cannot change the opacity of Background layers. You can adjust the background only if you transform it into a layer. Click Layer, New, and then Layer From Background. You can also double-click the background in the Layer palette, and a prompt will allow you to convert it to a layer.

Did You Know? ※

You can take a layer with a lower opacity setting and place its objects over another layer with lowered opacity settings; the overlapping areas have combined colors and higher opacity. Opacity is cumulative in multiple layers. You can make a layer with a yellow circle and a layer with a blue circle. Set both layers to 50 percent opacity and the circles to overlap half way. The overlapping colors combine into a more opaque green color.

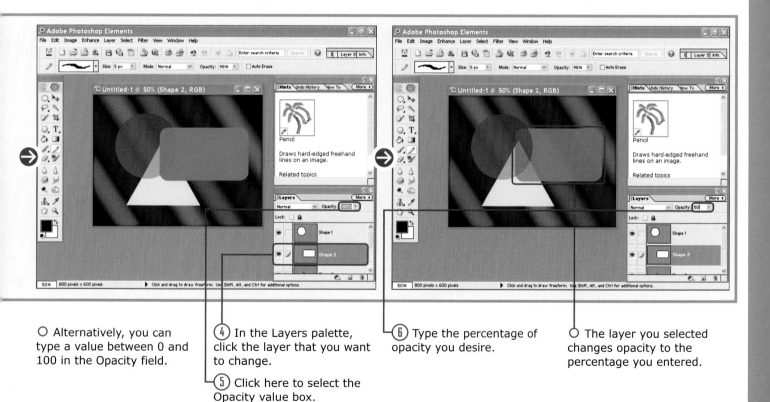

○ Alternatively, you can type a value between 0 and 100 in the Opacity field.

④ In the Layers palette, click the layer that you want to change.

⑤ Click here to select the Opacity value box.

⑥ Type the percentage of opacity you desire.

○ The layer you selected changes opacity to the percentage you entered.

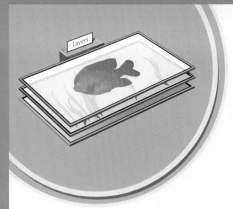

Use the blending modes to
BLEND LAYERS

You can use the Photoshop Elements blending modes to create special effects on your layers. The blend modes take the pixels of a layer and causes them to interact with the pixels of another layer. This affects the hues, tones, and saturations of the lower layer's image. There are several groups of blending modes you can use. Each mode has several variations of a basic effect form. Each blending mode defines how a layer interacts with other layers, mostly in the area of Highlights, Midtones, Shadows, and Color. Highlight-based filters ignore midtone and shadows,

and adjust only the lighter colored pixels. Shadow and Midtone blending modes affect dark tones and the middle range of tones, respectively. The color modes affect only the Hue, Saturation, and Color blends of the layer it modifies, leaving the contrast and tones alone.

You can experiment with each blending mode, and it is strongly encouraged, because each image has its own range of tones and color, and there is no way to predict how each blending mode affects the other layers.

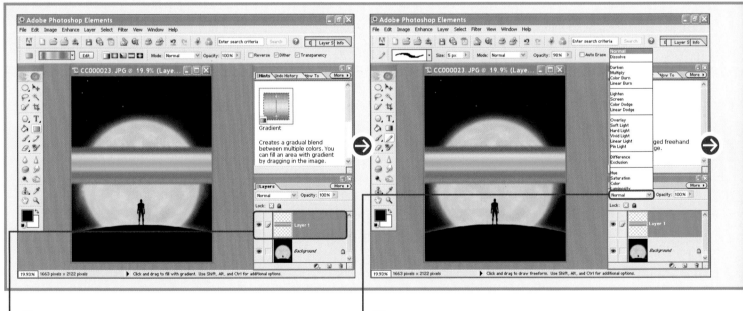

① In the Layers palette, click the layer that you want to blend.

② Click here to open Blending Modes menu.

Did You Know? ※

You can reset and adjust blending modes at any time. The blending modes are not permanent effects. However, they do affect all layers below the layer with the blending modes. When adjustments are made to a layer affect, the pixels of all the layers below it are affected. You can adjust the opacity to lessen and lighten the effects that the blending modes apply.

Did You Know? ※

You can use multiple blending mode layers for all types of different effects. Blending modes are cumulative, meaning they build upon each other as you apply them. For example, you have three layers, and the middle layer has one blending mode. Only the bottom layer is affected. If the top layer also had a blending mode applied to it, its blending mode would affect both the middle and the bottom layer, compounding or adding to the effect the middle layer was creating. It is best to experiment and see how each mode works.

 # 3

DIFFICULTY LEVEL

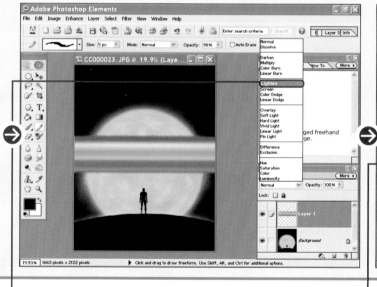

③ Select the blend mode.

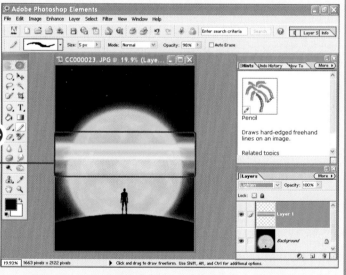

○ Elements blends the selected layer with the layers below it.

Add effects with
LAYER STYLES

You can improve the looks of your layers by using layer styles. Styles add dimension and special effects to your objects. You can apply styles to any layer except your Background layer. When you apply styles to a background, you are prompted to convert it to a regular layer before it can apply the style.

You have 14 layer style categories from which to choose. You can apply styles with a simple click of the button. Clicking more than one style can add to the current style or replace the current style completely.

Your basic styles, like the bevels, shadows, and glows, have specific uses. The Complex styles incorporate the bevels, shadows, and glows as well as patterns, color overlays, and other extras to create a truly original effect.

You can still edit text and shapes after you apply styles. Unlike most filters, styles can work on vector graphics such as text and shapes without requiring simplification first. This is a great advantage for later editing and corrections.

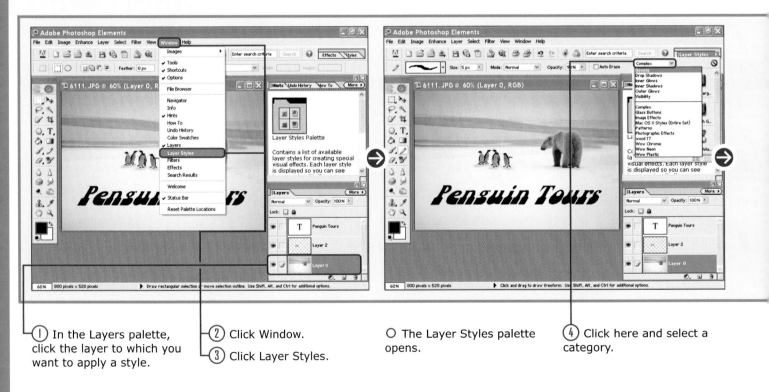

① In the Layers palette, click the layer to which you want to apply a style.

② Click Window.

③ Click Layer Styles.

○ The Layer Styles palette opens.

④ Click here and select a category.

Did You Know? ※

You can remove all layer styles from your layer by clicking the Clear Style button in the upper-right corner of the Layer Styles palette. Clearing the style can only be undone with the History palette.

Did You Know? ※

You can experiment with styles, however, the History palette does not show a record of the specific styles, only Apply Style. So keep track of what you use, so you can re-create the same effect later.

Customize It! ※

You can edit certain aspects of your layer styles. To start, click the *f* icon in the Layer Palette on the layer that has the style applied to it. A dialog box appears with sliders and adjustors for your active style effects. You can change the settings on the active effects and create a custom layer style for your project.

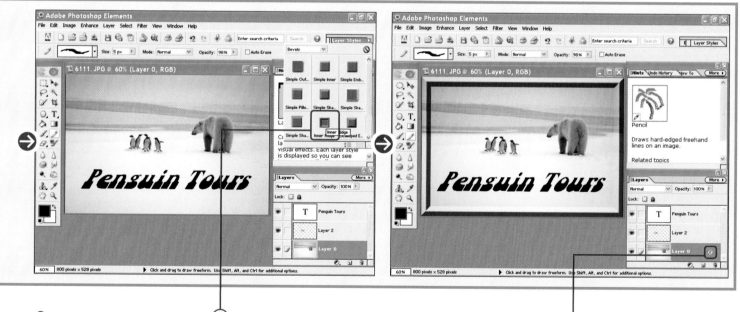

○ A list of layer styles appears.

⑤ Click the layer style you want to apply.

○ Elements applies the layer styles.

○ The *f* icon (⬚) appears in the layer indicating a layer style has been applied.

Work with
ADJUSTMENT LAYERS

You can alter the appearance of a layer using another layer with special properties. These types of layers are called *adjustment layers*. Adjustment layers affect one of several specific properties of the layers below the adjustment layer. Hue/saturation, levels, contrast, and other options are available.

The adjustment layer is versatile because it allows you to make dramatic changes to your image without irreversibly changing your original image. It is handy for enhancing color of an image, or increasing the contrast of faded photographs.

By default, the adjustment layers affect all layers below them. However, you can also specify the adjustment layer to affect only one layer by grouping it with a specific layer.

You can find many uses for adjustment layers in your everyday photographic or graphical use. They are excellent for making initial adjustments to digital camera imports or scans, or correcting improper color balances or poorly detailed contrast. The ability to make significant changes to your images without permanently damaging them makes adjustment layers almost irreplaceable for photo corrections.

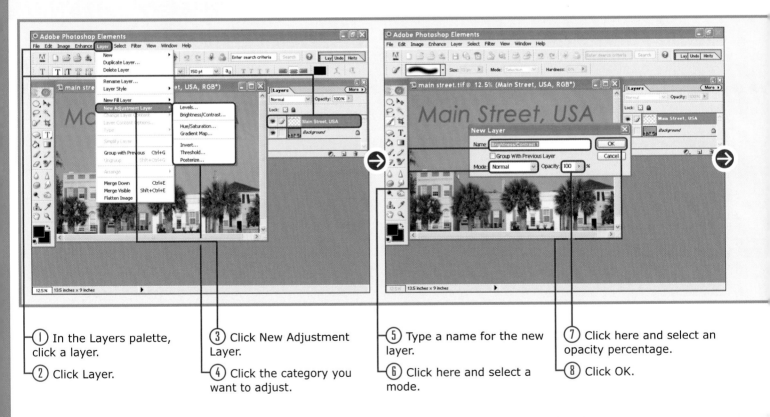

① In the Layers palette, click a layer.

② Click Layer.

③ Click New Adjustment Layer.

④ Click the category you want to adjust.

⑤ Type a name for the new layer.

⑥ Click here and select a mode.

⑦ Click here and select an opacity percentage.

⑧ Click OK.

Did You Know? ※

You can apply an adjustment layer to a selection of the image. You do not have to make a change to an entire layer. Just select the area with the Selection tool before you create your adjustment layer.

Did You Know? ※

To tweak the result of an applied effect, you can lower the opacity of an adjustment layer to soften the effects.

Did You Know? ※

You can use Adjustment layers to affect other Adjustment layers. Adjustment layers are cumulative and affect not only the regular layers, but the adjustment layers below as well. For example, two different color adjustment layers set at less than 100% opacity will complement each other, blending colors, and apply those colors to the regular layers below as well.

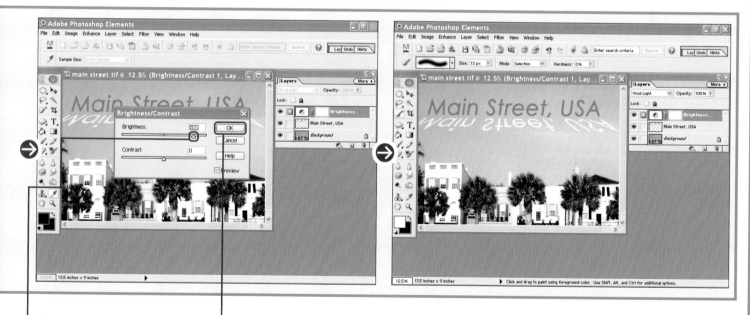

⑨ In the Brightness/Contrast dialog box, click and drag the sliders to make adjustments.

⑩ Click OK.

○ Elements applies the Brightness/Contrast settings.

○ Although image appears different, the original image remains unchanged because changes were done on the Adjustment layer.

Enhance your creativity by
IMPORTING LAYER STYLES

You can use many layer styles for all your custom work. They are useful and creative. There are other layer styles available online that you can import into Elements to expand your available tools and enhance your creativity.

You can visit many places online that have available layer styles for use in Photoshop Elements 2. Adobe Studio Exchange, hosted by the creators of Elements, has hundreds of styles available to choose from, most of which will work within Elements.

You can download and save these files into Photoshop Elements 2. You can save them to Elements' styles folder, and upon the next restart of Elements, the program will automatically load the styles into the available styles menu.

You can really expand your creativity with outside style. Although some of the features used in these imported styles may not be editable, many still are, such as the bevels, glows, and shadows.

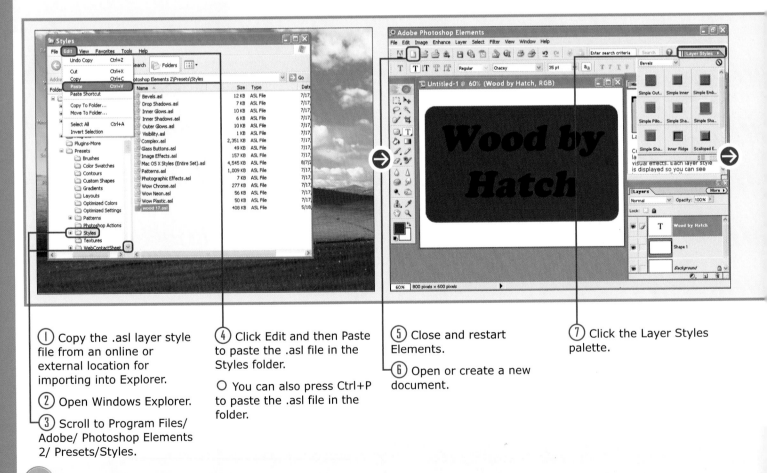

① Copy the .asl layer style file from an online or external location for importing into Explorer.

② Open Windows Explorer.

③ Scroll to Program Files/ Adobe/ Photoshop Elements 2/ Presets/Styles.

④ Click Edit and then Paste to paste the .asl file in the Styles folder.

○ You can also press Ctrl+P to paste the .asl file in the folder.

⑤ Close and restart Elements.

⑥ Open or create a new document.

⑦ Click the Layer Styles palette.

Did You Know? ※

Most layer styles that are available for the regular version of Photoshop are compatible with Photoshop Elements. This compatibility opens the door to many new and creative styles for your use in Elements, although some attributes of the newly imported styles you may not be able to edit.

Did You Know? ※

There are many places online with layer styles for your use. Go to http://share.studio.adobe.com, which is the open exchange forum for the graphics programs of Adobe. The Wood Styles used in this example are compliments of F. Hatcher at www.psxtras.com.

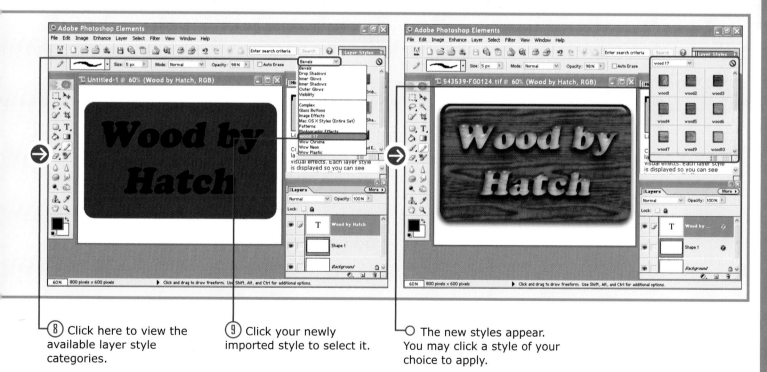

⑧ Click here to view the available layer style categories.

⑨ Click your newly imported style to select it.

○ The new styles appear. You may click a style of your choice to apply.

Master
ZOOMING

You can use the Zoom tool to increase the magnification of an area so that you can see it better. The Zoom tool works like a mini-magnifying glass, letting you move in and out on particular areas.

The Zoom tool is particularly handy because it lets you get up close to a specific area of an image and view the details. This is very useful with pixel-based images.

You can do very detailed manipulation of images by utilizing the Zoom tool. By magnifying the trouble spot of a photograph, for example a red-eye effect

on a portrait, you are able to use smaller brushes with more accuracy for making adjustments.

There are several handy tools with the Zoom tool. With the Zoom tool selected, the top toolbar changes to reveal zoom options. You can zoom in, zoom out, show the image at actual pixel size or print size, and even reset the zoom size to fit the available space on-screen.

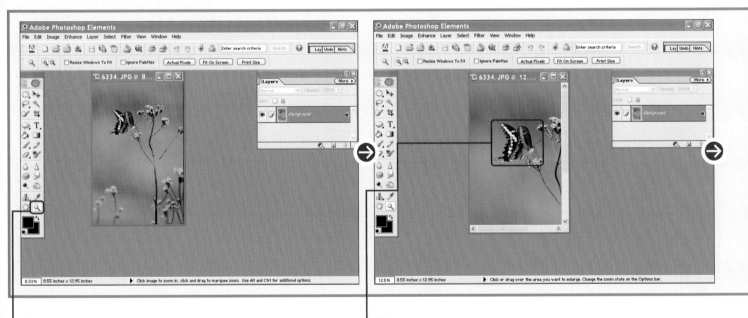

① Click the Zoom tool.

② Click the area in the image that you want to enlarge.

○ The area gets larger as you click.

Did You Know? ☀

You can click the status bar in the lower-left corner of the screen and type a zoom percent number instead to increase or decrease the magnification.

Did You Know? ☀

You use the Zoom tool even if you have another tool selected. Just press Ctrl+Spacebar to zoom in or Ctrl+Alt+Spacebar to zoom out.

Did You Know? ☀

You can double-click the Zoom tool icon in the toolbar, and Elements will automatically set the zoom amount to View Actual Pixels size. You can also double-click the Hand tool icon in the toolbars, and Elements will automatically set the zoom to Fit On Screen.

#7

DIFFICULTY LEVEL

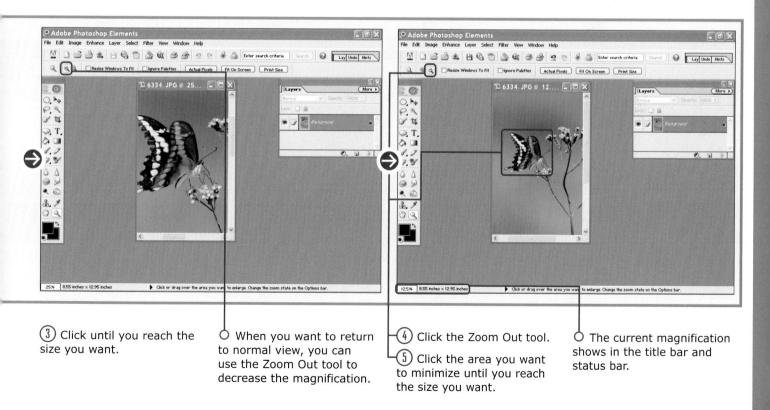

③ Click until you reach the size you want.

○ When you want to return to normal view, you can use the Zoom Out tool to decrease the magnification.

④ Click the Zoom Out tool.

⑤ Click the area you want to minimize until you reach the size you want.

○ The current magnification shows in the title bar and status bar.

Increase precision by activating
GRIDS AND RULERS

You can adjust your placement of text and images perfectly thanks to the grids and rulers Photoshop Elements offers. These tools are great for exact placements and layouts in your multi-layer images. You activate the grids and rulers under the View menu.

When you activate the rulers, ruler guides appear on the side and top of your image canvas. This helps to show sizes and placements within the image.

When you activate the grids, you turn on a grid-line overlay on the image that allows you to align and place objects at specific locations on your image.

This allows you to easily align your objects. You can set the grid and ruler sizes by clicking Edit, and then Preferences. In the Preferences dialog box, you can select options to change the ruler measurements, grid sizes and colors, and other options.

You can change the zero center point of your rulers by clicking and dragging from the upper-left corner and positioning it in your image. Double-clicking the corner again resets the zero point to the upper-left corner.

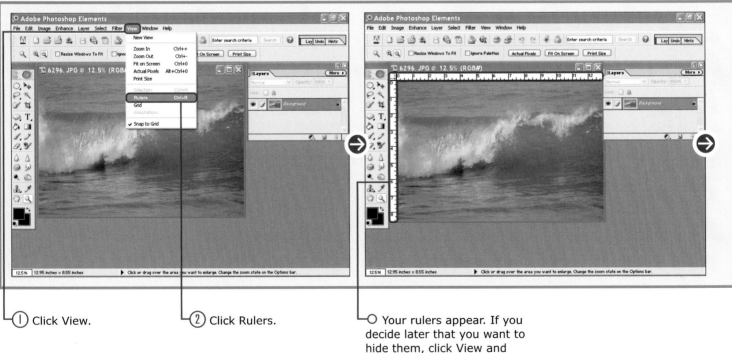

① Click View.

② Click Rulers.

○ Your rulers appear. If you decide later that you want to hide them, click View and then Rulers.

DIFFICULTY LEVEL

Did You Know? ※

You can use the grid to straighten photos. Open a crooked scanned photo. Turn on your Grid. Click Image, then Transform, then Free Transform. Use the Rotate function of the Free Transform tool to align the edges of your image to your grid.

Apply It! ※

You can access an option under the View menu called Snap to Grid. This option causes any relocated object to snap to the nearest gridline. You must have the grid on-screen for this to work.

Apply It! ※

You can change the ruler settings without going to the Preferences dialog box. Double-click the ruler. In the dialog box that appears, click the Ruler drop-down list in the Units section and choose your measurement unit.

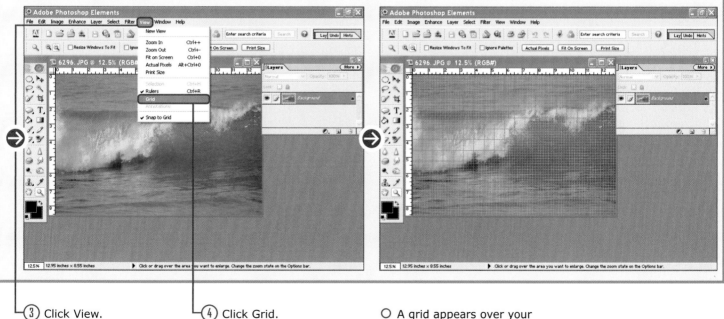

③ Click View.

④ Click Grid.

○ A grid appears over your image.

MOVE OBJECTS
in layers

You can take advantage of the great strength of layers and the mobility of its objects. The beauty of layers is that their contents are independent of the other layers. What you do to one layer does not affect the others, unless you intend it to.

You can place your layer objects wherever you want within the boundaries of the image. To adjust the position of your objects, you can use the Move tool.

Using the Move tool creates a bounding box around the individual object or objects within the layer. By clicking and dragging your object, you can place it

where you want. Alternatively, you can use the arrow keys on the keyboard for precise positioning.

You can click a different object to select it, or click any layer in the Layers palette to switch the Move tool to a new layer.

You can also switch layers by right-clicking anywhere in the image when using the Move tool. Any layers that overlap where you click will appear in a list that you can choose from to select that layer.

① In the Layers palette, click the layer that contains the object you want to move.

② Click the Move tool.

○ The Move tool automatically selects the objects in the currently selected layer by default.

#9

DIFFICULTY LEVEL

Did You Know? ☀

You can move multiple layers at one time if you link the layers. *Linking* the layers ties the layers together so that you can move them all at once using the Move tool. To link layers, click one layer, and then in the Layers palette click the empty box next to the Eye icon. A chain appears denoting the link.

Shortcut Keys! ☀

You can access the Move tool at almost any time by holding the Control key while using another tool. Most tools allow you to access this shortcut.

Shortcut Keys! ☀

When you use the keyboard to move an object, you can hold the Shift key while pressing the directional keys. This moves the object several pixels at a time, instead of one at a time. You can also press Ctrl+Down key to move one pixel at a time.

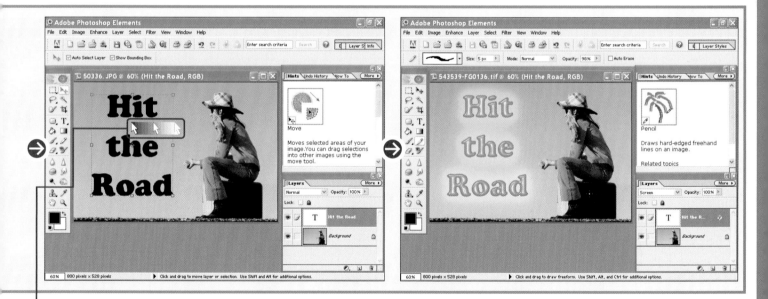

③ Click and drag the object you want to move to its new position.

○ Your object moves without affecting the other layers.

ORGANIZE LAYERS

You can shuffle layers in your image to make it more visually appealing. You can accomplish what seems like a major rearrangement with just a few clicks of your mouse in the Layers palette. Because layers are like sheets of paper, you can easily adjust the look and feel of your image by simply moving a layer up or down. Renaming the layer to something more descriptive is very beneficial, as well.

Each layer functions like its own file, meaning that the changes that you make to one layer do not affect all layers. However, special effects, such as a

blending mode, are intended to affect other layers. You can experiment to see how certain layers affect others.

You can use all regular layers when it comes to a move. Remember, you cannot move the Background layer. However, you can convert the Background layer into a regular layer if you need to move it.

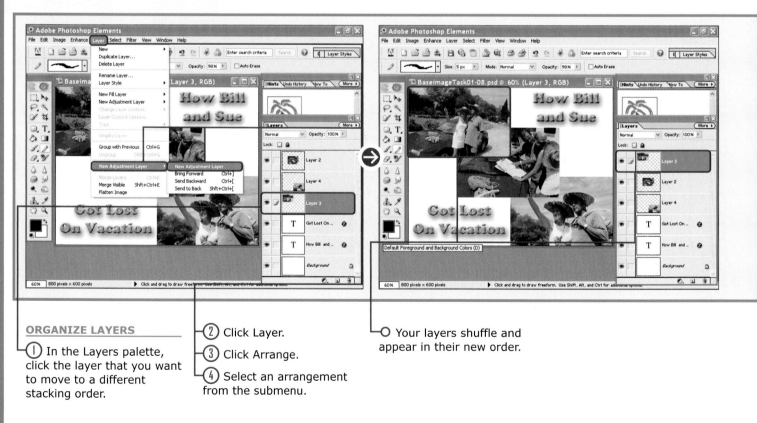

ORGANIZE LAYERS

(1) In the Layers palette, click the layer that you want to move to a different stacking order.

(2) Click Layer.

(3) Click Arrange.

(4) Select an arrangement from the submenu.

○ Your layers shuffle and appear in their new order.

Shortcut Keys! ☀

You can take advantage of a
few keyboard shortcuts to
rearrange your layers.

Shortcuts	Function
Ctrl+]	Moves a layer one level up
Ctrl+[	Moves a layer one level back
Shift+Ctrl+]	Moves a layer to the front
Shift+Ctrl+[	Moves a layer to the back

10

DIFFICULTY LEVEL

Did You Know? ☀

You can easily rename your layer. Click the layer you want to
rename. Click Layer and then Rename Layer. In the Layers
Properties dialog box, type a new name and click OK to rename
the layer. You can also double-click the layer in the Layers palette
to open the same dialog box.

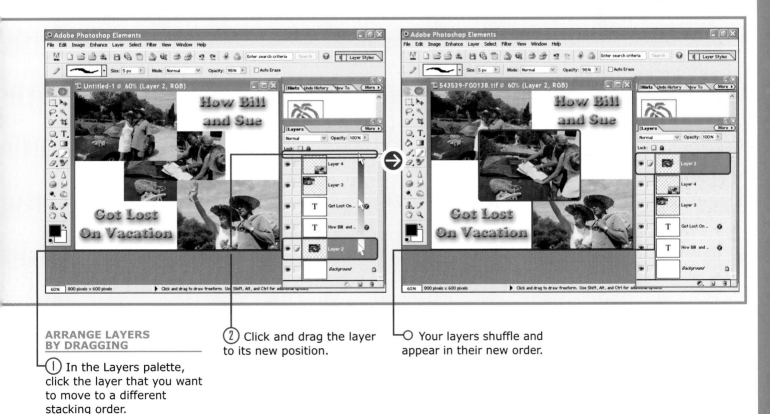

**ARRANGE LAYERS
BY DRAGGING**

① In the Layers palette,
click the layer that you want
to move to a different
stacking order.

② Click and drag the layer
to its new position.

─○ Your layers shuffle and
appear in their new order.

CHAPTER 2

Working with Selections and Masks

You can achieve amazing effects and results with Elements' selection tools and mask tools. Selection tools are essential to Elements users because of the nature of raster, or bitmap, graphics. When working with bitmaps, you are working with thousands of pixels, and to make any changes to these pixels, you must specify which ones you want to affect. The selection and masking tools are critical to this function. You can specify what areas or pixels you choose to change by selecting them from the image. You can do this with the selection and mask tools available in Elements.

When you make a selection, you are telling the program to change *these* selected pixels, and do *not* change *these* unselected pixels. The selection

tool creates a border around your selected area or areas. You see the border as a moving dotted line, or as *marching ants*. Anything within these borders is affected by your changes, while everything outside remains as is. Masks work similarly by telling the program that the colored areas are affected while the uncolored areas are not. Masks primarily affect the visibility of a pixel, whereas selections allow the adjustment of colors, size, design, and so on. You can use masks to create selections, and vice versa, which can be very useful.

Overall, selections and masks are vital to complex designs. In this chapter, you can discover many different methods of using these tools, and some of the best ways to get the most out of them.

TOP 100

Using the
MARQUE SELECTION
tool

You can make simple and fast selections with the Marquee Selection tools. There are several variations to choose from in the Marquee tools. You can choose rectangular or elliptical selection tools from the tool bar. The Marquee tool is excellent for quick selections in simple shapes.

You can create any size of selection, up to the size of the image. You just click and drag the cursor on the screen and the Marquee tool draws your rectangle or ellipse in the direction of your cursor. When you have reached the shape and size you

desire, release the mouse button, and the dotted line boundaries appear, marking your selection's outline. You can deselect your selection by clicking the mouse on the inside of a completed selection.

You can manipulate and edit the image pixels in between the edges of your selection after you have drawn your selection. Any pixels outside of the selected area are ignored, and are not affected. This is a very useful tool for general editing of an image or graphic, such as affecting color and contrast of a section of an image.

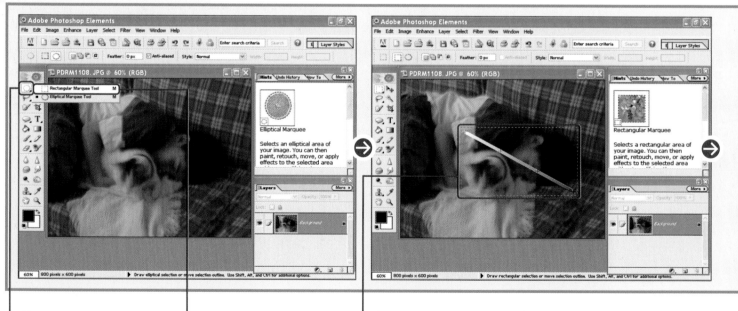

① Click and hold the cursor over the Marquee tool.

○ The Marquee tool selection bar appears.

Note: These selections also appear on the options bar at the top of the screen.

② Select a Marquee tool.

③ Click and drag to make a selection.

Customize It! ☀

You can feather your marquee selections before you use your Marquee tools. In the Options bar across the top of the screen, you can enter a value into the Feather box. That value feathers the edges of your selection, or creates a semitransparent blending edge that is less stark.

Did You Know? ☀

To constrain the dimensions of the Marquee tool, press and hold the Shift key while dragging the cursor. The relative size appears even, creating perfect squares or circles.

#11

DIFFICULTY LEVEL

○ Upon releasing the mouse button, Elements creates the selected area.

④ Click Enhance.

⑤ Click Auto Levels.

○ Elements applies the Auto Levels enhancement only within the selection area.

Note: To turn off your selection, click Select and then Deselect from the menu.

INVERT
your selection

You can invert a selection in Elements. You may have an image or graphic you want to adjust only part of. In Elements, you can make a selection of the area you want ignored. Then, you can invert the selected area. Now instead of Elements affecting only the selected area, that area becomes the only thing not affected by Elements.

If you have an image with multiple layers and objects, any selection you make on that layer will only affect the objects on that layer. This is useful when the item you want to change is on its own separate layer.

Inverting a selection can be a great time-saver. Instead of selecting a large portion of your image, you can instead select the smaller portion and invert it. This is especially helpful with smaller subjects you want excluded.

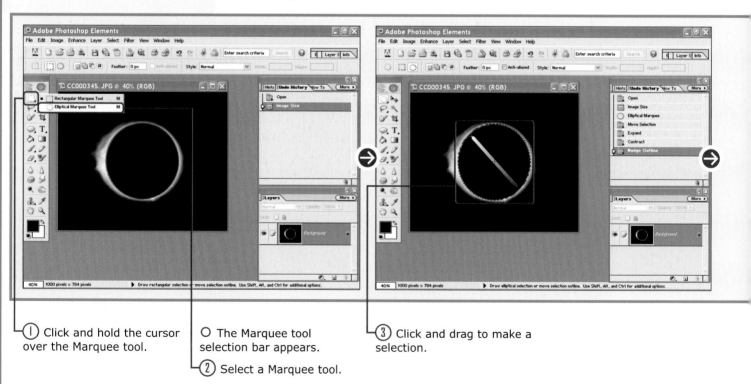

① Click and hold the cursor over the Marquee tool.

○ The Marquee tool selection bar appears.

② Select a Marquee tool.

③ Click and drag to make a selection.

Did You Know? ※

You can invert your selection and all the options as well. For example, if you choose to feather a selection with the Marquee tool options bar, and choose to invert the selection, the feathering also is inverted.

Did You Know? ※

When you load a selection from the Load Selection option in the Select menu, you can click a radio button to automatically select the inverted form of the saved selection.

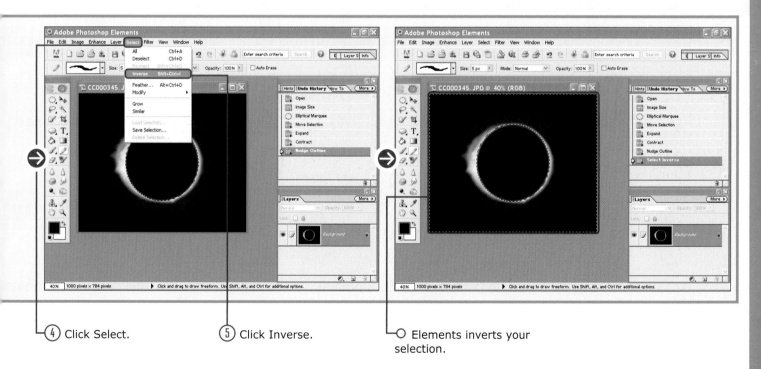

④ Click Select.

⑤ Click Inverse.

○ Elements inverts your selection.

SAVE
your selections

You can store your reusable or complex selections of your image for use later on. Elements has a feature that allows you to make a selection and save it within the document for you to return to later. This feature is a big time-saver, especially with complex selections. Trying to make a second selection on the same object can become tedious, but because you can save the selection, it saves you the effort.

Elements also allows you to save a selection within the image itself when saving it to the computer.

You can access the same selection by re-opening the image in Elements, going to the Load Selection command, and making the selection again.

You can load your selections easily, too. Inside the Select menu is the Load Selection command, where you can access any saved selections contained within that document. With the Save Selection command, you can save time from having to recreate your selections from scratch.

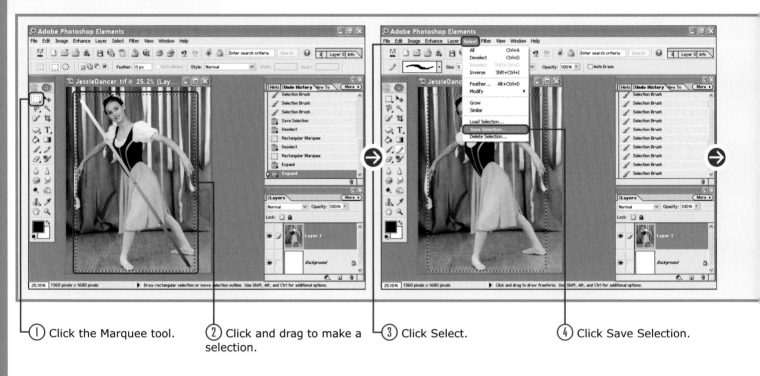

① Click the Marquee tool.

② Click and drag to make a selection.

③ Click Select.

④ Click Save Selection.

13

DIFFICULTY LEVEL

Did You Know? ※

You can load your selection back into your image quickly. To access the Load Selection command, click Select and then Load Selection. The Load Selection dialog box opens. You can click the drop-down menu of all available selections within the document. Click a selection and then click OK. You can see the saved selection reactivated again.

Did You Know? ※

You can save more than one selection per image. Repeat the steps for saving a selection to add each to the drop-down menu. Giving your selections detailed names will help you find them later.

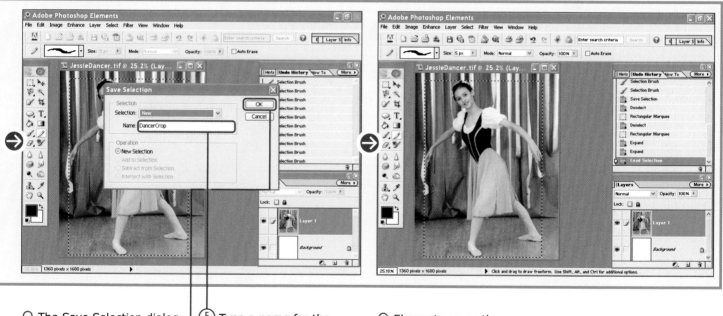

○ The Save Selection dialog box appears.

⑤ Type a name for the selection.

⑥ Click OK.

○ Elements saves the selection within the document.

Work with the
LASSO TOOL

You can make custom and complex selections with the Lasso tool. The Lasso tool is a selection method that allows you to draw any shape you desire with your mouse, and have that boundary become the selection. When you click and drag your mouse, a boundary line is drawn until you release the mouse button. If you place the mouse back at its origin point, the cursor adopts a small letter *o,* meaning the selection is enclosed. You can release the mouse button at this point. The drawn

selection appears laid out. Releasing the cursor sooner causes the endpoint to go directly to the origin, enclosing the selected area.

You can use your mouse to draw a complex selection without the limitations of the geometric shapes of the Marquee tools, making the Lasso tool flexible for the user. You can easily draw around any object. You can deselect your selection by clicking the mouse on the inside of a completed selection.

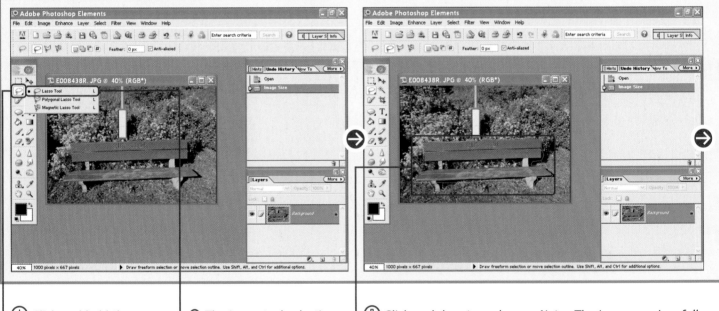

① Click and hold the cursor over the Lasso tool.

○ The Lasso tool selection bar appears.

② Select a Lasso tool.

③ Click and drag to make a selection.

Note: The Lasso requires fully encompassing boundaries, so draw with intent to return to the origin point.

#14

DIFFICULTY LEVEL

Did You Know? ☀

You can feather your selections before you use the Lasso tools. In the Options bar across the top of the screen, you can enter a value into the Feather box. That value will feather the edges of your selection, or create a semitransparent blending edge that is less stark. You can click the value box and enter a value, and use your Lasso tool as normal. When you are done, the selection will be feathered.

Customize It! ☀

You can add and delete sections of the selection after you complete it. Press and hold down the Shift key while making a selection to add to the current selection. Press and hold down the Alt key while selecting the area to erase from the current selection.

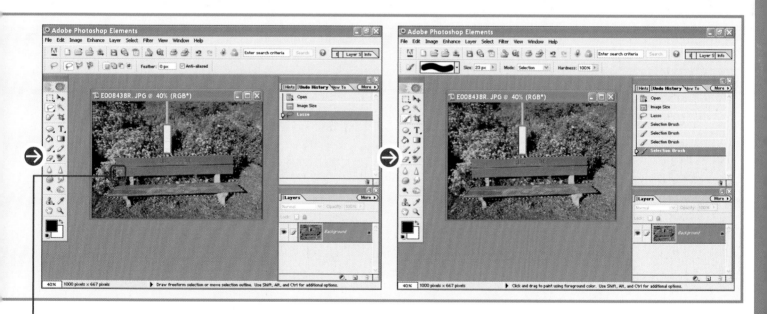

④ Position the cursor back to the origin point and release the mouse button.

○ A small letter *o* will appear by the cursor when the origin point is reached.

○ Elements generates a selection based on drawn boundaries.

Make selections with the
BRUSH SELECTION
tool

You can now make selections with a new tool in Elements 2. The Brush Selection tool is one of the easiest and most innovative selection tools Elements has to offer. The Brush Selection tool acts like the regular brush tool, except that when you draw with the Brush Selection tool, instead of pixels or colors, what is painted is selection. This allows you to make sophisticated and quick selections.

The Brush Selection tool shares access to the Brush's library of brush shapes. You choose your

brush, and when you begin painting your selection, the shapes, sizes, and options of that brush are all applied to the selection area.

You can adjust a hardness option that allows you to vary your brush edges from soft, or lightly feathered, to hard. This replaces the feathering option available on most of the other selection tools. You can deselect your selection by clicking the mouse on the inside of a completed selection.

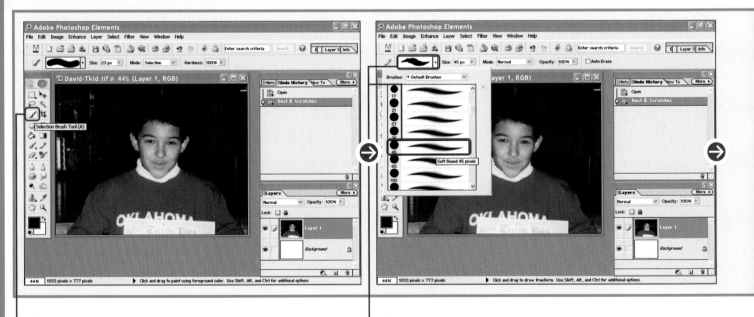

① Click the Brush tool.

② Click here and select a brush shape.

Did You Know? ※

You can erase areas of a drawing by pressing and holding the Alt key while drawing with the Brush Selection tool. This is a very nice corrective feature in case you select a mistaken area.

Did You Know? ※

You can manipulate your selection at different points of creation. You can alter the hardness of the brush or the brush shape while drawing your selections, allowing you more freedom of selection design. You can use the Select menu options to alter the current selection. You can continue working with the Brush Selection tool after these adjustments, and the brush continues to carry its current settings.

DIFFICULTY LEVEL

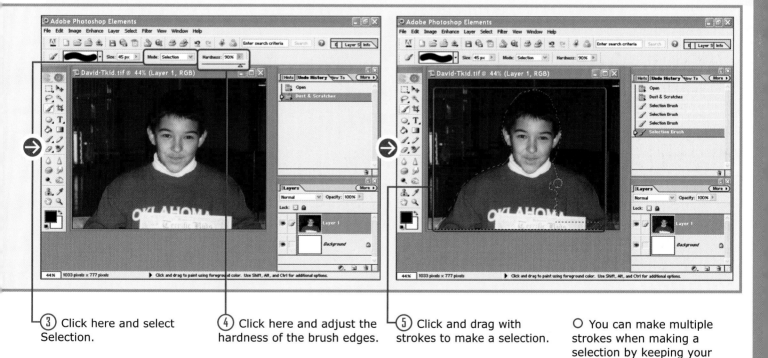

③ Click here and select Selection.

④ Click here and adjust the hardness of the brush edges.

⑤ Click and drag with strokes to make a selection.

○ You can make multiple strokes when making a selection by keeping your mouse pressed down.

MODIFY
your selections

You can adjust your selections after completing them. These modifications affect the size, structure, and edges. Two of the most commonly used of these are Contract and Expand. You can use these for size modifications to your selections. They are both excellent tools for working with complex shapes and Web site design.

You can alter the total area size of your selections with these tools. The Contract modification reduces the total scale of your selection by a specified number. You can enter a value to adjust a specific amount of pixels you contract in. The contraction is constrained, and equal in all directions. This is an excellent tool if you want to create an inner edge on an object. The Expand modification is similar to Contract, except it moves the pixel size outwards. You can use the Expand modification to create an outline or to ensure what you delete off an image leaves no lingering pixels. Both tools allow you adjustments, but excessive amounts of adjusting can cause the selection tool to lose its clarity.

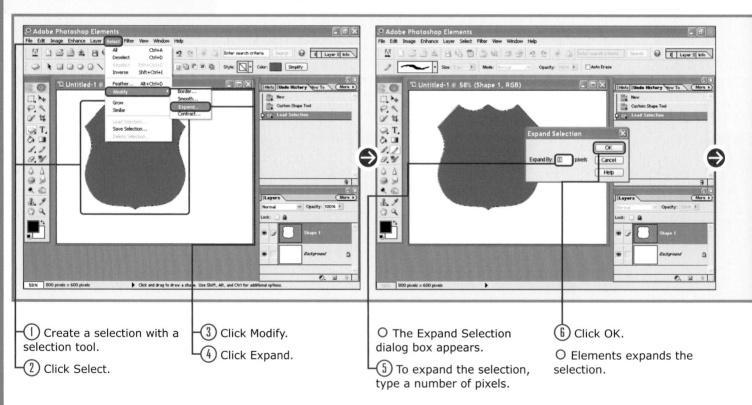

① Create a selection with a selection tool.

② Click Select.

③ Click Modify.

④ Click Expand.

○ The Expand Selection dialog box appears.

⑤ To expand the selection, type a number of pixels.

⑥ Click OK.

○ Elements expands the selection.

Customize It! ※

You can easily make an outline of any object. Make a selection of your object. Click Select, Expand, and then enter a number of pixels. Next click Edit, Fill, and set the Use type to Black. Click OK. Now, click Select, Contract, and enter the same number as before, and click OK. Then, press the Delete key and the selected object is deleted with a perfect outline remaining.

DIFFICULTY LEVEL

Did You Know? ※

Follow the outline tip mentioned here, but work on the selection on a new layer. This way, when you perform the Fill and Delete commands, they do not affect your original image.

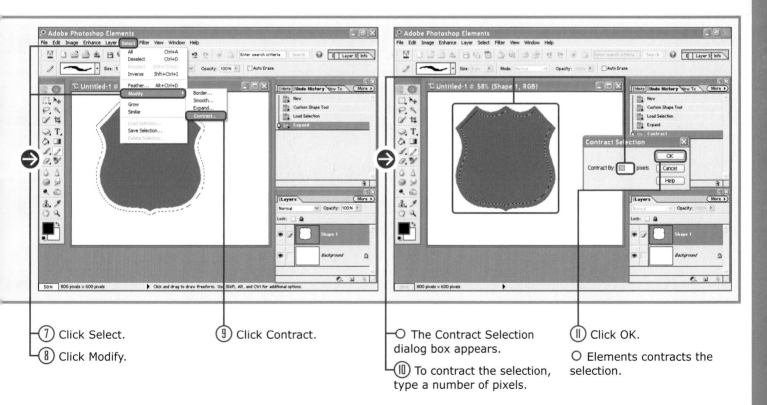

⑦ Click Select.

⑧ Click Modify.

⑨ Click Contract.

—○ The Contract Selection dialog box appears.

—⑩ To contract the selection, type a number of pixels.

⑪ Click OK.

○ Elements contracts the selection.

COPY
with selections

You can use the selection tools to copy and paste parts of an image. One of the most common uses for the selection tool is copying parts of a graphic or image from one image or layer to another. You can use the different selection tools to cut out your subject and place that subject on another layer or even into another complete document.

To copy with a selection is simple. You can use any of the selection tools available to create an outline around the subject. Elements does not recognize any part of the image outside of the selected area,

so by clicking Edit, and then Copy, you are copying only what is on the inside of the selection boundaries. You can then simply create a new layer and paste the clipboard copy of your selection onto the new layer.

You can use selections to copy important portions of an image you are about to manipulate in order to protect against permanent changes, or to create a specifically shaped selection for a special effect such as a double image.

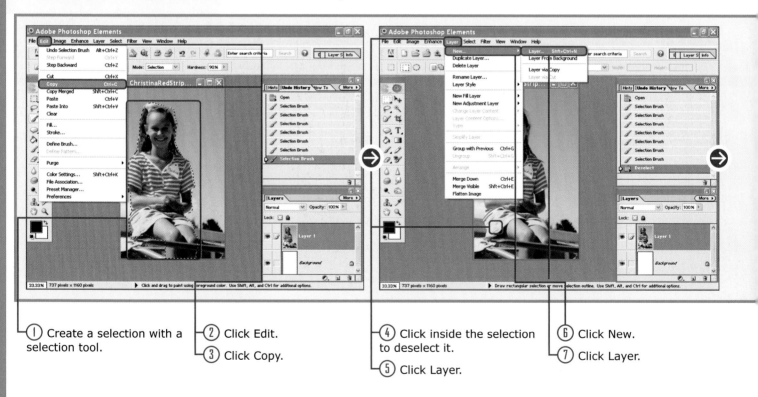

① Create a selection with a selection tool.

② Click Edit.

③ Click Copy.

④ Click inside the selection to deselect it.

⑤ Click Layer.

⑥ Click New.

⑦ Click Layer.

Did You Know? ※

You can copy all layers in an image when using selections. When you use the Copy command, you are only making a copy of the active layer. If you have a multiple layered document, you can use the Copy Merged command to create a selection copy of *all* the layers.

DIFFICULTY LEVEL

Did You Know? ※

You can place your copy in several different ways. If you do not deselect your selection, you can paste your copy directly into the original selection. If you did deselect, you can press and hold the Shift key while clicking Paste, and the object will appear in the exact center of the document.

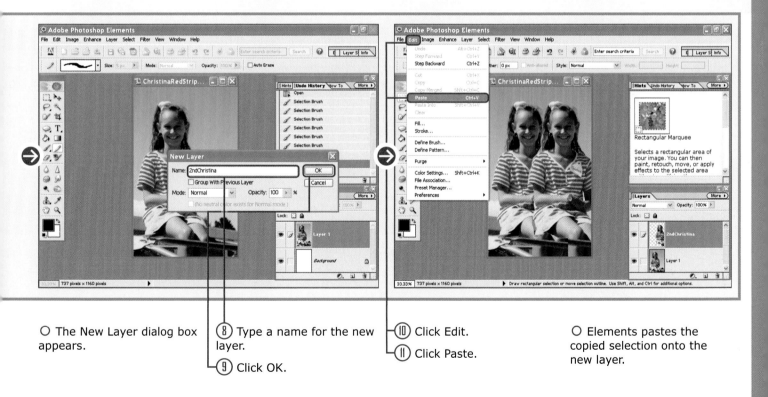

○ The New Layer dialog box appears.

⑧ Type a name for the new layer.

⑨ Click OK.

⑩ Click Edit.

⑪ Click Paste.

○ Elements pastes the copied selection onto the new layer.

TRANSFORM
your selections

You can manipulate selected areas with the Transform tool. Elements allows you to transform selections similar to transforming shapes and objects. You can also scale down and distort selections as needed. The changes you make affect only the area within the selection. This can ease workflow, by selecting a single item to transform.

You can design your selection boundaries around your transformation needs. For example, if you feather your selection, when you transform your selection area, those edges will also be feathered.

This may ruin the intended effect, or it may complement it by letting it blend in better with the surrounding areas. You can make selections with your transformation in mind to take advantage of this feature.

You click and drag the handles of the bounding box to make your changes. You can also Press and hold the Ctrl key while you click and drag to change the cursor into the Distort transform tool. You can press Enter or double-click the selected object to commit the changes.

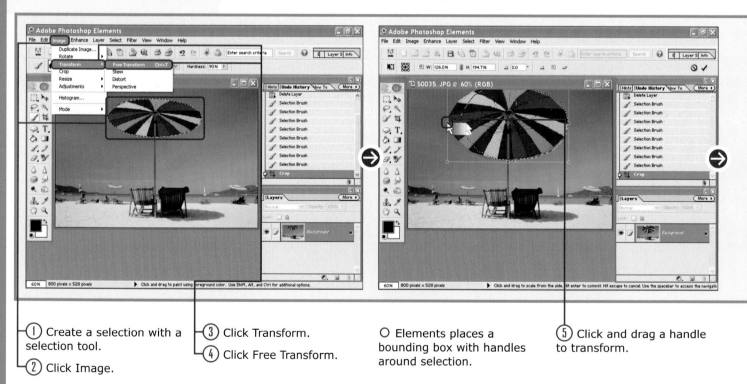

① Create a selection with a selection tool.

② Click Image.

③ Click Transform.

④ Click Free Transform.

○ Elements places a bounding box with handles around selection.

⑤ Click and drag a handle to transform.

Did You Know? ☀

You can apply transformations
equally horizontally or vertically
from your object midpoint. You can
press and hold the Shift key while scaling
it to constrain proportions to keep your
image in proportion to the original size.

Did You Know? ☀

You can free transform any object or layer, except
backgrounds. If you try to change a background, a
prompt will appear asking you to change the
background to a layer.

Did You Know? ☀

While you can also scale non-vector graphics, you
should exercise caution when doing so. Scaling a
JPG, BMP, or other pixilated formats, can result in
pixelation and loss of clarity.

DIFFICULTY LEVEL

⑥ Click here to commit
transformation.

○ Elements applies the
transformation.

⑦ Click inside the selection
to deselect.

Make a SELECTION FROM A MASK

You can use a special kind of tool, called a *mask*, to make selections in your images. When you use the selection tools, you are placing a border boundary around a specific area, and everything within those boundaries is in the selection. With masks, you can create your selection by painting over the areas you do not want seen. This makes for a very quick and easy selection tool even for complex selections, because you can paint over the areas you do not want selected. This Mask mode for selections is located in the Brush Selection tool's Mode drop-down menu.

When you use the Mask mode, you are erasing into transparency the area over which you paint. The painted area is represented by a semitransparent color, which is by default a red overlay. When you convert the masked area into a selection, any unpainted area is considered part of the selection, and the painted area is ignored and unselected. When you paint with the Mask mode, you have access to all the brush shapes in Elements.

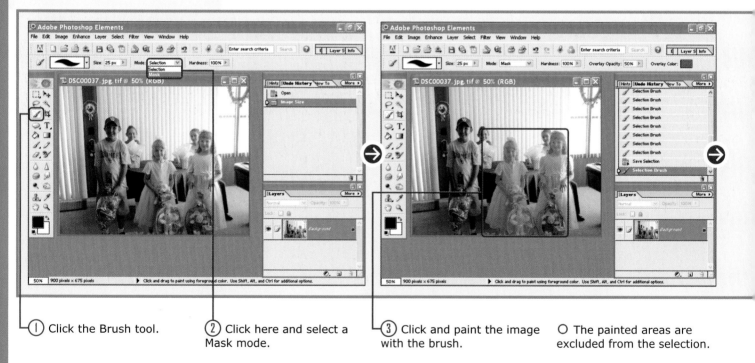

① Click the Brush tool.

② Click here and select a Mask mode.

③ Click and paint the image with the brush.

○ The painted areas are excluded from the selection.

Did You Know? ☀

You can also make mask
selections with the Type Mask tool
in the Type tool variations. Click the
Type Mask tool and your whole image
receives the red overlay from masking. You
can then type your text and it appears
normally. Click the Commit type button and your
masked text becomes a selection for filling, stroking,
or copying.

DIFFICULTY LEVEL

Did You Know? ☀

You can use any selection tool and turn it into
Mask mode. Click a selection tool, make a
selection, and click the Selection Brush tool. Click
the mode drop-down box and choose Mask. Your
image now gets the red overlay showing the mask of
all the current selections. This is useful to see clearly
what areas are affected.

④ Click here and select
Selection.

○ Elements converts the
Mask into a Selection.

FEATHER
your selections

You can create selections that have edges that are not cut and stark. Feathering an edge manipulates the selection edges to become semitransparent, or blend in the selection edges with the image behind it. You can really make use of feathered edges when dealing with copying and cutting selections from images. Feathering creates a smoother blend to the selection and less choppy and stark edges, which improve overall appearance.

Most selection tools have available feathering options that you can specify before you make a

selection. This builds the Feather option into your selection. If you do not have a feathering option or already have selection, you can access the Select menu and apply feathering there.

You can use feathering for removing elements from one image and placing them in another. You can also create framing effects, vignettes, and other edge effects. You enter the amount of feather to control the amount of blend and blur the edges of the selection receive.

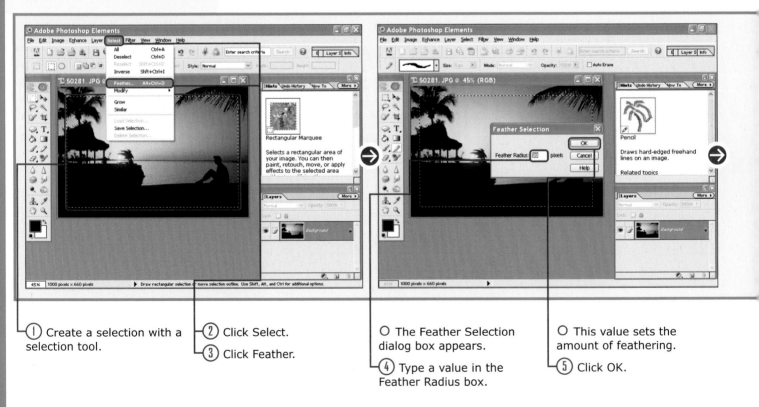

① Create a selection with a selection tool.

② Click Select.

③ Click Feather.

○ The Feather Selection dialog box appears.

④ Type a value in the Feather Radius box.

○ This value sets the amount of feathering.

⑤ Click OK.

Did You Know? ※

You can use the Feather option
for removing objects in layers.
Leave a slight outer pixel buffer around
your objects when you select them,
allowing the feather to work without erasing
or blurring the edges of your subject.

Did You Know? ※

You can feather your selections and still use
layer styles on your objects. Layer styles
recognizes a majority of the pixels involved
with the feathered edge, and applies the filter
to them as well. The result may also seem
semitransparent because of the feathering, but the
styles can still accent your graphics.

#20

DIFFICULTY LEVEL

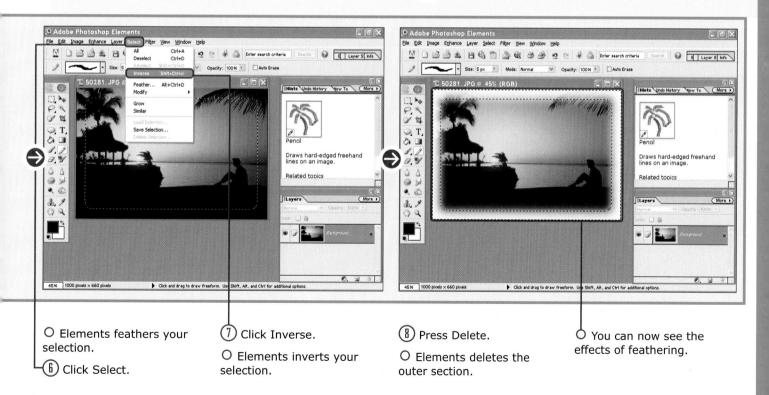

○ Elements feathers your selection.

⑥ Click Select.

⑦ Click Inverse.

○ Elements inverts your selection.

⑧ Press Delete.

○ Elements deletes the outer section.

○ You can now see the effects of feathering.

CHAPTER 3

Using Filters

Elements has a wide variety of filters that you can use for incredible effects. Although the information about filters could cover an entire book, this chapter explores some of the neater tricks. One thing to note: Filters usually permanently change the layer object or photo to which you apply them, so if you are using filters for the first time, try them on a duplicate of your image. Many filters have their own set of adjustments and settings that can completely change the final result. You can also apply filters on top of other filters to create new effects.

Filters range from simple blurs and sharpening to mimicking artistic painting styles. Distortions, sketch strokes, textures, and more are available to transform an ordinary image into an extraordinary image. In addition, you can install third-party plug-in filters to expand the abundant Elements filter collection even further. Some of these resources are discussed in Chapter 10.

This chapter covers some of the more popular and versatile filters, giving a sample of their possibilities. These techniques give you a clearer understanding of how you can use single and multiple filters to achieve your desired effects. However, experimentation is the best way to discover the uses and variety of filters, and the power they add to Photoshop Elements.

TOP 100

ADD MOVEMENT
with the Motion Blur tool

Today's cameras give you crisp, clear pictures, capturing even the most active moments. However, sometimes you want to show the movement and see the speed of motion. Magazine advertisements make frequent use of this trick, called a *motion blur*. You can take a selected object and give it a feeling of motion by creating a motion blur trailing along behind it.

Creating a motion blur involves combining several techniques, such as using layer objects and complex selections, and applying the Elements

filter and Motion Blur. The Motion Blur generates a *movement* effect on the object or image to which you apply it. When you are done, the object seems to speed across your image. When using these filters, you can click the Preview radio button to see it applied in your larger image.

To create a motion blur, start with an object on its own layer. The object can be a shape, text, or an element extracted from a selection.

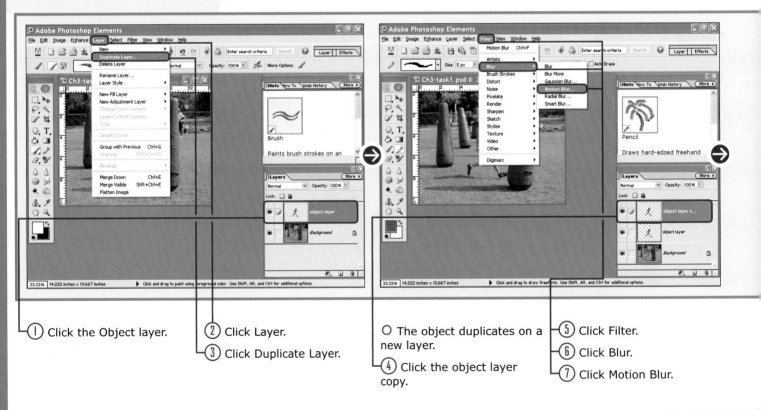

① Click the Object layer.

② Click Layer.

③ Click Duplicate Layer.

○ The object duplicates on a new layer.

④ Click the object layer copy.

⑤ Click Filter.

⑥ Click Blur.

⑦ Click Motion Blur.

DIFFICULTY LEVEL

Did You Know? ※

You can use the different Transform tools, available under the Edit menu, to further adjust the motion blur you just created. You can stretch the blur for a longer distance indicating more blur; change the angle of the blur to a different direction; and even distort the blur to create a perspective effect.

Did You Know? ※

The Gaussian Blur filter is also handy for softening photographs that are very grainy. A slight Gaussian blur can help blend in the pixelization you can get from some digital cameras or scanning older pictures. Gaussian blurs also help when creating glows or shadows that the Layer Styles cannot accommodate. A little goes a long way with Gaussian blurs, so start with smaller values.

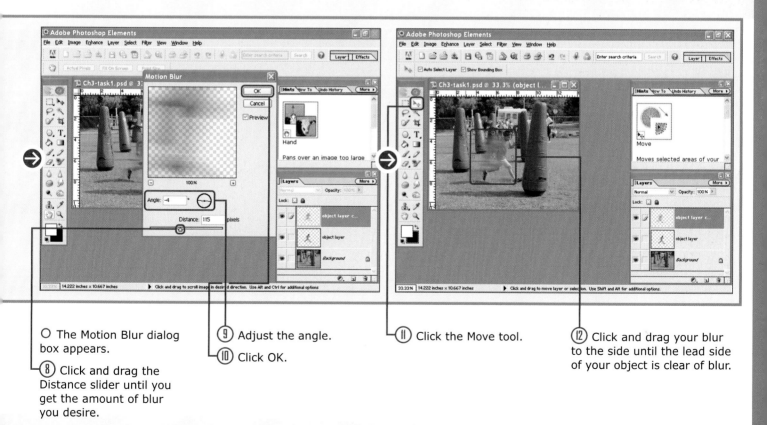

○ The Motion Blur dialog box appears.

⑧ Click and drag the Distance slider until you get the amount of blur you desire.

⑨ Adjust the angle.

⑩ Click OK.

⑪ Click the Move tool.

⑫ Click and drag your blur to the side until the lead side of your object is clear of blur.

SOFTEN HARSH EDGES
to create believable images

When you transfer objects from one photo to another, there are often rough or harsh edges on the object you relocate. Elements has filters and tools to help correct this and create a more believable assimilation into the photograph. By utilizing the Blur filters and the Blur tool, smoothing out the harsh edges is simple.

The Blur tools and filters take a contrasting set of connected pixels and balance out the colors and tones towards each other. For example, a black and white edge would change into a gray joining.

For colors, the Blur tools balance out the contrast, and create a color that is a combination of the two colors.

Ideally, a subject has high contrasting edges to the surrounding scene behind it. Elements' Blur tools blend its edges into its surroundings, making the image more believable. There is more than one way to soften harsh edges, but this trick is simple, quick, and one of the more effective methods.

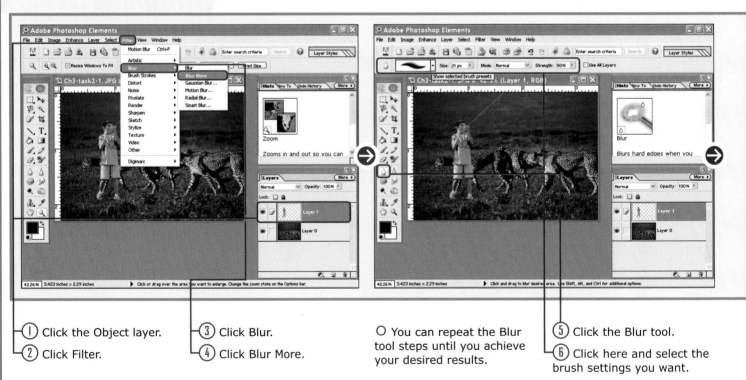

① Click the Object layer.

② Click Filter.

③ Click Blur.

④ Click Blur More.

O You can repeat the Blur tool steps until you achieve your desired results.

⑤ Click the Blur tool.

⑥ Click here and select the brush settings you want.

Caution! ※

The Blur tool, like many others, permanently affects the pixels it adjusts. Fine detail in an image can be lost rather quickly with these tools, so be cautious when using them. Do not use the Sharpen filter to attempt to recover detail in an image after using Blur, as it cannot recover the original data. You usually want to work on a duplicate image or save under a different name than the original, just to be safe.

DIFFICULTY LEVEL

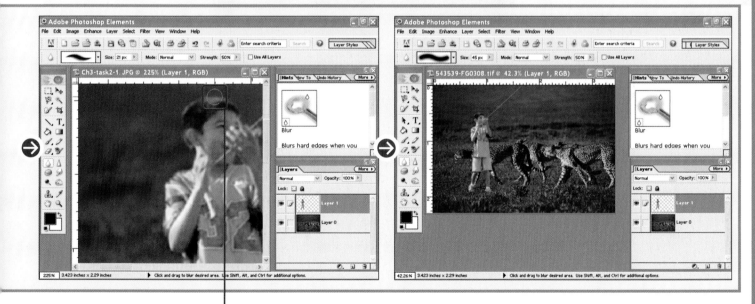

○ It may be helpful to use the Zoom tool to get closer to the edges you are blurring for better control. In this example, the Zoom tool was used to get closer to the subject.

⑦ Click and drag the Blur tool cursor along the edges of your object.

○ Elements blurs the harsh edge pixels to blend more smoothly with the surrounding image.

Use filters to
CREATE AN OLD NEWSPAPER PHOTO

You can transform your full-color photographs to resemble old newspaper photos with the filters in Elements. The process uses the Reticulation filter and the Equalize filter to create a black-and-white dot style photo, which resembles the old newsprint style of photograph. This is a neat effect for family photos and Web design.

The Reticulation filter simulates an unusual photo development technique, causing the ink to merge into dots instead of a smooth finish. These dots help recreate the photograph style of newspapers.

The Equalize tool takes the image's lightest and darkest tones, and evenly spreads all the remaining tones between them. This helps create a more neutral tone for the newspaper photo result.

It is best to work on larger-sized photos with the Reticulation tool to help keep the detail of the image. Smaller images can lose detail, especially photographs with finer features, such as human faces. Keep your image size larger to keep the details intact.

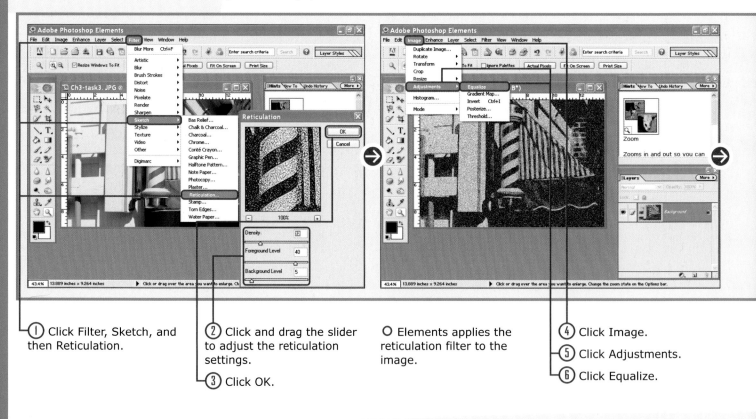

① Click Filter, Sketch, and then Reticulation.

② Click and drag the slider to adjust the reticulation settings.

③ Click OK.

○ Elements applies the reticulation filter to the image.

④ Click Image.

⑤ Click Adjustments.

⑥ Click Equalize.

Customize It! ※

You can create a color newspaper photograph by duplicating the original image layer and hiding it. Select the original layer and run the Old News Photo steps on it. Turn on the duplicate image layer, and make sure it is in position above the original layer in the Layers palette. Then, in the Blending mode drop-down menu of the Layers Palette, change the duplicate image's blending mode to Color. Changing the layer opacity makes the colors more faded out. This makes the photo look like a color newspaper image.

DIFFICULTY LEVEL

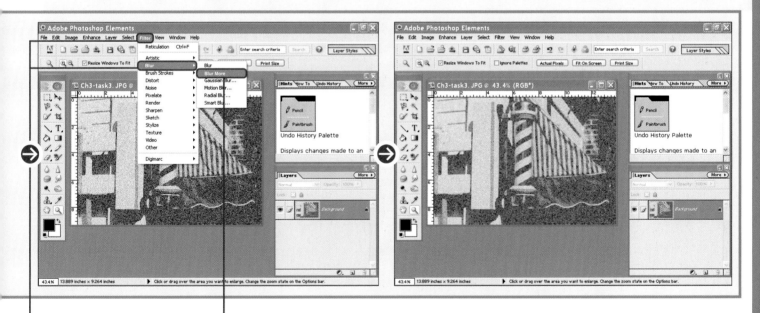

○ Elements applies Equalize to the image.

⑦ Click Filter.

⑧ Click Blur.

⑨ Click Blur More.

⑩ Repeat step **9** two to three times more.

○ Elements applies the Blur More, eliminating some of the graininess of the image.

Turn your photo into an
ARTIST'S SKETCH

Imagine taking a picture and drawing a sketch of it. By utilizing the Elements 2 filters, you can create the semblance of an artist's sketch from an ordinary photograph, a trick that you can do on almost any image. This also provides you with a base for creating items such as coloring books, trace patterns, and more.

This trick is not the only sketch transformation you can make. There are plenty of other options in the Filter menu for sketching and stylizing your art. There are filters such as the Conte Crayon,

Charcoal, and Graphic Pen, each which re-create other popular sketch styles. Experimentation is the key to discovering the value of these artistic filters.

The purpose for using the Enhance menu here is to desaturate, or remove, the colors of the image. The Enhance menu is also used to adjust the Levels of the image, which increase the clarity of the shapes within the image. This makes the Find Edges tool more accurate because the edges are clearly defined.

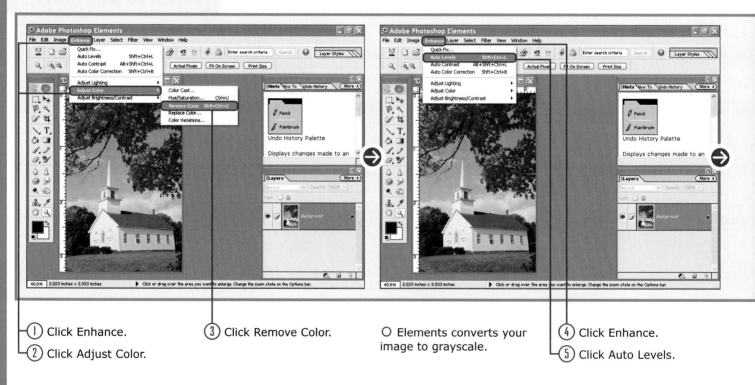

① Click Enhance.

② Click Adjust Color.

③ Click Remove Color.

○ Elements converts your image to grayscale.

④ Click Enhance.

⑤ Click Auto Levels.

Customize It! ☀

You can retain some color in your sketch by skipping the desaturation, steps **1** to **3** in this task. When you do this, Elements creates a colored pencil sketch effect that adds a completely different appeal to your final image.

DIFFICULTY LEVEL

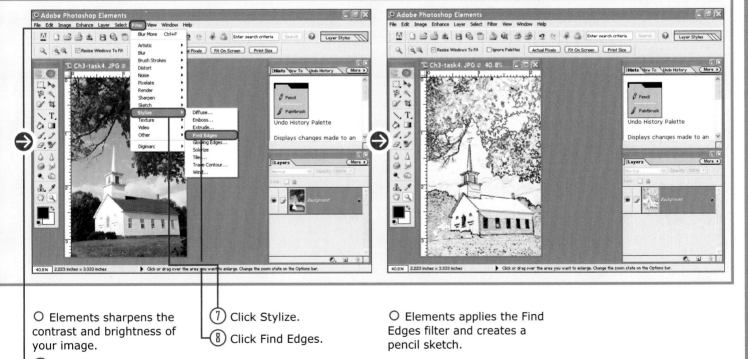

○ Elements sharpens the contrast and brightness of your image.

⑥ Click Filter.

⑦ Click Stylize.

⑧ Click Find Edges.

○ Elements applies the Find Edges filter and creates a pencil sketch.

Remove graininess and noise to
SHARPEN A PHOTO

Blur can really ruin an otherwise excellent photo. Elements has numerous tools that affect the photo's clarity and detail. By using these tools, you can re-create some of the crispness of the photo's details and improve the quality of the image.

Perhaps the most effective sharpening tool Elements offers is the Unsharp Mask tool. Too much sharpening on an image can result in intrusive noise and grain on an image, and the Unsharp tool gives you excellent precision in

balancing between clarity and clutter. It is unique in the sharpening tools because you are able to control the amount and quality of the sharpening.

The Unsharp Mask tool uses three options that affect the sharpening: Amount, Radius, and Threshold. The *Amount* specifies how much sharpening you desire, the *Radius* defines the thickness of the resultant edges, and the *Threshold* determines the relative distance in contrast the pixels must be to be affected. Together, these three allow you to maximize the sharpening of a photo or image.

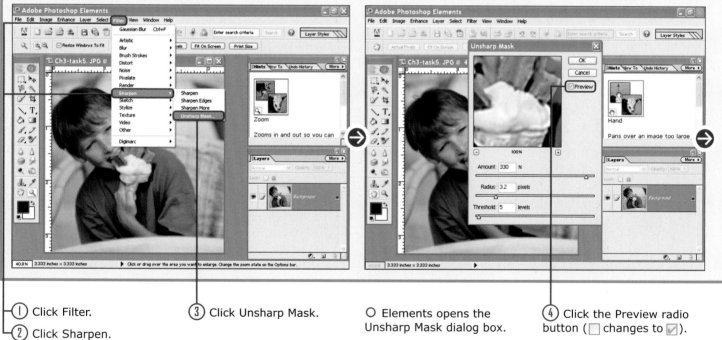

① Click Filter.

② Click Sharpen.

③ Click Unsharp Mask.

○ Elements opens the Unsharp Mask dialog box.

○ A full image preview is available in the dialog box.

④ Click the Preview radio button (☐ changes to ☑).

○ The main document will now reflect the changes you make as you make them.

Caution! ☀

The Unsharp Mask tool is very dramatic at the higher settings. In most cases, it is recommended that you use several passes of low settings on this tool to gradually sharpen a photo. Even with Undo History available, the Unsharp Mask will result in irreversible changes to your image after you save it. It is recommended that you use a duplicate of the original until you are completely satisfied with the results.

Customize It! ☀

You can use the Unsharp Mask on selections or layer objects. By simply creating your selection or selecting a specific layer, you can apply the Unsharp Mask to a specific area or item in your image. This is very useful when merging photo objects onto a separate photograph and the difference in clarity is notable.

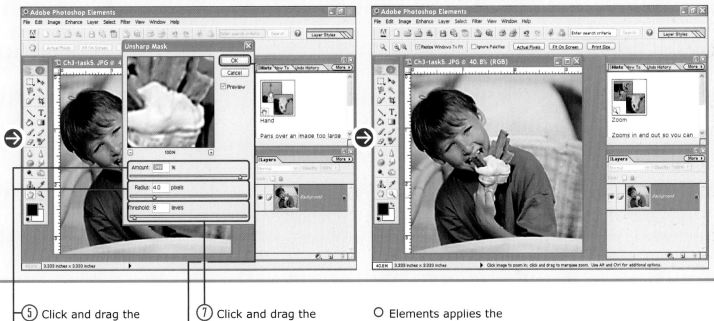

⑤ Click and drag the Amount slider to set your value.

⑥ Click and drag the Radius slider to adjust your setting.

⑦ Click and drag the Threshold slider to adjust your levels.

○ Each setting affects the other, so further adjustments may be necessary.

⑧ Click OK.

○ Elements applies the Unsharp Mask to sharpen the photo.

Use multiple filters to
CREATE A TEXTURE

Elements has numerous tools that can help you create a texture, whether it is mimicking a canvas, creating a chrome finish, or manufacturing a rock formation. The types and styles of textures are limited only to the imagination, and by using the filters in Elements, you can create textures for your own use and design.

By utilizing two filters, you can render a realistic-looking rock formation that you can use as a sandstone background texture, or a full-fledged rock outcropping for a more dynamic image.

This task introduces you to Render Clouds and Render Lighting Effects. Each of these filters has its own wide range of uses, but used together, they can create a great random texture. The Render Clouds filter generates a random mixed pattern of foreground and background colors. The Render Lighting filter is also very powerful. It can create lighting from customizable sources, and even create 3D texturing effects.

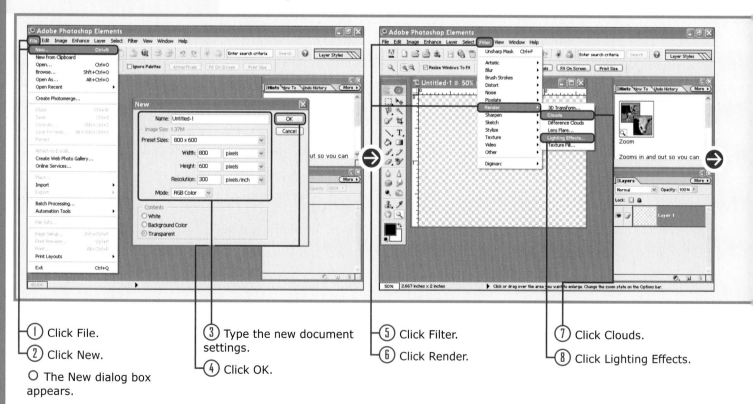

① Click File.

② Click New.

○ The New dialog box appears.

③ Type the new document settings.

④ Click OK.

⑤ Click Filter.

⑥ Click Render.

⑦ Click Clouds.

⑧ Click Lighting Effects.

Customize It! ☀

You can create textured 3D text. First, create a text layer and make a selection of your text. Then repeat steps **5** to **12** in this task and add a Bevel Style.

Customize It! ☀

You can simulate lighting on a colored surface by adjusting the colors in the Lighting Effects dialog box.

Customize It! ☀

You can achieve unique and fun effects by using other filters. After you Render Clouds, apply different filters on the results before Lighting Effects. Many filters affect the clouds, creating completely different textures.

Did You Know? ☀

You can use the Lighting Effects filter for color effects by adjusting the color boxes located in the dialog box, and selecting None in the Texture Channel menu.

#26

DIFFICULTY LEVEL

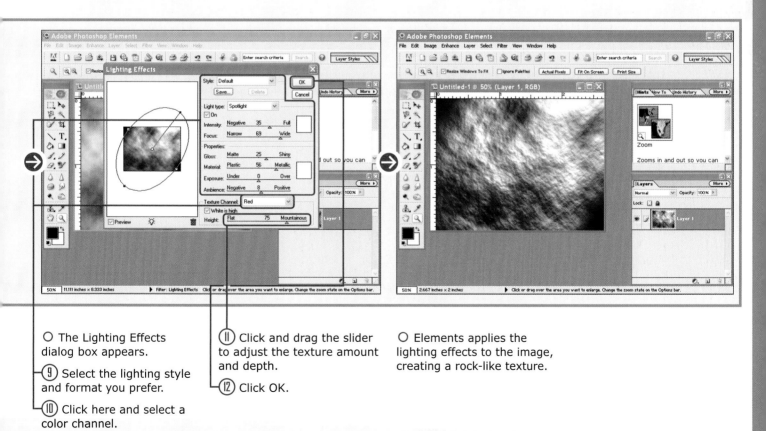

○ The Lighting Effects dialog box appears.

⑨ Select the lighting style and format you prefer.

⑩ Click here and select a color channel.

⑪ Click and drag the slider to adjust the texture amount and depth.

⑫ Click OK.

○ Elements applies the lighting effects to the image, creating a rock-like texture.

Turn your photos into
WATERCOLOR ART

You can transform a regular photograph into a watercolor by using two Artistic filters. Elements enables you to take a photograph and transform it into a different medium to look as if it were painted with oils or watercolors. In Elements, you can choose from several filters with multiple combinations that enable you to manipulate photos into different strokes and textures, and mimic other artistic mediums. The simplicity with which you can convert image to art is amazing, and the effects are easily changeable. Play with the different filter styles to see what kind of mediums you can re-create.

You can re-create a realistic watercolor painting style using the Watercolor filter, which mimics the soft saturated edges and posterized colors of a real watercolor painting. After a second repetition to emphasize the style, you can apply the Dry Brush filter to create the random stroke of a brush on canvas.

Repetitive use of the same filters can intensify the effects. Adding textures can mimic the effect of canvas to complete the illusion of a rendered watercolor painting. Experiment, as always, to learn more of the subtleties of filter interaction.

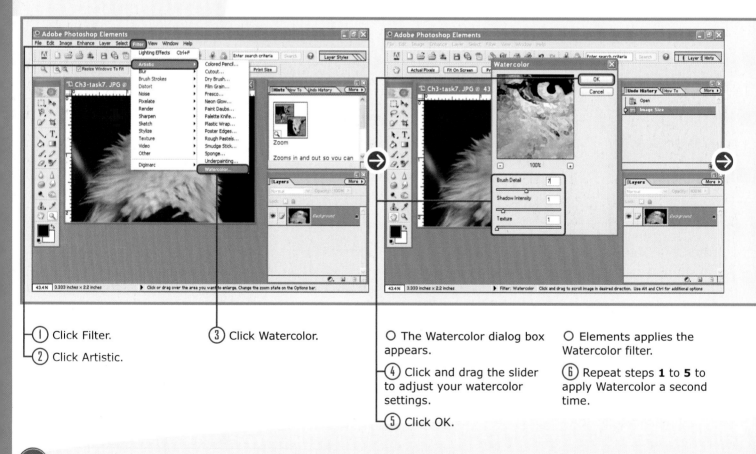

① Click Filter.

② Click Artistic.

③ Click Watercolor.

○ The Watercolor dialog box appears.

④ Click and drag the slider to adjust your watercolor settings.

⑤ Click OK.

○ Elements applies the Watercolor filter.

⑥ Repeat steps **1** to **5** to apply Watercolor a second time.

Put It Together! ※

You can convert an image to watercolor. Take the final product and apply the framing task #31. This technique combination can create fully-framed artwork worthy of hanging up, or sending online to family and friends.

Customize It! ※

You can click Filter, Artistic, and Cutout filter, or perhaps Image, Adjustments, and Posterize, or any of the Blur functions to reduce the amount of fine detail in the original photo for a more abstract effect to this technique.

#27

DIFFICULTY LEVEL

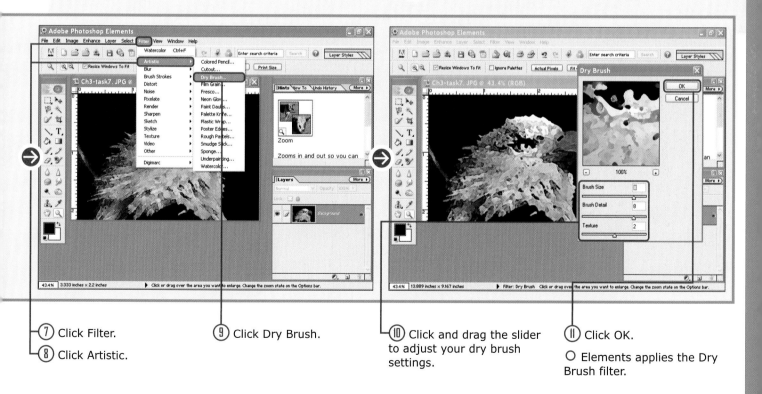

⑦ Click Filter.

⑧ Click Artistic.

⑨ Click Dry Brush.

⑩ Click and drag the slider to adjust your dry brush settings.

⑪ Click OK.

○ Elements applies the Dry Brush filter.

Add flair to 3-D text using
LIGHTING EFFECTS

You can create very sophisticated shading and texture effects in Elements. Making 3D type and shapes is not always as easy as applying a Bevel Style. The Lighting Effects filter is a very powerful Elements tool for creating 3D shading results. It can apply many different multidirectional lighting effects mimicking many different types of light, from a simple spotlight to a five-light parallel lighting strip. It also has multiple slider options that can intensify and affect the result.

There is also a Texture Channel option, where you can choose any one of the RGB channels of a color

photo, or the transparency channel of your layer. Select the Texture channel and set the amount of texture you want with the height slider. The Lighting Effects filter is one of the strongest filters Elements has to offer.

By using a Blur tool, and then rendering the Lighting Effects filter, you can cause the Texture Channel to create faux shading, and therefore your 3D effect. However, you have a much smoother and customizable definition of shading by using multiple layers.

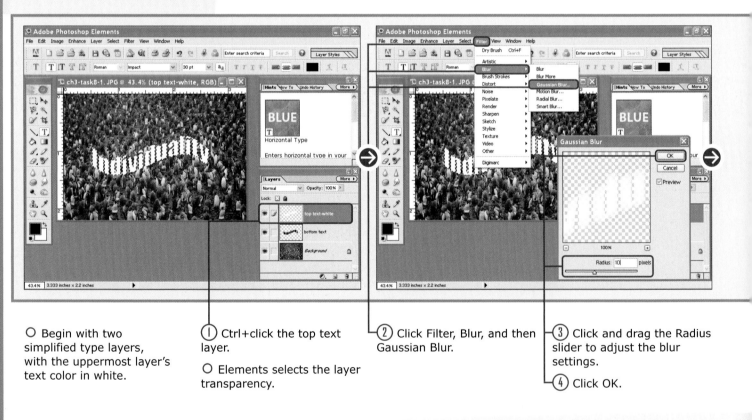

○ Begin with two simplified type layers, with the uppermost layer's text color in white.

① Ctrl+click the top text layer.

○ Elements selects the layer transparency.

② Click Filter, Blur, and then Gaussian Blur.

③ Click and drag the Radius slider to adjust the blur settings.

④ Click OK.

Apply It! ☀

You can create high-quality
3D effects easily by using multiple
layers and adding some color in the
Color options. You can also use this
technique with custom shapes and brushes.
You need to simplify shapes before you can use
some of the filters on them. Brushstrokes are
already simplified after you draw them. You can
apply filter effects right away.

DIFFICULTY LEVEL

Customize It! ☀

By selecting a different color of text for the
bottom text layer, you can completely change the
background color of the text. Because the top
layer is blurred, the color shows through on the
edges. This is not a similar effect to what a colored
lighting effect would do, but adds color to the text
base layer.

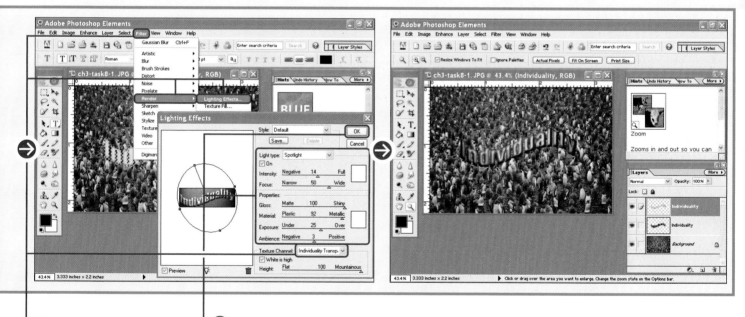

○ Elements applies the blur.

⑤ Click Filter, Render, and then Lighting Effects.

⑥ Click here and select Layer Transparency.

⑦ Click and drag the slider to adjust the Light type and Properties options.

⑧ Click OK.

○ Elements will apply the Lighting Effects filter.

ADD GHOSTLY OVERLAYS
to your image

Elements filters can help you create ghostly overlays of one image over another. You start with each image on its own layer. By using the Gaussian Blur and Diffuse Glow filters, and the Layer Opacity, you can adjust one of the images to seem ghostly and faded into the background. This can result in an ethereal and subtle backdrop to the central object in the photo.

Semi-transparent overlays generate dozens of different uses, from simple overlays for artistic effect, to subtle reflections on a polished surface, to faded imagery on textured surfaces. You can even use it to actually generate a ghost-like effect for spooky layouts.

① Click Filter, Distort, and then Diffuse Glow.

② Click and drag the slider to adjust the Diffuse Glow settings.

③ Click OK.

○ Elements applies the Diffuse Glow filter.

④ Click Filter, Blur, and then Gaussian Blur.

⑤ Click and drag the Radius slider to adjust the blur amount.

⑥ Click OK.

Customize It! ※

By using the Enhance menu, you can alter the image in many ways before applying ghostly overlays. Desaturating the image before you blur and distort the photo object can create a more subtle or withdrawn effect, as can creating a duotone color on the image. See task 70 for more on duotones.

Customize It! ※

You can use the Wave filter or the Liquefy tool to alter the basic shape of the photo overlay into a more ethereal looking image for more ghostly effects. You can desaturate the object to eliminate color, and then distort the object with the Liquefy tool. Apply an Outer Glow Layer style, like Blue Ghost, to achieve a truly spectral effect.

○ Elements applies the Gaussian blur.

⑦ In the Layer palette, click Opacity.

⑧ Click and drag the Opacity slider to adjust the amount.

○ Elements lowers the opacity of the object to achieve your desired effect.

Combine images to
CREATE A SEAMLESS BACKGROUND

You can use Elements to create a seamless background from images. Seamless backgrounds are very useful, from Web pages to texturing a large object. Elements contains tools that you can use to alter textures or images to turn them into seamless backgrounds.

Elements has a filter called Offset that shifts image pixels up, down, and side-to-side. There are several options for shifting pixels, which produce various effects when shifted outside the boundaries of the image. The Set to Background option replaces the empty space with the background color. The Repeat

Edge Pixels repetitively duplicates the edge pixels as far as the offset is defined. Wrap Around shifts pixels, leaving the image on the corresponding spot on the opposite side; for example, the bottom-right corner pixels moving down and right would end up in the upper-left corner.

With the Clone Stamp tool, you can replace pixels with pixels from a spot elsewhere in your image. You define that area using the Alt key with the tool. When you move your brush, the defined spot moves in tandem with your brush, reproducing the corresponding pixels.

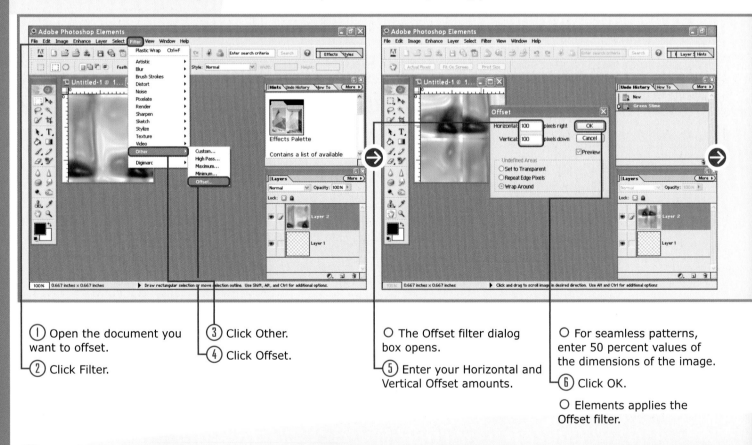

① Open the document you want to offset.

② Click Filter.

③ Click Other.

④ Click Offset.

○ The Offset filter dialog box opens.

⑤ Enter your Horizontal and Vertical Offset amounts.

○ For seamless patterns, enter 50 percent values of the dimensions of the image.

⑥ Click OK.

○ Elements applies the Offset filter.

#30

Did You Know? ※

The best seamless backgrounds are items that are easily repetitive, such as beans, stucco, or geometric shapes. Singular items or evenly spaced items that do not overlap the edges of the document can also make good backgrounds. Full photos of a skyline with a sunset, or similar images, are awkward and difficult to pattern seamlessly and tend not to make a good background as a pattern nor do any images that have high contrast.

Apply It! ※

Place a perfectly symmetrical object such as a circle or square, centered on a plain square background. Because the object and image are symmetrical, a 50 percent Offset will result in ¼ of the object perfectly placed in each corner with the center of the image now empty. You can add to the center, or leave as is, and it is already seamless!

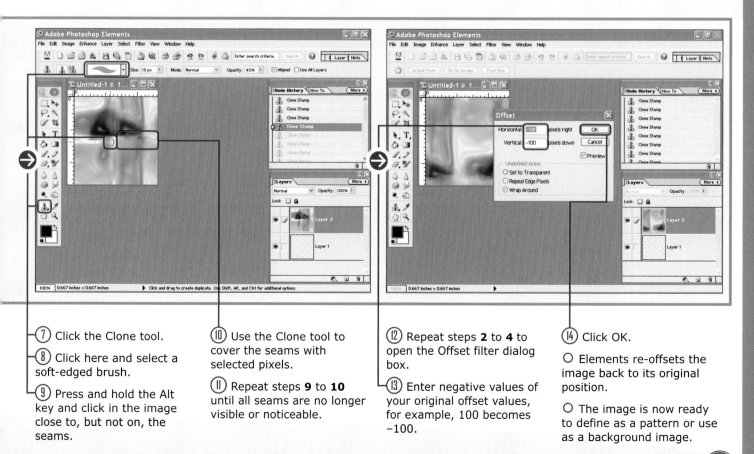

⑦ Click the Clone tool.

⑧ Click here and select a soft-edged brush.

⑨ Press and hold the Alt key and click in the image close to, but not on, the seams.

⑩ Use the Clone tool to cover the seams with selected pixels.

⑪ Repeat steps **9** to **10** until all seams are no longer visible or noticeable.

⑫ Repeat steps **2** to **4** to open the Offset filter dialog box.

⑬ Enter negative values of your original offset values, for example, 100 becomes −100.

⑭ Click OK.

○ Elements re-offsets the image back to its original position.

○ The image is now ready to define as a pattern or use as a background image.

CHAPTER 4

Work with Effects and Styles

In addition to Filters, Elements contains a wide variety of other image and text enhancers called *Effects* and *Styles* that you can apply to your photos, shapes, and text. You can use these effects for a wide variety of uses and results, from applying a brick wall to creating a glassy beveled text. Effects and Styles are located in two separate palettes — the Window menu and in the docking area. Elements uses Effects and Styles to create and enhance your photographs and layered objects, taking them from plain and ordinary to dynamic and exciting.

You can apply the dozens of different results from the Effects palette to text, photos, and shapes. The Effects palette even has a separate section for effects that you can apply specifically to text layers. The Layer Styles palette has 14 different categories of styles available, and you can use each of them on text, shapes, and images.

There is a key difference between Effects and Styles. You can apply an Effect and it will change your object irreversibly with its special effect. You cannot edit Effects after they are applied. With layer styles, you can edit the text or shape directly, changing font, size, and more and the layer style will adjust itself to your new text or shapes. You can also edit certain aspects of the Layer Style itself. You can get amazing results on your graphics with these powerful tools.

TOP 100

FRAME
your pictures

You can quickly create a framed wall of photos for your digital photo albums and other graphics projects easily with Elements 2. Not every photograph needs a frame, but some shots just cry out for it. From family walls to digital photos on a Web site, photograph frames are commonplace. Elements has many neat ways to create frames.

You can create frames by using the Stroke command, which draws pixels in relation to a selection's boundary. Several options change this

effect for a variety of uses. After the stroke is placed, you can use Layer Styles to create a custom carved look.

You can also make frames using the Effects palette built-in frame effects in its Effect menu. You can use these quick, easy, and effective frame styles for a wide variety of effects on your photographs.

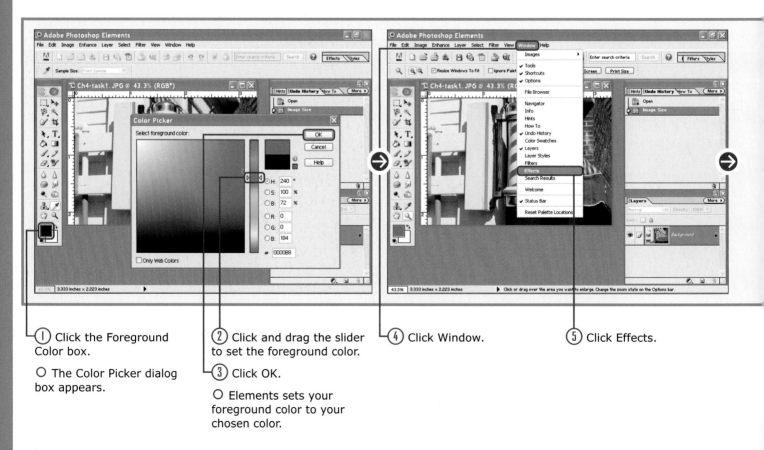

① Click the Foreground Color box.

○ The Color Picker dialog box appears.

② Click and drag the slider to set the foreground color.

③ Click OK.

○ Elements sets your foreground color to your chosen color.

④ Click Window.

⑤ Click Effects.

31

DIFFICULTY LEVEL

Customize It!

You can adjust the layer styles by double-clicking the little *f* icon ( ) on any layer that contains one. This opens a dialog box, which allows adjustments to the particular layer effect you chose. Try increasing the size of the bevel and see what happens.

Caution!

You can use many of the frames and still be able to affect and adjust your photo. Most frame effects do not alter your original image. However, some directly change your image, and after you save the file, you cannot undo the changes. You can use these effects on a duplicate of your photo to prevent any accidental mishaps from ruining your pictures.

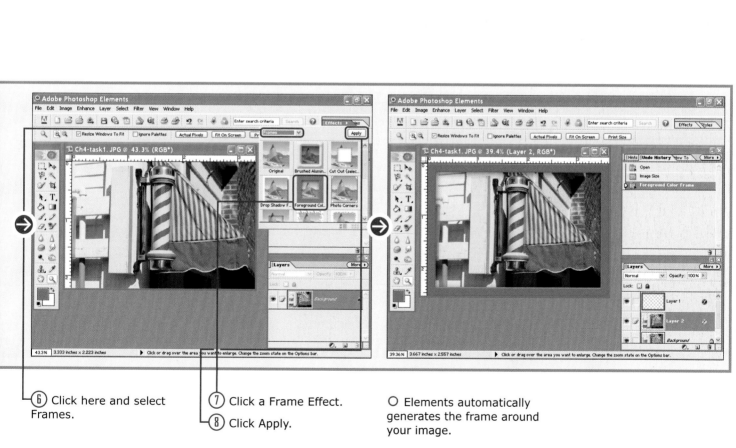

⑥ Click here and select Frames.

⑦ Click a Frame Effect.

⑧ Click Apply.

○ Elements automatically generates the frame around your image.

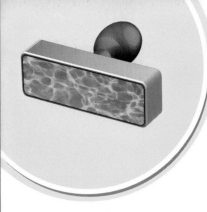

CREATE A SNOWSTORM
in your image

You can make it snow in your photographs. Elements has a great effect available that can make it snow anytime, anywhere, and on anyone. You can find the Blizzard effect in the Effects palette under the Image effects section. It generates, using a preset combination of filters and tools, a realistic looking scene of snow falling. You can use this to add snow to your winter photos, or even make it snow on the beach.

A benefit of this effect is that it does not affect the original image or selection. It creates its own layer, generates the blizzard, and sets the layer-blending mode to Screen. The Screen blending mode ignores the midtones and shadows of the blended layer, and accentuates the highlights, or in this case, the white snow. If you do not like the effect, you can make the layer invisible or delete it altogether, and it will not affect your original image.

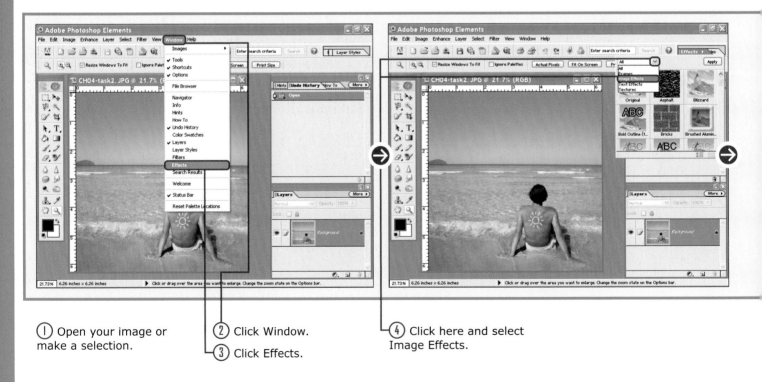

① Open your image or make a selection.

② Click Window.

③ Click Effects.

④ Click here and select Image Effects.

Customize It!

You can make an even heavier snowstorm on your image. Select your image layer and apply the Blizzard effect a second time. Running the effect again creates another snow layer, doubling the effect of the snow. Because the Blizzard effect creates a random snow pattern each time, it will make the storm look fiercer rather than having duplicate snow patterns.

Apply It!

You can make it snow inside a home or other impossible place. Find a photo that contains a large window to a summer morning or an open door leading to a visible room inside the home. Make a selection based on the windowpanes or the open door and apply the Blizzard effect to it.

⑤ Click Blizzard.

⑥ Click Apply.

○ Elements applies the Blizzard effect.

Create a
WATER REFLECTION

You can flip your text and generate a random wavy warp to the letters to simulate waves on water with the Water Reflection effect. Elements has taken a popular text effect and turned it into an easy trick. Water reflections have been the inspiration for untold numbers of paintings, photographs, and drawings, and now with Elements Effects palette, you can re-create that effect with your text.

You can generate a text layer, apply the Water Reflection effect, and Elements duplicates the text as if it were reflected in front of the text itself, in

whatever color text you created. You can take this one step further and add a layer style to the text as well, so that the result is a more stylized reflection. It is a great way to add more realism to the reflection.

You can apply the Water Reflection and all other text effects only on text layers. These effects do not work on regular photos, selections, or simplified objects.

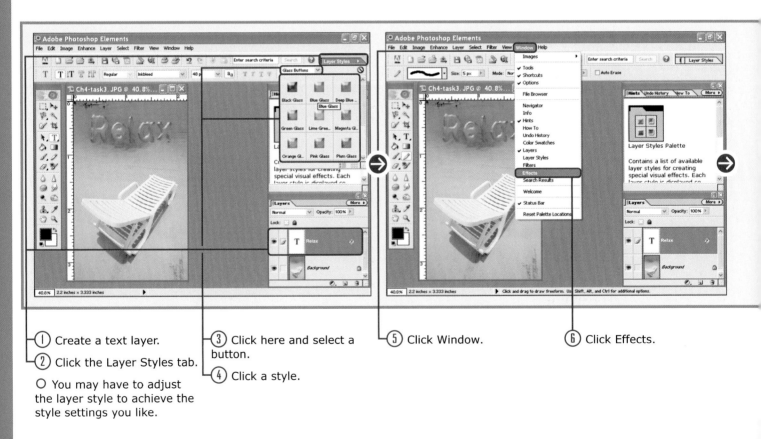

① Create a text layer.

② Click the Layer Styles tab.

○ You may have to adjust the layer style to achieve the style settings you like.

③ Click here and select a button.

④ Click a style.

⑤ Click Window.

⑥ Click Effects.

DIFFICULTY LEVEL

Customize It!

You can apply any kind of layer style or text alteration before applying the Water Reflection effect, as long as it does not simplify the text layer. If the text layer is simplified, the text effects will not work. You can use the Text Warp tool to apply a Flag or Bloat distortion to the text, and then apply the Water Reflection effect.

Caution!

After you apply a text effect, Elements simplifies your text layer, and you can no longer edit it or change the font, size, or color. Try these effects on duplicate layers of your text, or hold off until last to try the effects so you can go back into the Undo History menu and undo the last application. After you save, the effect is permanent.

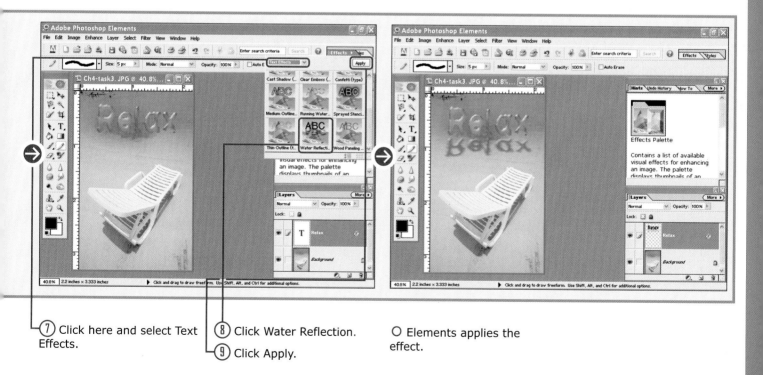

⑦ Click here and select Text Effects.

⑧ Click Water Reflection.

⑨ Click Apply.

○ Elements applies the effect.

Add
CHROME
to text and shapes

You can use Elements to create a metallic shine to your text and shapes. Elements knows how useful and popular chrome effects are and designed multiple layer styles to mimic different blends and styles of chrome. You can find the WOW Chrome in the layer styles palette. It contains several variations of chrome effects that are useful to have.

You can adjust the WOW Chrome styles, as with any layer style. You can make dramatically different results by adjusting bevels and shadows. Double-clicking the *f* icon in the layer with the style will open the Layer Style Adjustment dialog box.

layer styles are easy to apply to text and shapes alike. You can edit shapes and text until you simplify them, any changes made to the base shape or text, will automatically have the style effect adapt and apply to them. You can use this to your advantage because you can make edits and changes while still retaining the original shapes clarity, and the chrome effect will be just as clear.

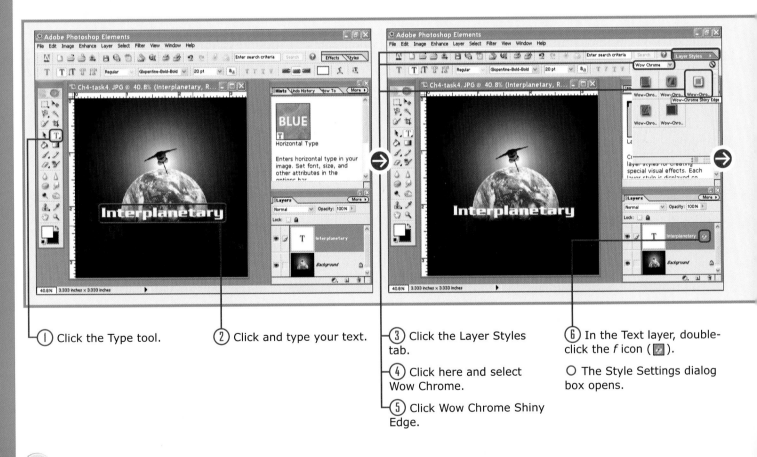

① Click the Type tool.

② Click and type your text.

③ Click the Layer Styles tab.

④ Click here and select Wow Chrome.

⑤ Click Wow Chrome Shiny Edge.

⑥ In the Text layer, double-click the *f* icon ( ).

○ The Style Settings dialog box opens.

Customize It! ⁂

You can add some real flair to the chrome effects with the brush tools. Create a new layer above the others. In the Brush palette, select one of the Star brushes, set your foreground color to white, and you can add light gleams shining off the chrome to enhance the shiny new effect you just created. The final image in this example has Star brushes applied to it.

Did You Know? ⁂

You can merge the layer and style together. Create a blank layer directly below the layer with a style applied. Select the layer with the style and link the two layers together in the Layers palette. Click Layer, and then Merge Layers. This combines the layers together, flattening the layer style onto the other layer.

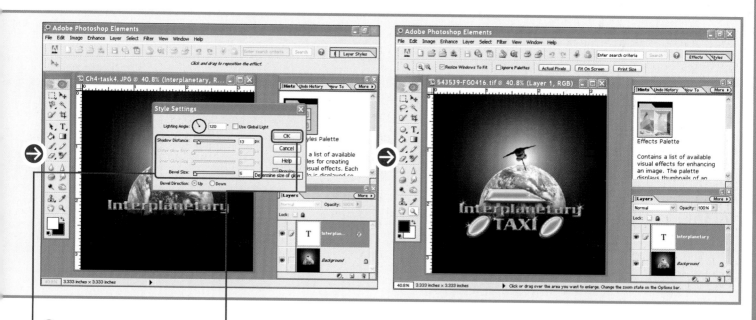

⑦ Click and drag the slider to adjust each setting.

⑧ Click OK.

○ Elements applies adjustments.

○ The text and shapes appear coated in chrome.

○ You may add other text and custom shapes as desired by repeating steps **3** to **8**.

Make a
RUBBER STAMP

You can create a personal mark that you can use like a rubber stamp on your projects. Elements has a nice effect called *Rubber Stamp*, and it creates a square-edged stamp out of whatever image you put forth. Higher quality, higher resolution images, such as complex photographs, do not make good stamps, simply because during the effect process, colors are flattened and posterized to a single color, ruining the details. Gradients do not survive this trip very well, either. You can make effective rubber stamps by keeping your original image simple in colors and design.

One nice touch here is that you can use the Rubber Stamp effect and convert the result into a custom brush. This is very handy for personal marks on protected images or digital documents. By defining the image as a brush, you can use it in any document you create in Elements, or even create a small image that you can insert into a word processing document or spreadsheet.

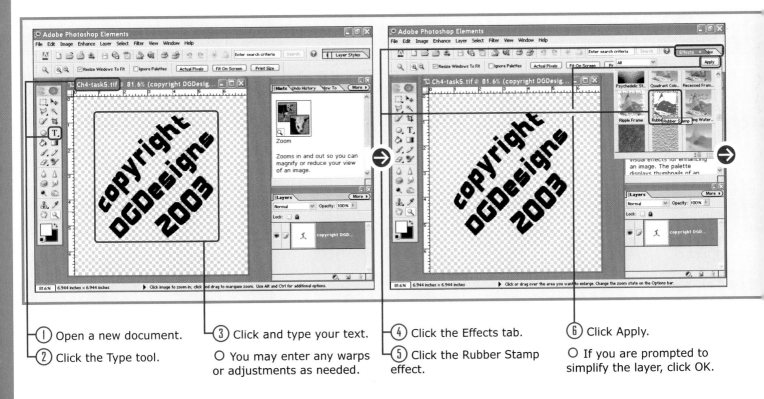

① Open a new document.

② Click the Type tool.

③ Click and type your text.

○ You may enter any warps or adjustments as needed.

④ Click the Effects tab.

⑤ Click the Rubber Stamp effect.

⑥ Click Apply.

○ If you are prompted to simplify the layer, click OK.

Customize It!

You can make versatile
variations of your rubber stamp.
Before you apply the Rubber Stamp
effect, duplicate your image and resize it.
Apply the Rubber Stamp to the resized
image. You can duplicate and resize several
different copies of your original image, and when
you finish, you can define them each as a brush,
too. This gives you different sizes you can use in
almost any sized document or image. Resizing applied
brushes results in pixilated edges and loss of clarity.

Did You Know?

Even though the Rubber Stamp tool makes the result in red,
the brush always defaults to the foreground color you select
when using it, unless your image is in grayscale mode.

#35

DIFFICULTY LEVEL

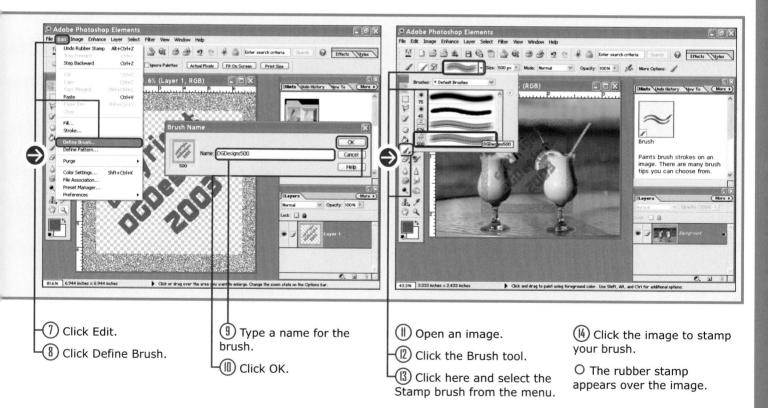

⑦ Click Edit.

⑧ Click Define Brush.

⑨ Type a name for the brush.

⑩ Click OK.

⑪ Open an image.

⑫ Click the Brush tool.

⑬ Click here and select the Stamp brush from the menu.

⑭ Click the image to stamp your brush.

○ The rubber stamp appears over the image.

BLUR THE BACKGROUND
to make an image stand out

You can use blur to bring an object to the center of attention. The Blur tool has many uses, and it usually results in the loss of focus, drawing attention away from the content. Some images have a very strong character object that can get lost in the detail surrounding it. Professional photographers use dozens of different camera filters to get a blurred edge frame surrounding their subject. You can use Elements to re-create this effect using filters and selections, mimicking the vignette blur filter for cameras.

The method is straightforward. You select the object you want as the focus of the image, and blur everything else around it. How much and in what manner you blur around the object can define the mood of the final image as well. The method here is dynamic and works well on active subjects. Blurring the surroundings is a very effective method of focusing attention on a specific subject that you can use easily.

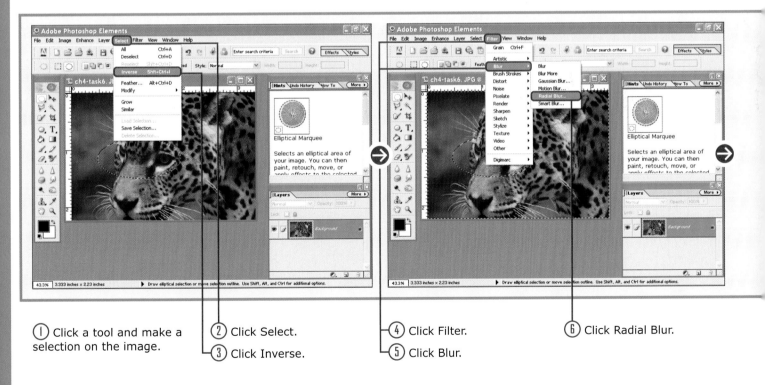

① Click a tool and make a selection on the image.

② Click Select.

③ Click Inverse.

④ Click Filter.

⑤ Click Blur.

⑥ Click Radial Blur.

Customize It!

You can accomplish many variations by using the selection tool adjustments. When making your initial selection, try feathering the edges, so that when you run the Blur effect, it blends smoothly with the edges of the un-blurred section. In addition, using symmetrical shapes can add additional focus to an object as shown in our example, but custom selections are great for complex subjects, such as people and nature.

Customize It!

The types and amount of blurs you use can also impact your result. Using the Zoom filter as above adds a dynamic effect to the results. Using the Gaussian blur instead creates a softer effect, allowing the subject to be the mood-creating object. Try using the motion blur to generate a directional movement, which accents active subjects as well. Experimentation is the key here to discovering how a blur can focus attention.

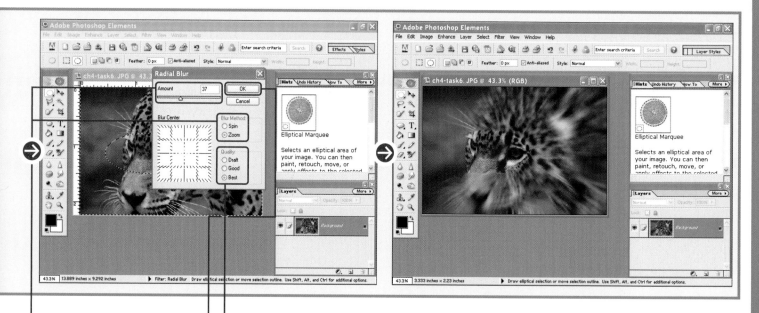

○ The Radial Blur dialog box appears.

⑦ Select a Blur Method (○ changes to ◉).

⑧ Click and drag the Amount slider to adjust the setting.

⑨ Select the Quality (○ changes to ◉).

⑩ Click OK.

○ Elements applies Radial Blur.

Note: To turn off your selection, click Select and then Deselect from the menu.

Add a
STUDIO TARP EFFECT
to a background

You can make your object or photo subject look like they are standing in front of a photographer's canvas backdrop. Studio photographers have dozens of different backdrops for their photo subjects to stand in front of, and usually the fabric nature of the backdrop is obvious. Elements can take a real or inserted image backdrop for an object and make the photo look like a painted tarp hanging behind a subject. This tarp effect is a humorous effect that can be used in Web photo albums or advertising.

To re-create this effect, you can use any photo with a clear subject. Simply make a selection of your object, invert the selection to get the entire backdrop, and apply an artistic paint effect and a texture to mimic the studio props. You can feather your selection for a less crisp edge to the subject, if you wish. This effect is just one way to separate the subject and its surrounding environment to direct focus in the image.

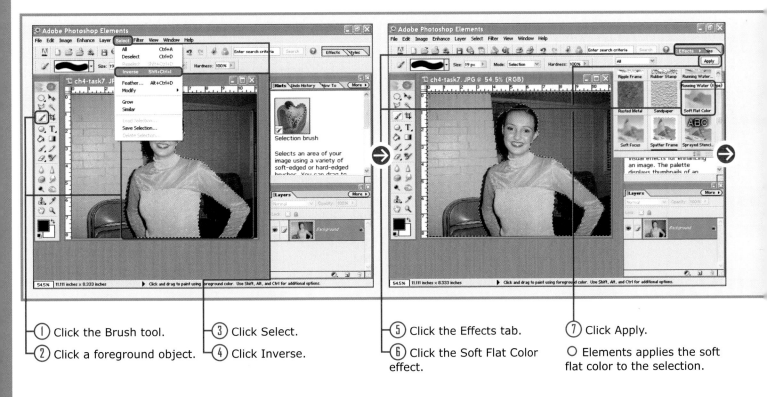

① Click the Brush tool.

② Click a foreground object.

③ Click Select.

④ Click Inverse.

⑤ Click the Effects tab.

⑥ Click the Soft Flat Color effect.

⑦ Click Apply.

○ Elements applies the soft flat color to the selection.

Customize It!

Instead of changing the
background of the actual image,
try cutting out your selected object
and placing it on a very unlikely or
unusual background image. How about
putting your daughter on the moon, or making
a Christmas photo from a snapshot in a bathing
suit? This can make your photos look like a studio
portrait shot with a fully customizable backdrop.
Experimentation can lead to some very unusual results.

DIFFICULTY LEVEL

Caution!

This trick irreversibly changes the background of an image.
Data and pixel information are transformed permanently, so it
is recommended that you duplicate your original image before
you apply these effects, just to be safe.

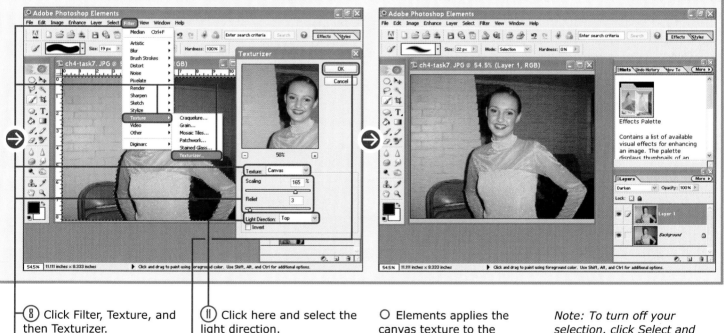

⑧ Click Filter, Texture, and
then Texturizer.

⑨ Click here and select the
Canvas texture.

⑩ Click and drag the sliders
to adjust the scaling and
relief.

⑪ Click here and select the
light direction.

⑫ Click OK.

○ Elements applies the
canvas texture to the
background.

*Note: To turn off your
selection, click Select and
then Deselect from the
menu.*

Change
DAY INTO NIGHT

You can use Elements to take a daytime photograph and transform it into a nighttime photograph. Elements has tools and effects that can simulate a change in time, and place you in the evening with a beautiful sunset. You can take a photograph that is captured during the day and create the illusion of being at sundown.

You can do this with the Sunset effect. You accomplish the effect by removing the sky from your image and replacing it with a colorful, deep sunset generated

by this tool in the Effects palette. You can then select your foreground and use brightness and contrast tools to darken the overall tone. The result is that you have shifted the hours, from dawn to dusk, in no time at all.

You can apply this technique to any image with a skyline. You can also adapt it for scenes through a window. By substituting a daytime sky and lightening the foreground, you could create a sunrise effect as well.

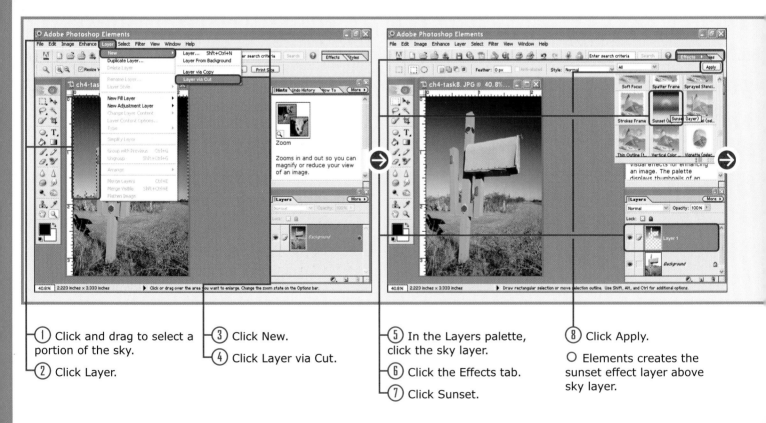

① Click and drag to select a portion of the sky.

② Click Layer.

③ Click New.

④ Click Layer via Cut.

⑤ In the Layers palette, click the sky layer.

⑥ Click the Effects tab.

⑦ Click Sunset.

⑧ Click Apply.

○ Elements creates the sunset effect layer above sky layer.

Apply It!

You can use the Lighting Effects filter, see task 28, to create sunset style lighting on your objects. In the Lighting Effects dialog box, click the color selection boxes and select colors close to your backdrop. Select your lighting style and apply it. You can use this setting to imitate sunset lighting, or the back lighting of an object in silhouette to a colorful sunset.

Customize It!

You can apply different backgrounds for different effects. You can also use Cloudy skies instead of clear, or starry night with a full moon, or even a dark storm cloud. Take your new backdrop, copy it, and paste it in its separate layer above the background layer for a new sunset.

DIFFICULTY LEVEL

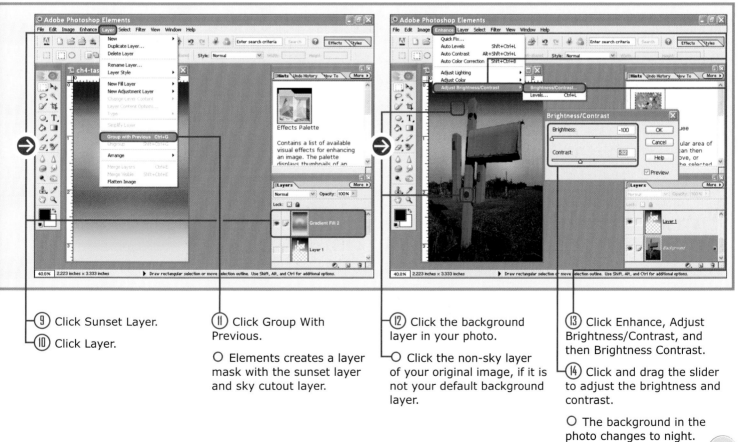

⑨ Click Sunset Layer.

⑩ Click Layer.

⑪ Click Group With Previous.

○ Elements creates a layer mask with the sunset layer and sky cutout layer.

⑫ Click the background layer in your photo.

○ Click the non-sky layer of your original image, if it is not your default background layer.

⑬ Click Enhance, Adjust Brightness/Contrast, and then Brightness Contrast.

⑭ Click and drag the slider to adjust the brightness and contrast.

○ The background in the photo changes to night.

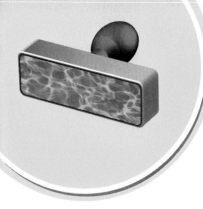

NEON EFFECTS

You can re-create the unique lighting styles of a neon light with a little help from Elements. Neon lights shine brightly with clearly defined boundaries, but are soft enough to view with the eyes. Elements has layer styles that can re-create this effect on your text or even your shapes.

The three keys to this effect are the color of your text and the use of an outer glow layer style and an inner glow layer style. It is best to use a round

edged font, preferably a thin one as well, to best emulate the thin tubing associated with neon lights. Shapes are best when they are tube lines forming an outline, similar to the layout on a neon sign. Intensity is a trademark of most neon lighting, and you can achieve that by duplicating the image and magnifying the glows. When you are finished, the product is bright and eye-catching.

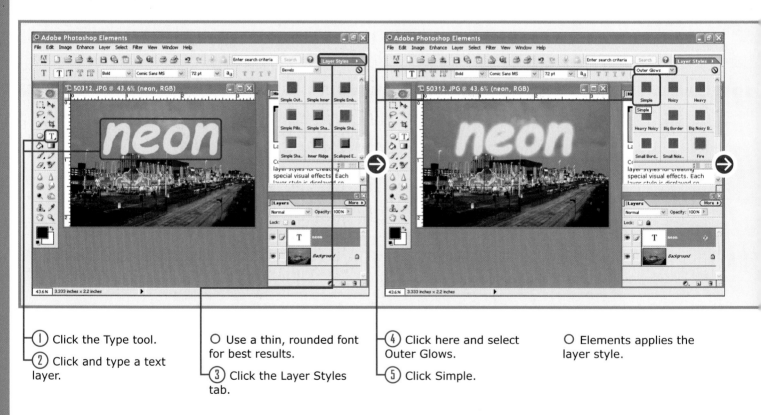

① Click the Type tool.

② Click and type a text layer.

○ Use a thin, rounded font for best results.

③ Click the Layer Styles tab.

④ Click here and select Outer Glows.

⑤ Click Simple.

○ Elements applies the layer style.

Did You Know? ✳

Duplicating layers can intensify many effects. You can create a glow effect with a semitransparent "cloud" of pixels surrounding the central object. Because of their low opacity, whenever you duplicate the image, you are multiplying the glow effect by doubling the opacity of the glow. This is useful to intensify the effect for the illusion of brightness.

Customize It! ✳

You can duplicate the layer that contains your text. Simplify the layer and make a selection of it. Contract the selection a few pixels, invert the selection, and delete the outer pixels you just contracted out of the selection. Now you can reapply the effects above for a more intense effect within the neon light. You can also take your new text selection, lighten the color closer to white, so after you complete the effects, the neon has a brighter center.

DIFFICULTY LEVEL

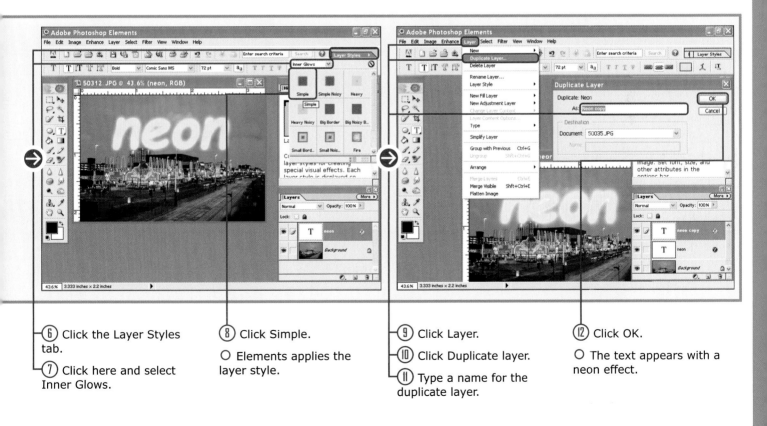

─⑥ Click the Layer Styles tab.

─⑦ Click here and select Inner Glows.

⑧ Click Simple.

○ Elements applies the layer style.

─⑨ Click Layer.

─⑩ Click Duplicate layer.

─⑪ Type a name for the duplicate layer.

⑫ Click OK.

○ The text appears with a neon effect.

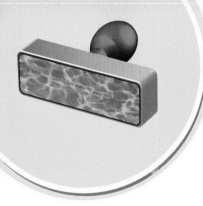

Make a
POLAROID PICTURE

You can create your own Polaroid camera picture right in Elements. The very popular picture form from the seventies is instantly recognizable. Using layer styles, you can re-create the same effect with any digital or scanned photo you have on your computer.

This is a different style of frame that is created with layer styles instead of the frame effects in the Effects palette. It is customizable, like all layer styles are, and you can still edit or transform the shape of

the frame. With this, you also have the foundation to add and transform your frame into any width, shape, or size.

To achieve this, use the layer styles. Sometimes the neatest effects are the ones that are the simplest, and this is no exception. Two layer styles applied to a layer with a framing shape around a photo and you have achieved this effect. It is easy, quick, and effective.

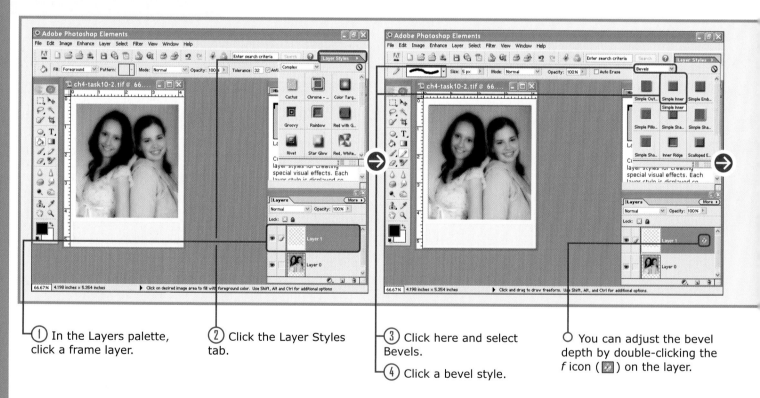

① In the Layers palette, click a frame layer.

② Click the Layer Styles tab.

③ Click here and select Bevels.

④ Click a bevel style.

○ You can adjust the bevel depth by double-clicking the *f* icon ( ) on the layer.

Customize It!

You can adjust the background frame shape of your image to resemble the shape of a regular slideshow slide. This trick is neat for online photo albums and Web sites. Use your Custom Shapes tool to create a rounded rectangle. Use the Square Marquee tool and delete a square section out of your shape. You now have the basic cutout shape of the classic slide.

Customize It!

You can now make a realistic looking slide. After you complete the slide effect, you can click your image layer. Then click Image, Adjustments, and then Invert. The image now resembles a film negative, so that your slide really does look like a slide before you put it into a projector.

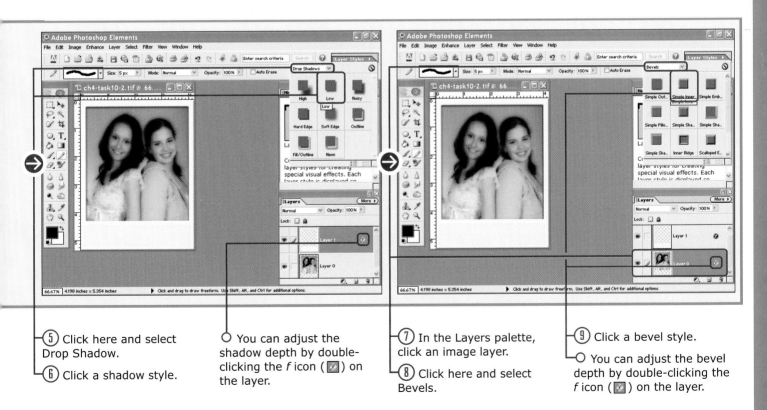

⑤ Click here and select Drop Shadow.

⑥ Click a shadow style.

○ You can adjust the shadow depth by double-clicking the *f* icon (▨) on the layer.

⑦ In the Layers palette, click an image layer.

⑧ Click here and select Bevels.

⑨ Click a bevel style.

○ You can adjust the bevel depth by double-clicking the *f* icon (▨) on the layer.

CHAPTER 5

Mastering Type, Brushes, and Shapes

The fact that you are working in Photoshop Elements 2.0 does not mean that you are limited to working with just photographs. On the contrary, you have a virtual cornucopia of tools at your disposal. Not only can you create work with photographs in Elements, but you can also take advantage of a variety of cool features, such as text, brushes, and shapes.

Adding type comes in particularly handy when you want to create a Web page, add a caption, or simply label or headline your photograph. Just create your text, and you can now jazz it up with patterns, styles, and special effects, such as beveling and drop shadows.

Text is not the only special tool at your disposal. In Elements, you can use custom brushes to personalize your photos or Web pages. Elements offers 12 sets of brushes for you to choose from, and you have the option of creating your own custom brushes. Whatever your artistic skill level, drawing with Elements' brushes is exciting.

You can also add shapes to your photographs, which function wonderfully as buttons on your Web page. Just as you can add three-dimensional effects to text, you can bevel your shapes in the same way, creating buttons that seem to "pop out" at your Web page visitors. You can also create custom shapes.

Fortunately, customizing Elements is not difficult — it is just a matter of knowing the proper steps to take, which you discover in this chapter.

TOP 100

Create
SEMITRANSPARENT TEXT

You can adjust the Opacity setting of your text layer to achieve semitransparent text. *Semitransparent* in Elements means that you are able to see objects and pixels that lay behind your object, but through the object itself. By making text semitransparent, you are able to view what is underneath your type while still being able to read your text.

Semitransparent text is a popular design method for graphics. It lends subtlety to the text, and depth to the image. Many times, it is not the focus of the image, but a bit of extra character to the design that

conveys a simple message related to the image. Fully opaque text can dominate an image and draw attention away from the center subject. You can create some excellent effects with semitransparent text.

You can create some text using the Type tool. When you use the Horizontal Type tool, your text appears on its own layer, which enables you to work with the text without worrying about affecting the underlying image.

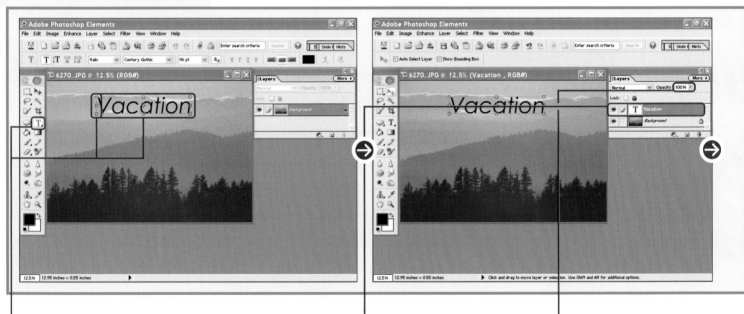

① Click the Type tool.

② Click where you want to place the text.

③ Type your text and press Enter.

○ You may change the font, style, size, and color of the text by clicking the down-arrow and making a selection.

④ In the Layers palette, click the Text layer.

⑤ Click here to display the Opacity slider.

Did You Know? ※

You can reset the opacity of semitransparent text and change it without hurting the image. You can adjust it as your needs change.

Did You Know? ※

You can also apply layer styles to a semitransparent text layer. If you have applied layer styles to a text layer, and then change it to semitransparent text, the layer styles will also change to semitransparent. Semitransparency affects the entire layer and all applied effects.

DIFFICULTY LEVEL

○ The Opacity slider appears.

⑥ Click and drag the Opacity slider to make adjustments.

○ Your Text layer lightens based on where you drag the slider.

○ Alternatively, you can type a value between 0 and 100 in the Opacity area and press Enter.

○ Your semitransparent text appears in your photo.

Add
TEXT PATTERNS

You can do quite a bit with text besides express the words you type. You can also apply layer styles, colors, effects, and patterns of repetitive graphics. With text, patterns are also graphical overlays that define and give character to your text. Patterns are shapes, colors, or even clips of an image. Using patterns is an excellent way to emphasize the word content or complement surrounding graphics in your design.

The pattern fill always generates a new layer and is handled three ways. You can design a pattern as a full-sized layer design, apply it to a selection, or group it with a layer. Grouping with a pattern layer might utilize a full-sized layer of the pattern, but it is only applied to the grouped objects. For example, with a text layer, only the text shows the pattern. With grouping, you can apply a pattern to any shape or text, and it does not cover anything but the shape or text.

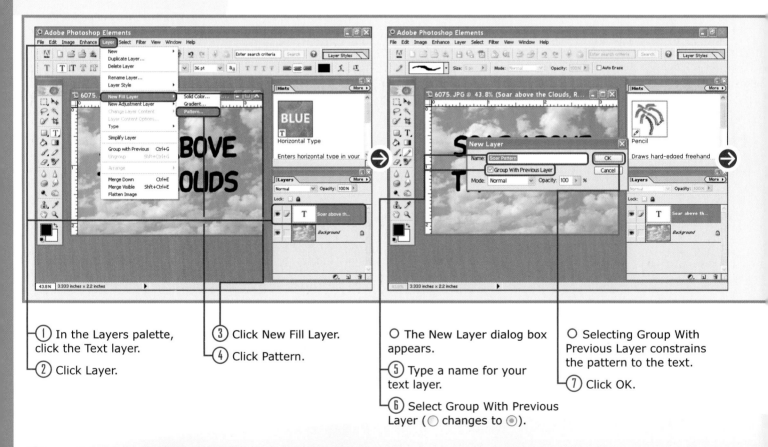

① In the Layers palette, click the Text layer.

② Click Layer.

③ Click New Fill Layer.

④ Click Pattern.

○ The New Layer dialog box appears.

⑤ Type a name for your text layer.

⑥ Select Group With Previous Layer (○ changes to ◉).

○ Selecting Group With Previous Layer constrains the pattern to the text.

⑦ Click OK.

Did You Know? ※

You can choose a font that
shows your applied pattern
clearly. Choose a font that is large
and wide enough so that the pattern is
clearly visible. If you use too thin of a font,
you will not be able to define or appreciate
the pattern you applied.

Put It Together! ※

You can really spice up your text by applying
other special effects, such as type effects that
make the text appear three-dimensional. Click
the Layer Styles palette, select Bevels from the
drop-down menu, and apply a bevel effect to your
patterned text. Be careful of which layer styles
you use; some have built-in patterns that will
erase yours.

DIFFICULTY LEVEL

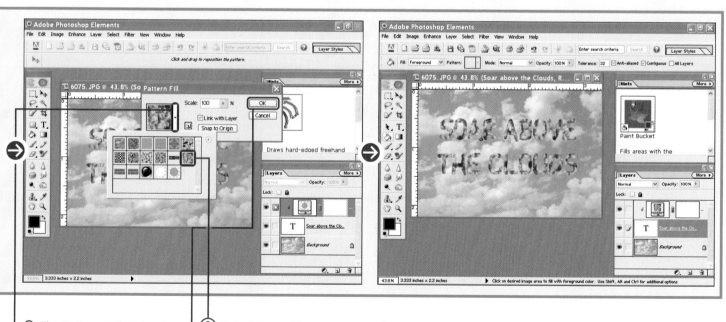

○ The Pattern Fill dialog box appears.

⑧ Click here to display the sample patterns.

⑨ Select the pattern you want to apply.

⑩ Click OK.

○ Your new pattern appears within your text.

Apply
TEXT MASKS

You can use a tool called *masks* in Elements to make changes to only part of an image. You can create a mask that affects objects, shapes, or in this case, text layers. A Layer Mask is a strong tool for adding special effects and overlays. Text made up of a photograph in the shape of words is an example of a text mask at work.

You can define two things with text masks. The text, which you type, and the overlay, which can literally be anything you can put on a layer. When you put the two together with a mask, the overlay shows only where the text is.

Masks work by defining visible and invisible areas in the layer. Whatever is considered empty on the mask shows through the mask and is visible on-screen. If the mask is filled, it considers that area invisible, and it is not visible on-screen, although it is not erased. You can use the contents of a layer as the mask, and the transparent areas are invisible.

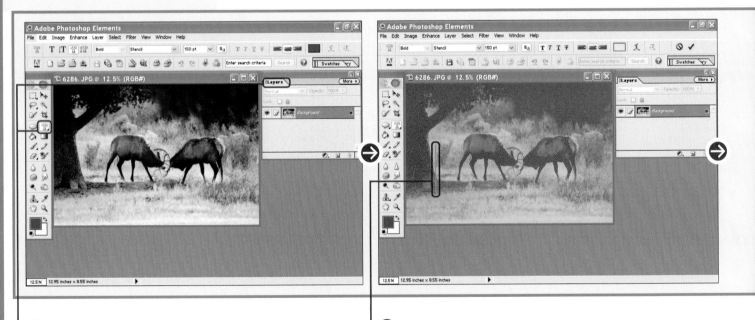

① Open the Layers palette.

② Click the Horizontal Type Mask tool.

○ To create vertical text, click the Vertical Type Mask tool.

③ Click where you want to place the text.

○ The screen turns red, indicating the text is masked.

#43

Did You Know? ✳

You can use masks to create the illusion of an object that is cut out and defined, while the overlay material is not damaged or affected in any way. This keeps the original image intact and clean. Open any photograph, create a mask layer of your subject, and group the two together. This causes your subject to appear removed from the image, while the image is not altered or damaged.

DIFFICULTY LEVEL

Did You Know? ✳

Masks are defined by grayscale colors. Black reveals the image and white conceals the image below. Shades and gradients create a feathered edge, with semitransparency. You can click your mask layer, draw on it in black to create a new mask shape, or you can draw in white to edit or erase your mask.

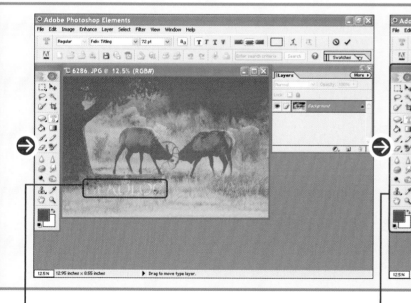

④ Type your text.

○ Unlike the rest of the photograph, the text you are typing does not appear in red. Instead, you can see the natural color of the photograph through the letters.

⑤ When you are finished typing, click the Commit Text button, or click a different tool.

○ Your text appears as see-through type with dotted lines surrounding it.

Change
TEXT ATTRIBUTES

You can change many attributes of your text, such as color, size, alignment, style, and font. *Font* refers to the type's unique standard width, weight, and style.

The best time to change these attributes is before you start typing. After you select the Type tool, you can then set your attributes before typing. However, if you type and then decide that you would like to make a change, you can still do so, as long as the

Type tool is active. You can even change just certain parts of your text — such as certain letters or words — by selecting it with the Type tool.

In addition, there are several Faux options available for you. You have Faux italic, bold, strikethrough, and underline. These are available in the Type tool options bar. These are especially useful when you are using a font that has no built-in italic or bold font styles.

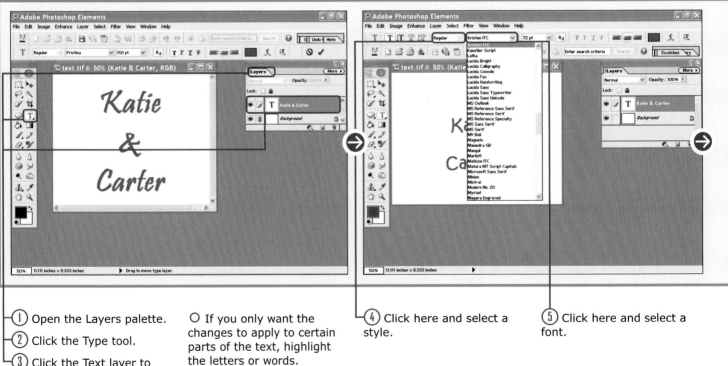

① Open the Layers palette.

② Click the Type tool.

③ Click the Text layer to apply the changes to all the text.

○ If you only want the changes to apply to certain parts of the text, highlight the letters or words.

④ Click here and select a style.

⑤ Click here and select a font.

#44

DIFFICULTY LEVEL

Did You Know? ※

You can make the edges of your text smoother by using *anti-aliasing*. Anti-aliasing is a feature you can turn on when working with type to avoid jagged type. To turn on this feature, click the Anti-Aliased button located in the Type options bar, next to the font size. It is denoted by two different lowercase *A*'s.

Did You Know? ※

You can add new fonts to Elements by simply installing them on your computer. Elements draws all of its available fonts from the default C:Windows/Fonts folders located in your computer. Be careful when sharing PSD files with unsimplified text. If your destination computer does not have the font installed, Elements uses the closest substitution in the font sets available, which can change the effect.

⑥ Click here and select a type size.

⑦ Press Enter.

○ Your formatting changes appear on-screen.

Create a textured
TYPE EFFECT

You can make your text appear to jump out of your photos by applying a 3D effect to your type. Elements has a very nice variety of special text effects available for use within its Effects palette. These effects create everything from simple depth to wood paneling.

You can only use these effects on an unsimplified text layer. No other layer style or object is able to utilize these, which makes them unique effects. When you use them, your text layer automatically

becomes simplified and therefore, no longer is editable. If you want to retain editable text, either create a duplicate layer, or use Layer Styles to create text effects.

You can experiment to discover text effects and their diverse range of results. They have effects that create transparent text with a shadow, a watery reflection, and even an outline of the text. There are plenty of options for creative text designs for you to utilize in your creative designs or projects.

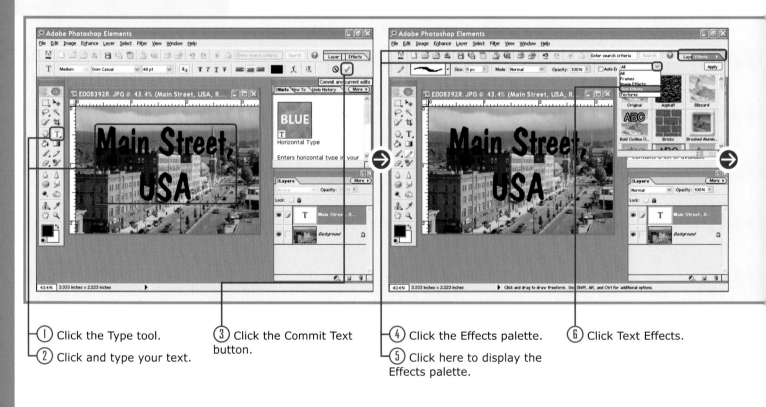

① Click the Type tool.

② Click and type your text.

③ Click the Commit Text button.

④ Click the Effects palette.

⑤ Click here to display the Effects palette.

⑥ Click Text Effects.

DIFFICULTY LEVEL

Did You Know? ※

You can experiment with the different text effects to see which one you like best by clicking a different option in step **7**. Just remember to click Edit and then Undo immediately to remove the effect if you do not like it.

Did You Know? ※

You can look in the Layer palette after you apply the effects and see if the layer has the Layer Styles *f* icon on it. Some of the text effects are changed through the Layer Styles. If applicable, you can double-click the *f* icon (▣) and edit certain aspects such as bevel, glow size, and shadows.

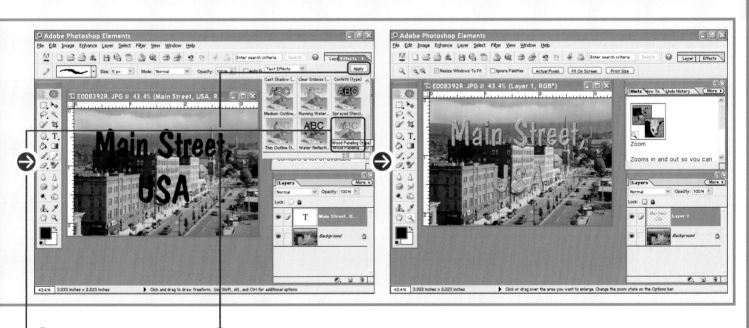

⑦ Click Wood Paneling.

⑧ Click Apply.

○ Elements applies the Wood paneling effect so text appears 3D and textured.

Design your own
CUSTOM BRUSHES

You can choose from more than 280 brushes to do your artwork and designs in Photoshop Elements. You can use a variety of shapes, designs, and styles. You can access these easily through the Brushes palette. Sometimes you may want a different design or size of brush. Elements lets you create custom brushes for your specific designs. You can edit the size, feather, and angle of your brush.

You also have available special options that allow you to change the fade-out point of a brush, similar to when placing a stroke with a paint brush — it

begins dark and full, and as the paint runs out, the stroke fades away. This fade function is a great addition to brushes in Elements. Other options include spacing, allowing you to create dotted lines instead of solid, and color jitter, which affects the color and placement of your brush dots. Overall, you can do much more with Elements' native brushes than ever before.

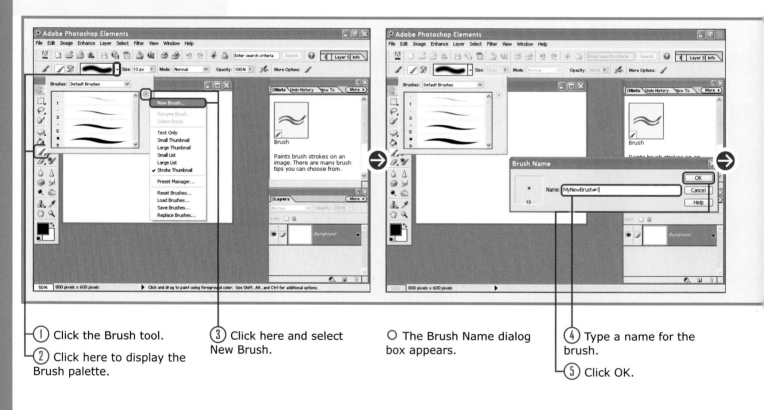

① Click the Brush tool.

② Click here to display the Brush palette.

③ Click here and select New Brush.

○ The Brush Name dialog box appears.

④ Type a name for the brush.

⑤ Click OK.

Customize It! ※

You can make your cursor
take the shape of the brush you
are using. Open the Preferences
dialog box and select Display & Cursors
from the drop-down menu that appears. In
the Printing Cursors area, click the Standard
radio button and then press Enter. You can see
exactly the size and shape of your current brush
before you draw with it, which allows you better
control and placement.

#46

DIFFICULTY LEVEL

Did You Know? ※

You can draw straight lines using your brush by clicking
in the image where you want your line to begin, moving
your Brush to where you would like the line to end, and
then pressing Shift+click. A straight line appears between
the two points using the current brush selection.

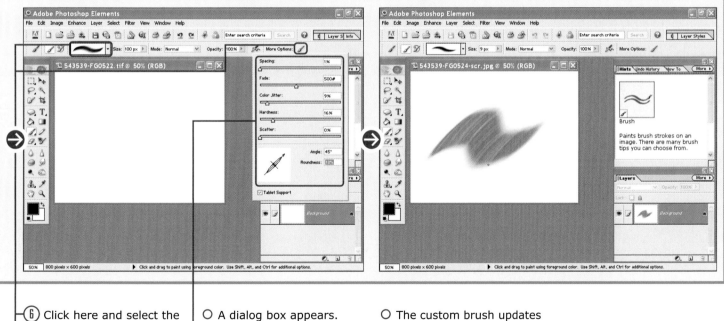

(6) Click here and select the style of brush that you want.

(7) Click the More Options button.

○ A dialog box appears.

(8) Click and drag the sliders to adjust the values.

(9) Press Enter.

○ The custom brush updates in the menu.

Work with
SHAPES

You can use the Shape tools to create geometric shapes. Elements has a library of shapes available for you to use in your graphics. The Custom Shape sets are filled with many different shapes, from animals to fancy ornament shapes. You can select your shape from the menu, and then click and drag your cursor to the size and dimensions of the shape you want.

You have six different Shape tools at your disposal in Elements 2.0: Rectangle, Rounded Rectangle, Ellipse, Polygon, Line, and the Custom Shape tool.

The first five deal with your basic geometric shapes. The Custom Shape tool has specialty shapes for other uses. See task #49 for more on custom shapes.

The five basic geometric shapes are shapes that may be difficult to reproduce by hand. You can create a hexagonal shape, but it could take a while to create six equilateral lines laid out into shape. The Shapes tool shortcuts that for you. You can create simple shapes with a click and drag very easily in Elements.

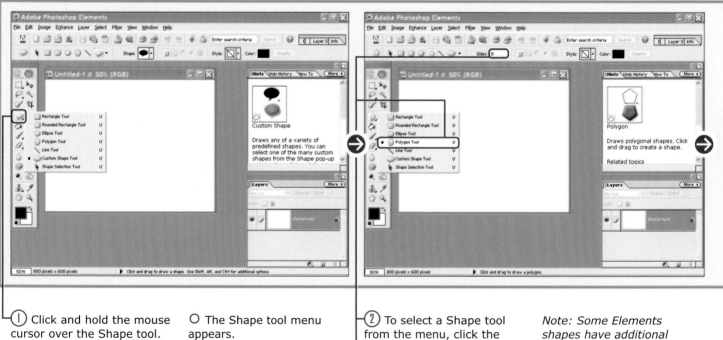

① Click and hold the mouse cursor over the Shape tool.

○ The Shape tool menu appears.

② To select a Shape tool from the menu, click the tool.

③ Click here and type an option, if applicable.

Note: Some Elements shapes have additional options on the option bar.

Customize It! ※

Your shape appears in the same color that you have selected as your foreground color. If you decide that this color is not for you, click the Color box in the options bar and select a new color from the Color Picker that appears. You can also set your foreground color before drawing with the Shape tool.

Did You Know? ※

Several of the geometric shapes available have additional options in the Option bar. Click the Rounded Rectangle shape, and you can set the radius of your rounded corners. The Polygon Shape tool allows you to determine the number of sides your shape has, from 3-sided to 100-sided.

#47

DIFFICULTY LEVEL

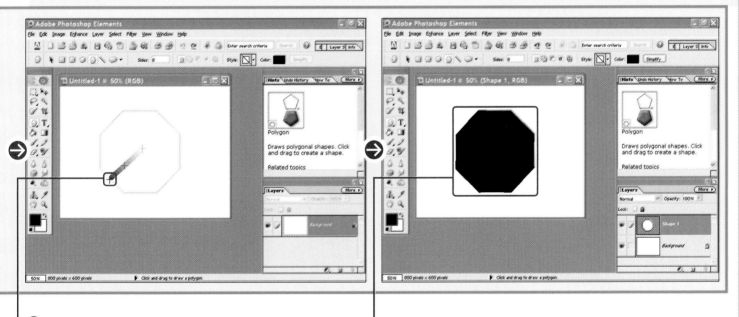

④ Drag the tool to create the shape you want.

○ Press and hold the Shift key while dragging to constrain shapes to equal proportions, like squares and perfect circles.

○ Your shape appears on-screen.

Add
SHAPE STYLES

You can use layer styles to creatively enhance your shapes. The layer styles palette has different style categories from which to choose, producing a large range of results. You can apply these to any shape design you create, allowing you to add bevels, shadows, glows, and more to add depth and pizzazz to your graphics.

With Elements, you can also add complex layer styles, which give more detailed and complicated results to your shapes, like chrome, glass, and even

cactus patterns. These styles are useful to provide character to the shapes, even more so than basic bevels and shadows mentioned above. You can create dynamic graphics with the large library of complex layer styles.

After you apply a style, you can click the *f* icon in your shape layer and adjust the components of the applied layer style. This is very useful for adjusting the scale of your styles to fit different sized shapes.

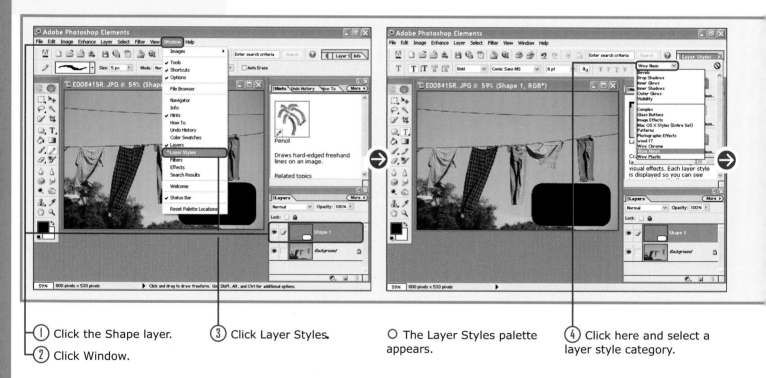

① Click the Shape layer.

② Click Window.

③ Click Layer Styles.

○ The Layer Styles palette appears.

④ Click here and select a layer style category.

Customize It! ※

You can transform your
shapes. Click the shape layer and
then from the menu click Image,
Transform Shape, and then a transform
command. Drag the bounding box handles
to scale and transform your shape.
Transforming lets you add perspective and resize
the shape to fit your needs.

Did You Know? ※

You can add shape styles as you draw your
shape. In the Shape tool option bar is a
drop-down box marked Styles. Click the
Styles box and the Layer Styles palette opens.
Click your choice of category and style
design to customize your shape at the
time you are drawing.

DIFFICULTY LEVEL

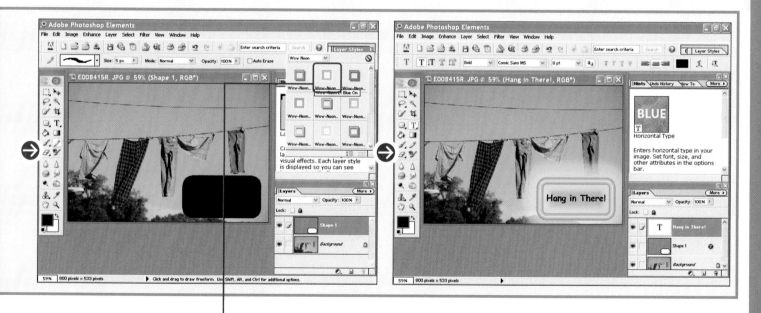

○ The layer style category
list appears.

⑤ Click a layer style.

○ Elements applies the layer
style to your shape.

Design with
CUSTOM SHAPES

You can use your Shape tool to generate some useful basic geometric shapes. Sometimes, the shapes are limited for the project on which you are working. You can access the Custom Shapes palette to allow you to use a wide variety of new, irregular shapes. Things like animal shapes to fancy ornamental shapes are available to use. You can choose from 16 different categories within Elements, each of which has it own unique set of designs. This large library of custom shapes opens the door for more creative designs, logos, Web page buttons, or whatever your graphical needs.

These custom shapes act just like the regular geometrical shapes in that they are vector graphics and can accept layer styles. You can access the dozens of layer styles to enhance the custom shapes for your projects. Like all shapes, any filters or effects you run on them forces the shape to become simplified and pixel-based.

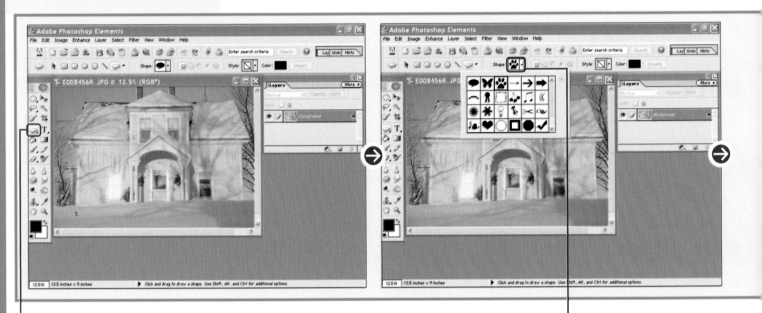

① Click the Custom Shape tool.

○ The Shape menu appears.

② Click and select a shape from the Shape palette.

#49

DIFFICULTY LEVEL

Caution! ☀

Because vector graphics are
so versatile for resizing and
editing, it is strongly recommended
that if you need to apply a filter, shape,
or other simplifying action, that you do so
on a duplicate layer. After you simplify a vector,
it becomes a pixel-based graphic and can pixelate
or become damaged by any editing or resizing
processes you apply to it afterward.

Did You Know? ☀

You can use custom shapes as great masks for other
graphics. Place a document-sized texture or image
above a shape layer. Click Layer and then Group
with Previous. The shape is a mask that reveals
only your document-sized image in the outline of
the custom shape.

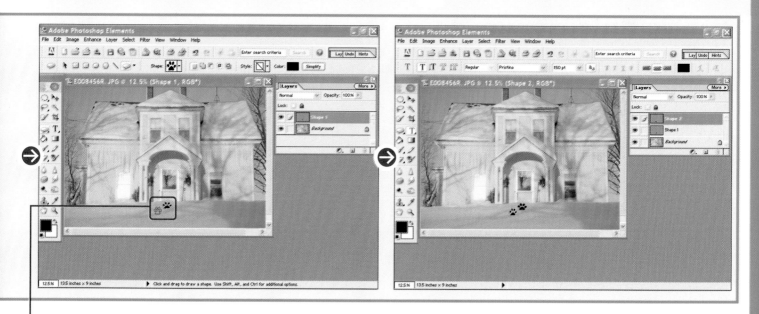

③ Click and drag to draw
your custom shape.

④ Release your mouse
cursor.

○ Your custom shape
appears.

Import
ADDITIONAL BRUSHES AND SHAPES

You can import brushes and shapes from outside of Photoshop Elements 2 for use inside the program. Many sites offer custom brushes and shapes that you can use inside of Elements. This is a great way to get all new designs and shapes.

You can import these custom sets by copying their files into the appropriate directory. When you start Elements, the program automatically loads the brushes, shapes, and other presets found within the default folders.

Brush files have the extension ABR, and Shape files have the extension CSH. You can tell you have the correct folders by the similar files within. By default, you can find both Brushes and Custom Shapes folders in this file location: C:\Program Files\Adobe\Photoshop Elements 2\Presets. After you load them, click the Shape selection options menu to load your new set, or click Load Brushes in the Brush selection menu options.

You can find incredible brushes and shapes available at many different locations online. For more information about online resources, see Chapter 10.

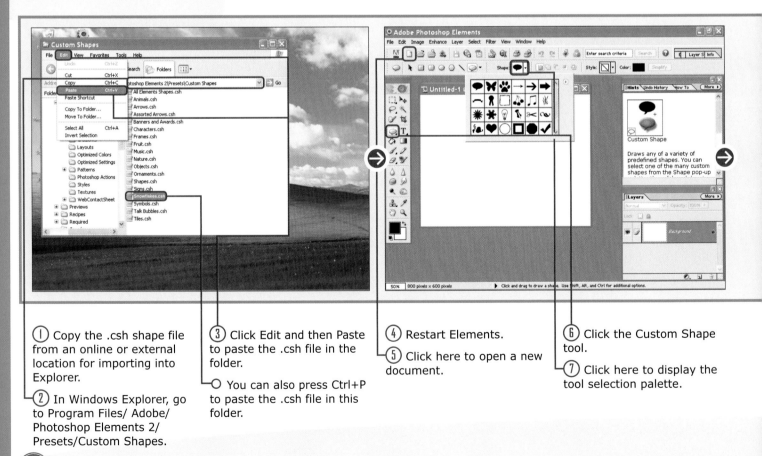

① Copy the .csh shape file from an online or external location for importing into Explorer.

② In Windows Explorer, go to Program Files/ Adobe/ Photoshop Elements 2/ Presets/Custom Shapes.

③ Click Edit and then Paste to paste the .csh file in the folder.

○ You can also press Ctrl+P to paste the .csh file in this folder.

④ Restart Elements.

⑤ Click here to open a new document.

⑥ Click the Custom Shape tool.

⑦ Click here to display the tool selection palette.

Did You Know? ※

You can easily install your imported brushes. Paste your ABR file in the Preset/Brushes folder. Restart Elements, and in the Brush selection menu options, click Load Brushes. You can open the brush file from the selection in the resulting Open dialog box by clicking the file and then OK. You can now use your new brush set by clicking the Brush selection drop-down menu.

Did You Know? ※

You can always return to your original brush and shape sets. In the Brush selection drop-down menu is an option to Reset Brushes. In the Shape selection drop-down menu is a Default shapes setting. Clicking either of these two choices resets the corresponding tool's default sets.

#50

DIFFICULTY LEVEL

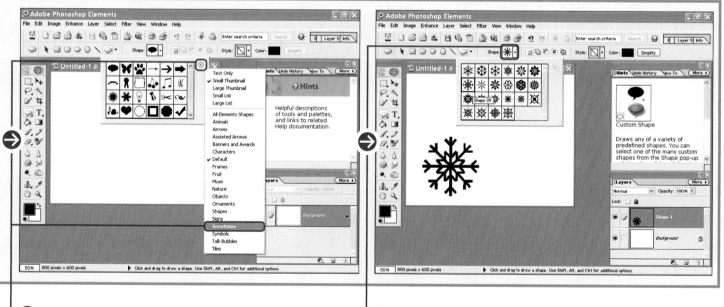

⑧ Click here and select a shape set.

⑨ Click here to view the new shape selections.

CHAPTER 6

Working with Photos

As the *photo* in its name suggests, Photoshop Elements includes a variety of features designed specifically for fixing or enhancing digital photographs.

One of the most common uses of Photoshop Elements is to correct and optimize photographs shot with a digital camera. This chapter introduces you to a versatile interface for accomplishing this — the Quick Fix dialog box. The dialog box gives you easy access to tools that enable you to apply exposure, color-correction, and other tools to fix digital photos.

Scanned photographs offer another set of challenges, and this chapter features tips that enable you to tackle them as well. Using the Grid feature, you can straighten photos that have been scanned in crooked.

You can also remove dust, scratches, and other artifacts — which can be introduced during the scanning process — by using the Clone Stamp tool.

Several tasks in this chapter show you how to use Photoshop Elements to combine separate photographs into a final composition. You can use the Photomerge feature in Photoshop Elements to stitch several images together into a single panoramic image. When you use the Photomerge feature, you identify your source photos, and then Photoshop Elements attempts to create the panorama for you automatically. You can also arrange several photos onto a single canvas to create a digital montage. Photoshop Elements makes it easy to create a montage by organizing the pasted images into separate layers.

TOP 100

APPLY A QUICK FIX
to a photo

You can apply exposure, color-correction, and other enhancement tools to your images using the Quick Fix dialog box. All of the tools in the dialog box are accessible through other Photoshop Elements commands. The Quick Fix dialog box simply gathers the tools under one convenient, easy-to-use interface. As you apply the Quick Fix tools, you can compare an original version of your photo with a version with the enhancements applied.

The Brightness tools available in the dialog box give you several ways to fix photos that have been underexposed or overexposed. The Auto Contrast

and Auto Levels tools offer simple one-click adjustments for bad lighting, while the Brightness/ Contrast tool offers sliders for more interactive fine-tuning.

The Quick Fix dialog box also features Focus tools for photos that are blurry, and Rotate tools for pictures that need to be flipped or rotated. Enlarging or shrinking photos in Elements can result in blur, while taking pictures in different orientations with a digital camera can require rotating.

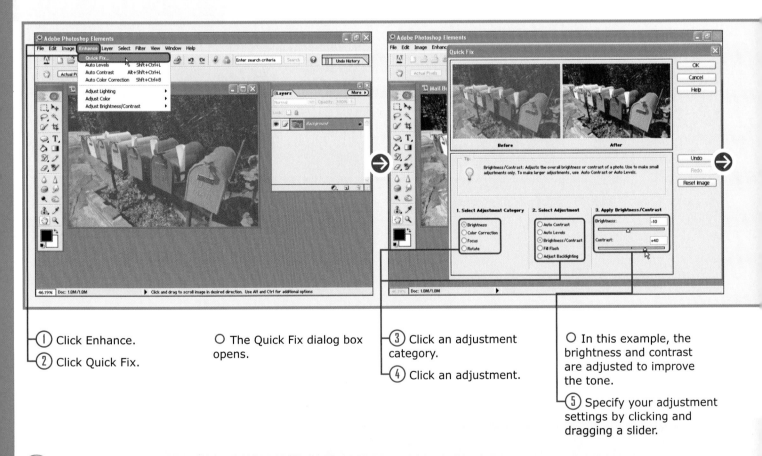

① Click Enhance.

② Click Quick Fix.

○ The Quick Fix dialog box opens.

③ Click an adjustment category.

④ Click an adjustment.

○ In this example, the brightness and contrast are adjusted to improve the tone.

⑤ Specify your adjustment settings by clicking and dragging a slider.

Did You Know? ☀

There are several ways to undo the changes you apply in the Quick Fix dialog box. You can click Undo to undo the most recent Quick Fix adjustment. Clicking Undo a number of times will undo multiple adjustments, if you have made them. You can redo an adjustment that was just undone by clicking the Redo button. Clicking Reset Image reverts the image to the state it was in when you opened the Quick Fix dialog box.

Customize It! ☀

You can also use the Quick Fix dialog box to make fixes to specific parts of your photos. Just make a selection before opening the dialog box. The adjustments will be applied only to the selected pixels.

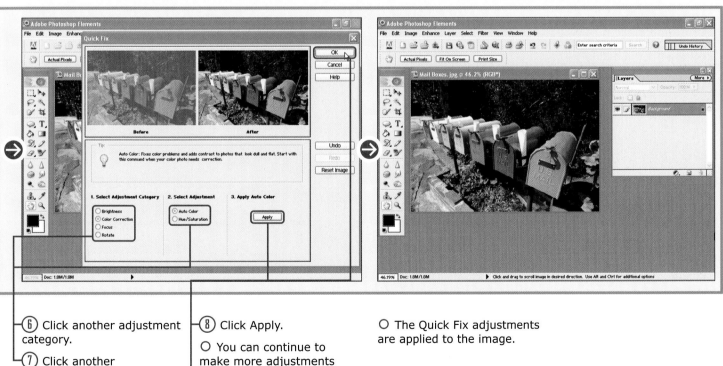

⑥ Click another adjustment category.

⑦ Click another adjustment.

○ In this example, Auto Color is selected to enrich the color in the photo.

⑧ Click Apply.

○ You can continue to make more adjustments from other categories.

⑨ Click OK.

○ The Quick Fix adjustments are applied to the image.

Use the grid to
STRAIGHTEN A PHOTO

You can use the Grid feature to straighten photos in a Photoshop Elements composition. Turning on the grid overlay creates an evenly spaced set of perpendicular lines over the top of your image. Using the Free Rotate Layer tool, you can reorient a photo so that it abuts the edges and corners of the grid, making the edges of the photo parallel with the outside of your image. This trick can come in handy with hand-scanned photos, which often times can come out crooked.

The Free Rotate Layer tool enables you not only to rotate the selected layer of your image, but also freely move it by clicking and dragging up and down and side to side, similar to the Move tool. This can be handy when orienting your photo. You can also make precise adjustments to the element being rotated using the arrow keys. Pressing the arrow keys moves your object one pixel at a time.

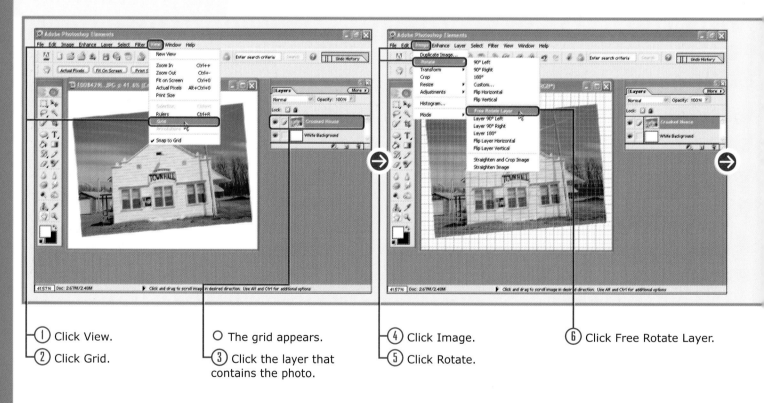

① Click View.
② Click Grid.

○ The grid appears.
③ Click the layer that contains the photo.

④ Click Image.
⑤ Click Rotate.

⑥ Click Free Rotate Layer.

Customize It! ※

You can customize the grid in Preferences. Click Edit and Preferences. In the Preference dialog box, select Grid from the top drop-down menu. Here you can change the color of the grid lines; pick from line, dashed, or dotted styles; and specify the line widths and number of subdivisions.

Did You Know? ※

By default, objects in your image when dragged near the lines of the grid will automatically snap to the lines. This comes in handy when using the grid to align objects. However, it can be annoying when you are arranging non-rectangular shapes, or want a more freeform way of arranging elements in your image. You can turn off the Snap to Grid feature under the View menu.

#52

DIFFICULTY LEVEL

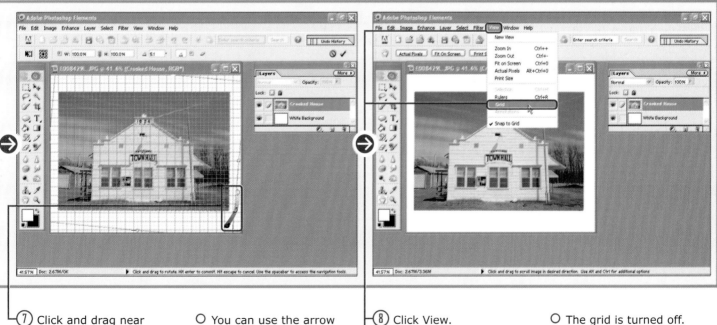

⑦ Click and drag near the corner of the layer to rotate it.

○ You can click and drag in the middle of the photo to move it vertically or horizontally.

○ You can use the arrow keys to nudge the image a pixel at a time.

○ Orient the photo along the grid lines.

⑧ Click View.

⑨ Click Grid.

○ The grid is turned off.

○ The photo is straightened.

Create a
PANORAMIC PHOTO

You can use the Photomerge feature in Photoshop Elements to stitch several images together into a single panoramic image. Panoramic images are usually much wider than they are tall and enable you to display more scenery in a single image than is usually possible in a normal photograph.

When you set up a Photomerge composition, you identify your source photos, and then Photoshop Elements attempts to create the panorama for you automatically. After the panorama is complete, you can still make changes to the placement of the

individual source photos. This enables you to correct alignment mishaps that can occur during the merge process.

The Photomerge dialog box helps you create the panoramic compositions. The dialog box includes tools for manipulating the source photos, a lightbox for organizing source images that are not in use, and a work area for assembling the panorama. There are also settings for adjusting perspective in the completed image.

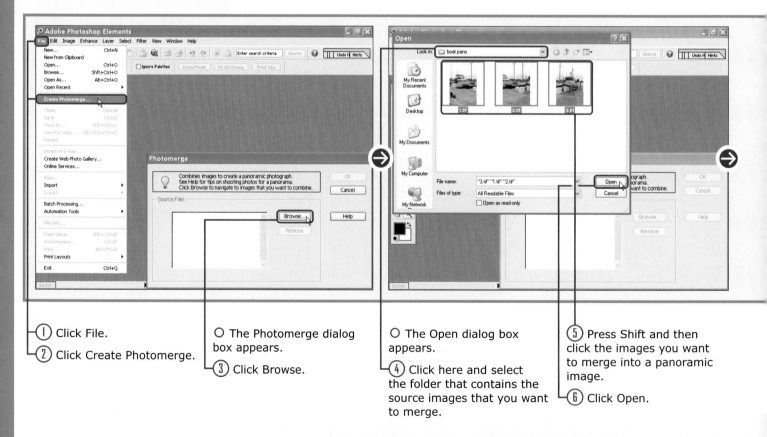

① Click File.

② Click Create Photomerge.

○ The Photomerge dialog box appears.

③ Click Browse.

○ The Open dialog box appears.

④ Click here and select the folder that contains the source images that you want to merge.

⑤ Press Shift and then click the images you want to merge into a panoramic image.

⑥ Click Open.

Did You Know? ☀

Wide-angle lenses can help you maximize the field of view attained in your source photographs as well as your resulting panorama. However, fisheye lenses should be avoided when creating panoramas, because they can distort your photographs and make it harder for the Photoshop Elements software to combine your images with one another.

Did You Know? ☀

Consistent exposure throughout your set of source photos is key to creating nice-looking panoramas. For example, using flash in some of the photos but not in others can make blending them together difficult; it can also result in a panorama in which the lighting shifts oddly across the picture.

CONTINUED

○ The filenames of the images appear in the Source Files list.

⑦ Click OK to build the panoramic image.

○ Elements attempts to merge the images together into a single panoramic image.

○ Thumbnails of the images that it cannot merge appear in a lightbox area.

○ You can click and drag the slider to zoom the panoramic image in and out.

Create a
PANORAMIC PHOTO

While you create your panorama, you may need to reposition an individual source file, or rotate a file in your composition in order to achieve consistent blending. The editing tools in the Photomerge dialog box help you work with your panorama. You can also zoom in and out to better see the alignment of each file.

You can save time and help avoid having to make adjustments by using source photos that have the right amount of overlap. For best results, source

photos should overlap one another approximately 15 percent to 40 percent. If the overlap is less, Photomerge may not be able to automatically assemble the panorama.

After your panorama is complete, you can edit and make adjustments to it just like any other Photoshop Elements image. This can include making exposure adjustments to the seams where the source photos were combined.

CONTINUED

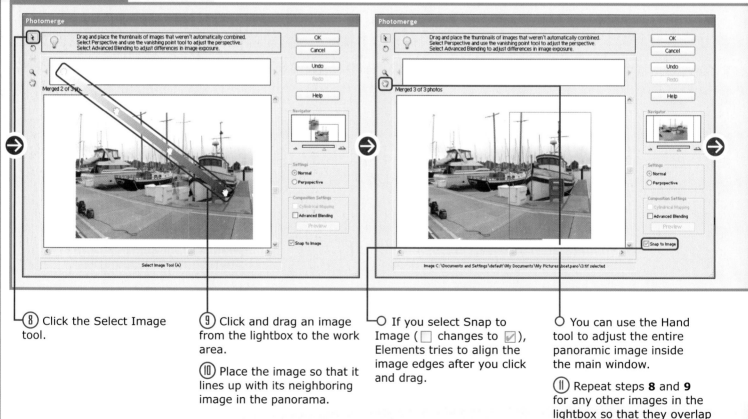

⑧ Click the Select Image tool.

⑨ Click and drag an image from the lightbox to the work area.

⑩ Place the image so that it lines up with its neighboring image in the panorama.

○ If you select Snap to Image (☐ changes to ☑), Elements tries to align the image edges after you click and drag.

○ You can use the Hand tool to adjust the entire panoramic image inside the main window.

⑪ Repeat steps **8** and **9** for any other images in the lightbox so that they overlap and match one another.

Did You Know? ☀

The more level your photographs are relative to one another, the easier they will be to merge into a single panorama. Using a tripod when shooting your photos will help make them as level as possible.

Did You Know? ☀

While most of your panoramas will most likely be comprised of horizontal arrangements of photos, you can also use Photoshop Elements to create vertical panoramas. To create a vertical panorama, first rotate your source photos 90 degrees. This will allow you to merge them together as if they were a horizontal panorama. Rotate the resulting panorama 90 degrees in the opposite direction and you have your vertical panorama.

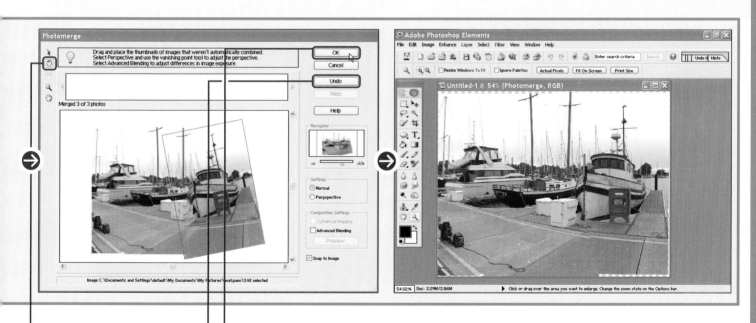

─O You can click the Rotate Image tool and click and drag with it to align image seams that are not level with one another.

⑫ Click OK.

─O You can click Undo to undo your Photomerge commands one at a time.

O Elements merges the images and opens the new panorama in a new image window.

Sepia TONE A PHOTO

You can sepia tone a photo to give it an old-fashioned look. Photos that are *sepia* colored have a brownish gray to dark olive brown hue. In the non-digital world, sepia toning is a photo-developing technique where print makers add extra silver sulfide solution while developing their photographs. This helps the photos stand up to light and last longer.

You can create a sepia-toned photo in Photoshop Elements by first removing all the color in the photo.

Then you add the brownish tint by adjusting the Hue, Saturation, and Lightness components of the photo. Achieving a sepia tone that looks authentic requires decreasing the Hue and Saturation values, and then adjusting the lightness so the photo is pleasing to the eye.

To add an additional old-fashioned effect, you can surround your photo with one of the vintage frames that is included with Photoshop Elements. To add a frame, see task #31.

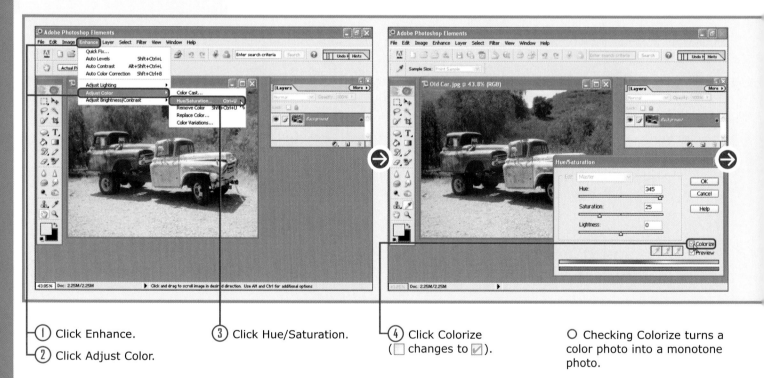

① Click Enhance.

② Click Adjust Color.

③ Click Hue/Saturation.

④ Click Colorize
(☐ changes to ☑).

○ Checking Colorize turns a color photo into a monotone photo.

Customize It! ☀

Sepia is just one of the color tones you can apply to your photo. By choosing different Hue settings, you can alternatively add yellow, green, blue, purple, red, or any other color in the spectrum.

Did You Know? ☀

If you already have a scanned, old-fashioned sepia tone photo and want to add real color to it, see task #66.

Did You Know? ☀

If you want to create a sepia tone version of your color photo, but also want to keep the original color version, create two identical layers of your photo. Then apply sepia toning to one of the layers. You can hide and unhide the original and sepia tone layers to compare the before and after versions.

DIFFICULTY LEVEL

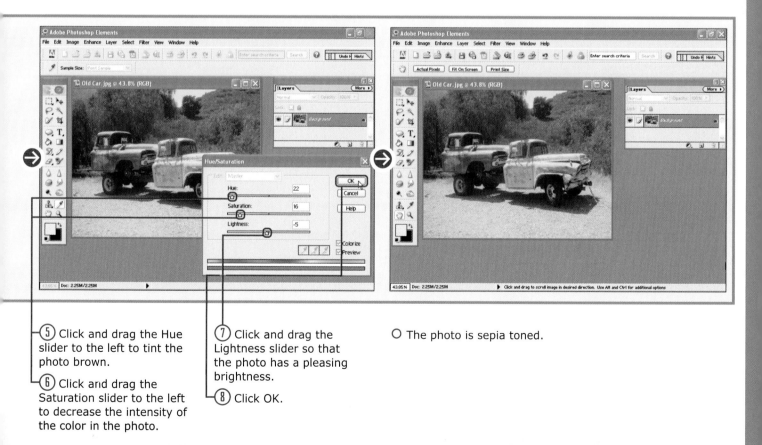

⑤ Click and drag the Hue slider to the left to tint the photo brown.

⑥ Click and drag the Saturation slider to the left to decrease the intensity of the color in the photo.

⑦ Click and drag the Lightness slider so that the photo has a pleasing brightness.

⑧ Click OK.

○ The photo is sepia toned.

Create a
PHOTO MONTAGE

You can arrange several photos onto a single canvas to create a digital *montage*. Photoshop Elements makes it easy to create a montage by enabling you to copy and paste images into a central image window, organize the pasted images into separate layers, and move them relative to one another with the Layers palette and Move tool.

The first step to making a montage is to create the canvas on which to combine the different photos. The canvas should be large enough to accommodate

all the content you plan on adding in the montage. It is usually a good idea to make the canvas larger than needed at first — you can later crop the montage to an appropriate finished size.

As you copy and paste each of the montage photos into the central canvas, each is automatically placed onto its own layer. This is convenient, because you can then move the photos independently of one another by selecting a layer and then moving the photo with the Move tool.

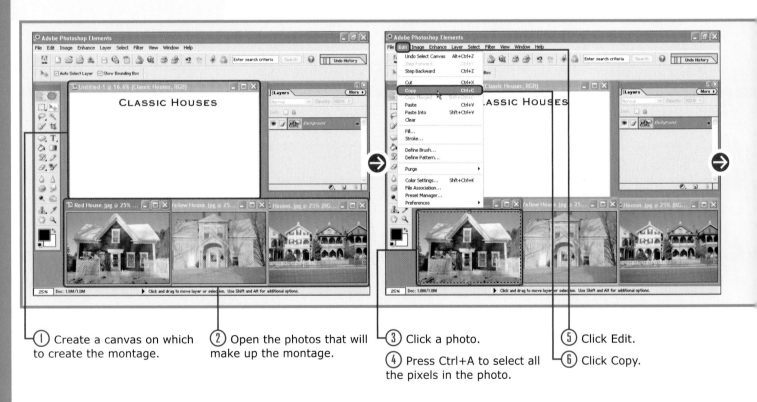

① Create a canvas on which to create the montage.

② Open the photos that will make up the montage.

③ Click a photo.

④ Press Ctrl+A to select all the pixels in the photo.

⑤ Click Edit.

⑥ Click Copy.

DIFFICULTY LEVEL

Did You Know? ※

Changing how the different photos in the montage are stacked relative to one another is as easy as clicking and dragging the different layers. Click and drag a layer up in the Layers palette to place it above other layers in the montage, and drag it down to place it below other layers in the montage.

Put It Together! ※

You can easily title or add text effects to your montage by mixing type layers among the photo layers. You can move and shuffle type layers like the image layers. For more information about adding interesting type effects to your montage, see tasks #41 and #42.

id You Know? ※

You can hide and unhide the different photos in your montage by clicking the Eye icon (⬚) in the Layers palette. This enables you to see how the montage looks with certain photos present or missing.

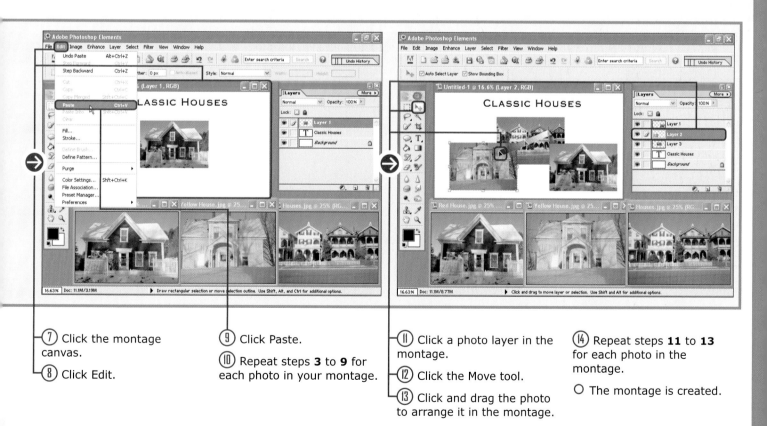

⑦ Click the montage canvas.

⑧ Click Edit.

⑨ Click Paste.

⑩ Repeat steps **3** to **9** for each photo in your montage.

⑪ Click a photo layer in the montage.

⑫ Click the Move tool.

⑬ Click and drag the photo to arrange it in the montage.

⑭ Repeat steps **11** to **13** for each photo in the montage.

O The montage is created.

REMOVE OBJECTS
in a photo

You can use the Clone Stamp tool on your photographs to remove scratches, dust specks, and other objects that you do not want in your scenes. The tool works by copying a different area of your photo, where objects are not present, over the unwanted objects. If the copied area is similar enough to the background around the unwanted objects, the results can be seamless — no one will know the objects were ever there.

It can be useful to first constrain the area around the unwanted objects with a selection tool before applying the Clone Stamp. That way, scenery near

the unwanted objects is not affected by the tool. Most often, you will want to use the Lasso selection tool, which makes it easy to select objects with curved or soft edges.

Sometimes it can be advantageous to use a combination of different textures, brushes, and backgrounds in the scene to cover up the unwanted objects. Such a tactic can make it less obvious that objects were removed.

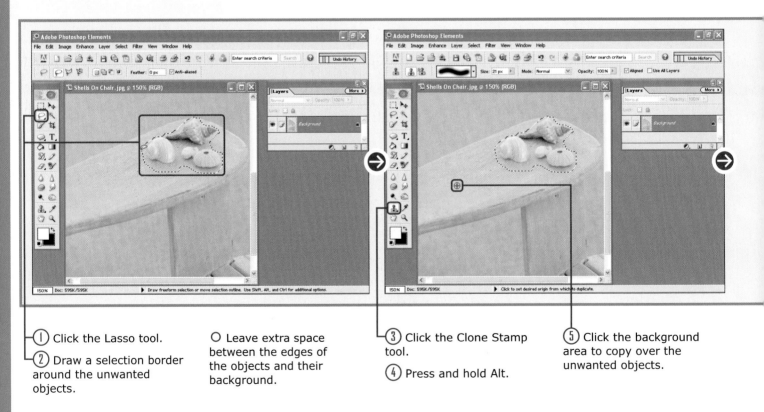

① Click the Lasso tool.

② Draw a selection border around the unwanted objects.

○ Leave extra space between the edges of the objects and their background.

③ Click the Clone Stamp tool.

④ Press and hold Alt.

⑤ Click the background area to copy over the unwanted objects.

56

DIFFICULTY LEVEL

Customize It! ※

In a perfect photo, there will be plenty of scenery to choose from to erase the unwanted objects and the scenery will have a consistent color and lighting. If this is not the case, for example, if the only scenery available is of a slightly different color or shading, you can use the opacity setting of the Clone Stamp tool to your advantage. By adjusting the setting to less than 100 percent, you can clone semitransparent copies of different areas of the scenery to make up for areas that do not exactly match.

Customize It! ※

You can change the size of the Clone Stamp tool using the menu on the Option bar or by pressing the opening and closing bracket keys ([ ]).

⑥ Click and drag inside the selection to copy the background over the unwanted objects.

⑦ If necessary, repeat steps **5** and **6** until the unwanted objects are covered up.

⑧ Press Ctrl+D to deselect the selection.

○ The unwanted objects are removed.

PASTE AN OBJECT
in another photo

You can cut an object out of one Photoshop Elements image and insert it into another. Using this technique, you can make seamless changes to a photo to rewrite history, or mix and match odds and ends in a scene to create a composition that is whimsical or surreal.

One of the key ingredients for creating realistic photographic collages is using source photos that have similar color tones and lighting. For example, combining imagery from two photos taken on overcast days will look more genuine than combining objects from a photo taken indoors with scenery from a photo taken in the midday sun.

Another important element to consider is the tool you use to cut out your objects. Unless your object is a nearly perfect rectangle or oval, you will most likely want to use one of the Lasso tools for this task. The regular Lasso tool is a good choice for objects that have edges that are curved or not well defined; the Polygonal Lasso tool is useful for objects that have straight edges; and the Magic Lasso tool can be convenient if your object has edges that contrast highly with the background.

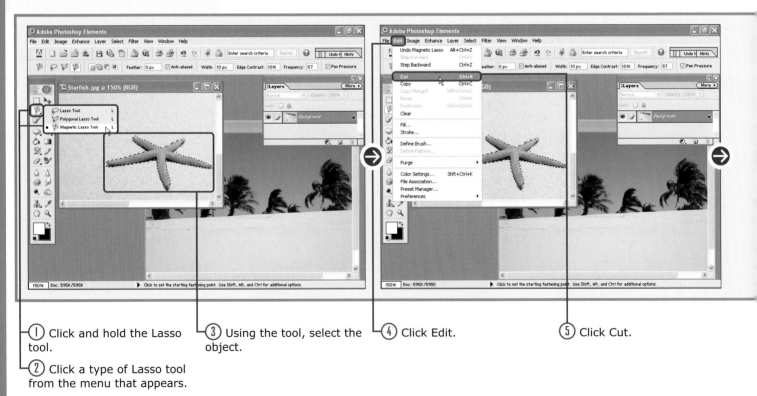

(1) Click and hold the Lasso tool.

(2) Click a type of Lasso tool from the menu that appears.

(3) Using the tool, select the object.

(4) Click Edit.

(5) Click Cut.

57

Customize It! ※

Sometimes a project requires multiple copies of an object in your image. You can easily create multiple copies by pasting the object once, which creates a new layer with the object in it, and then duplicating the new layer. You can rearrange the copies of the object using the Move tool ( ) to move the different layers.

Did You Know? ※

If you are cutting out a solid-color object from a photograph, you can use the Magic Wand tool ( ) to quickly select it. Adjust the Tolerance of the tool so that it selects all the object without selecting any of the surrounding background.

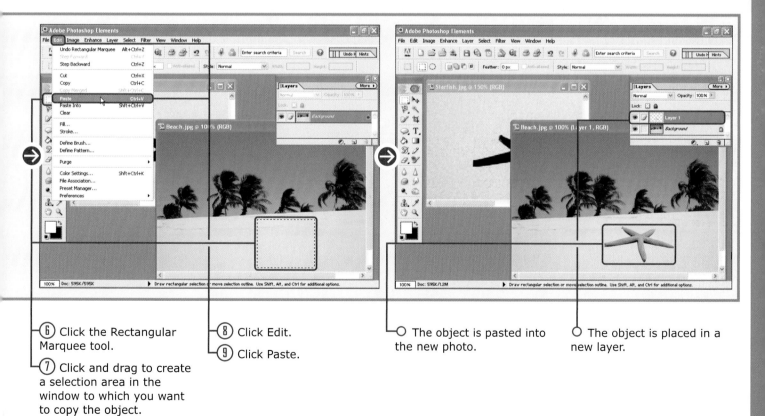

6 Click the Rectangular Marquee tool.

7 Click and drag to create a selection area in the window to which you want to copy the object.

8 Click Edit.

9 Click Paste.

○ The object is pasted into the new photo.

○ The object is placed in a new layer.

FIX RED EYE

Red eye is the eerie effect that occurs when the camera flash reflects off of the inside of a photo subject's eye, or retina. Red eye often occurs when you take flash photos in darkness or very low light. You can quickly and easily get rid of red eye from a photo using the Red Eye brush.

By placing the brush over the affected eye and clicking, Elements samples the reddish pixels in the area and adjusts them based on a predefined replacement color. The Red Eye brush changes the hue of the affected eye, without changing the brightness. This allows the Red Eye brush to remove the redness without getting rid of lightness or contrast.

An important setting for the Red Eye brush is the Tolerance. This specifies how close to the sampled color a pixel has to be before it is affected. A low tolerance setting may not remove all of the red in the eye, while a high setting may overly darken the eye, making it look even stranger than before.

① Click the Red Eye Brush tool.

② Click here and select a brush.

○ You can hold the circular brush over an eye in the image to match the brush to the eye size.

③ Click here and select First Click, which replaces the eye color you click in the image.

○ You can click Current Color to replace the color in the Current box instead.

Apply It! ✳

The Red Eye brush can help fix other photographic situations, not just red eyes. For example, you can use it to remove braces from a smile — just make sure you set the replacement color to white instead of black.

Did You Know? ✳

You can quickly decrease or increase the size of the Red Eye brush by pressing the [and] keys. Remember, the closer the brush size is to the size of the affected red eye, the better the results.

Did You Know? ✳

The Red Eye brush can be less useful for instances where the redness extends into the white of a subject's eye. Alternatives to using the Red Eye brush to fix such instances are some of the techniques covered in tasks #62 and #63.

#58

DIFFICULTY LEVEL

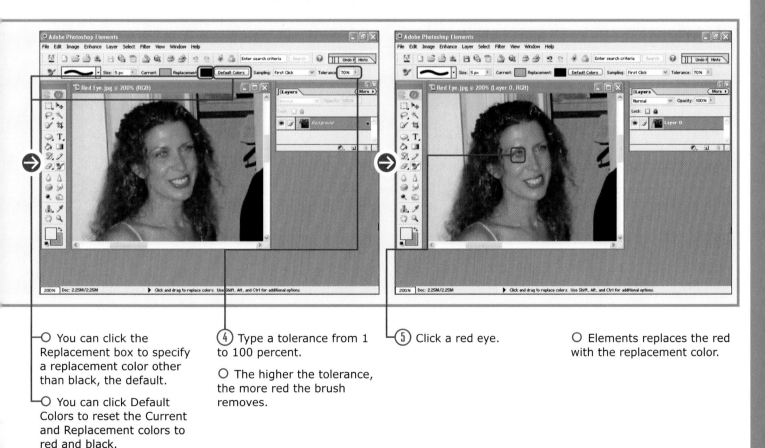

○ You can click the Replacement box to specify a replacement color other than black, the default.

○ You can click Default Colors to reset the Current and Replacement colors to red and black.

④ Type a tolerance from 1 to 100 percent.

○ The higher the tolerance, the more red the brush removes.

⑤ Click a red eye.

○ Elements replaces the red with the replacement color.

Turn a photo into a
JIGSAW PUZZLE

You can turn a photograph into a realistic looking jigsaw puzzle using the Texturizer filter. You can then print out your finished composition and carefully cut out the pieces to create a puzzle that you can take apart and put back together again.

There are several ways to customize your puzzle. You can scale the puzzle pieces that are applied on top of your photo. This lets you control how many total pieces are in the finished puzzle. You can also adjust relief and light direction settings to determine whether the pieces in your puzzle have edges that are bold or faint.

When you open the Texturizer filter, the jigsaw puzzle texture does not appear as an option in the dialog box. You must navigate to the Presets directory inside the Photoshop Elements 2 directory and select the Puzzle.psd file. The Puzzle.psd file is a separate Photoshop file that contains outlines for prearranged puzzle-piece shapes. When you apply the texture, the file is scaled and then merged with your photograph.

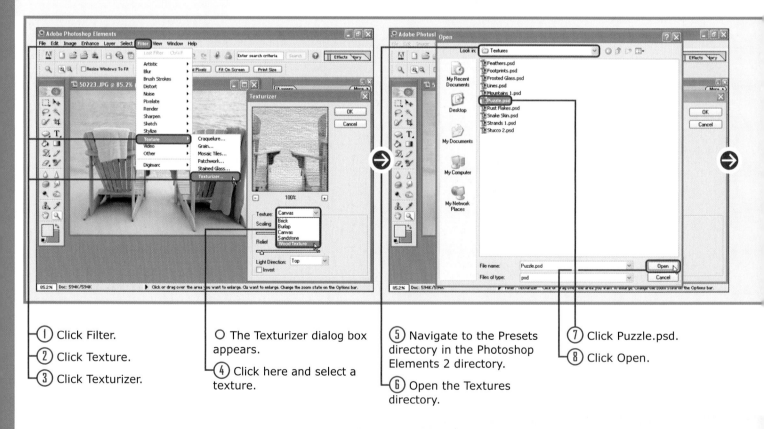

-① Click Filter.

-② Click Texture.

-③ Click Texturizer.

○ The Texturizer dialog box appears.

-④ Click here and select a texture.

⑤ Navigate to the Presets directory in the Photoshop Elements 2 directory.

-⑥ Open the Textures directory.

-⑦ Click Puzzle.psd.

-⑧ Click Open.

Customize It! ※

After building your photographic jigsaw puzzle, you may want to cut out the pieces digitally in Photoshop Elements and place the pieces in their own layers so that they can be easily manipulated. A quick way to do this is to insert a blank white layer on top of your jigsaw puzzle, and then re-create an identical set of white jigsaw puzzle pieces in that layer with the Texturizer filter. You can then select the outline of each puzzle piece by clicking inside this new layer with the Magic Wand tool ([✎]). After creating each selection outline in this way, you can then go back to the original puzzle layer to cut out the corresponding piece.

59

DIFFICULTY LEVEL

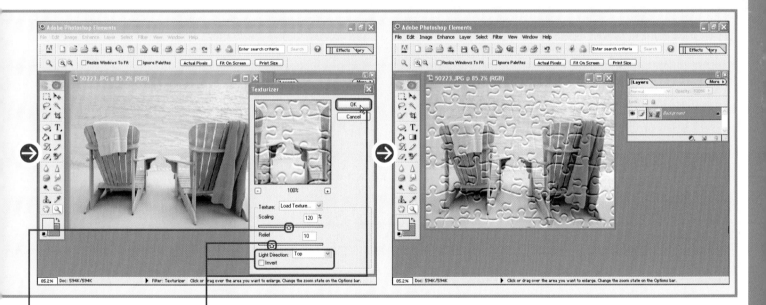

⑨ Click and drag the Scaling slider to specify how many puzzle pieces appear on your photo.

○ The higher the value, the fewer the number of pieces.

⑩ Click and drag the Relief slider to determine the boldness of the puzzle piece edges.

○ You can adjust the Light Direction and Invert settings to specify how the piece edges are lighted.

⑪ Click OK.

○ The jigsaw-puzzle effect is applied to the photo.

CROP PHOTOS
creatively

You can trim areas of your photo using the Crop tool. Trimming areas from the sides of your photos can help give particular objects in your photos more or less prominence. Cropping can also remove unneeded image content and thereby lessen the file size of the final image. This can be important if you are using the image on a Web site, where a smaller file size can result in faster downloading.

You can also use the Crop tool to add extra space around your image to give it a distinctive framed appearance. To add extra space, you must first

increase the area of the canvas window so that the Crop tool can extend beyond the boundaries of the image. Dragging the Crop tool outside the boundary and then executing the crop in this manner increases the canvas size.

Note that cropping an image affects all the layers in the image, including layers that are currently not selected or visible.

CHANGE THE FOCUS OF A PHOTO

① Click the Crop tool.

② Click and drag inside the photo to define the cropping boundary.

③ Click and drag the crop handles to fine-tune the cropping boundary.

④ Press Enter.

○ The photo is cropped.

Did You Know? ☀

You can also perform a crop using the rectangular marquee. First, click and drag with the rectangular marquee to select the area to crop. Click Image, and then click Crop. This method of cropping is less flexible than using the Crop tool (🔲) because you cannot adjust the cropping area after you have selected it.

Customize It! ☀

You can use the dialog boxes in the Options bar to specify the dimensions and resolution of the resulting image. Enter values in the Height, Width, and Resolution boxes. You can automatically add the dimensions and resolution of the current image by clicking the Front Image button (🔲).

DIFFICULTY LEVEL

ADD EXTRA SPACE

1 Click and drag the corner of the image window to add extra space around the photo.

2 Click and drag the Crop tool to define the cropping area.

3 Click and drag the handles to extend the cropping area outside of the boundary of the photo.

4 Press Enter.

○ The photo is cropped.

○ Extra space is added to the edges of the photo.

○ The extra space is filled with the current background color.

CHAPTER 7

Working with Color

Accurate, vibrant color is crucial to almost every successful digital photography project. Therefore, it should come as no surprise that many of the more powerful tools in Photoshop Elements have to do with adjusting and optimizing color.

With the Color Variations tool, Elements offers a powerful yet user-friendly way to adjust the overall color balance of your digital photographs. The Color Cast tool gives you the ability, with a single click, to remove unnatural tints that can permeate an image. With these two tools, Elements makes correcting the colors in your digital photographs a snap.

Elements also offers tools to precisely affect specific colors in your image. Using the Replace Color tool, you can quickly and easily select all the instances of a given color, and then shift it to a different hue or change its brightness or intensity. Combining Elements' various selection tools with the color adjustment tools, you can pinpoint objects in your image and customize their colors as well — or remove color from them altogether.

Need to find just the right color for painting? The Color Swatches palette offers you any easy way to pick out colors from across the spectrum, or pick only from colors that show up accurately on all Web browsers.

You can also affect the colors in your image using fill and adjustment layers. *Fill* layers let you quickly add color, pattern, and gradient elements to an image, while *adjustment* layers let you make color and tonal changes.

TOP 100

Adjust the
COLOR VARIATIONS
of an image

You can adjust the color balance, contrast, and saturation of an image using the Color Variations dialog box. As you make successive adjustments to your image, you can compare its current state with the state of the image when you opened the dialog box. When you are satisfied with your changes and click the OK button, the adjustments are applied to the photo in the image window.

You can use the Color Variations feature to adjust the color or exposure of a flawed image that was shot with a digital camera or digitized with a

scanner. You can also use it to match the look of two different photos so that they both have similar color content and overall lighting.

The settings in the dialog box allow you to affect a specific range of colors in your image — for example, just the colors in the shadowy or bright parts of the image. They also enable you to tailor the strength of the tool.

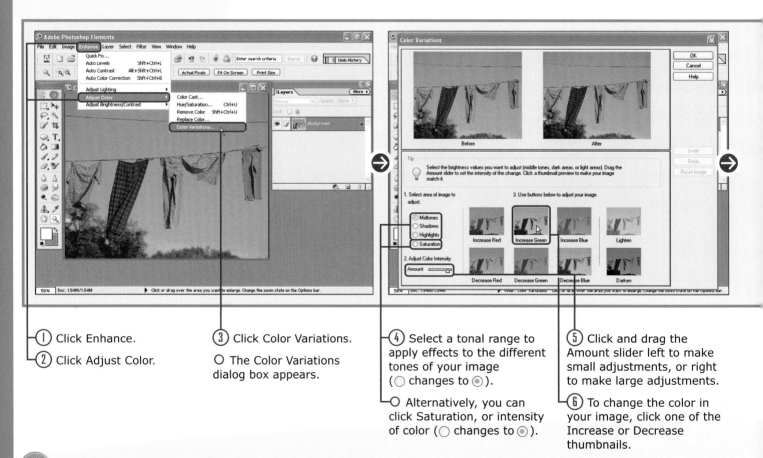

① Click Enhance.

② Click Adjust Color.

③ Click Color Variations.

○ The Color Variations dialog box appears.

④ Select a tonal range to apply effects to the different tones of your image (○ changes to ◉).

○ Alternatively, you can click Saturation, or intensity of color (○ changes to ◉).

⑤ Click and drag the Amount slider left to make small adjustments, or right to make large adjustments.

⑥ To change the color in your image, click one of the Increase or Decrease thumbnails.

#61

Did You Know? ☀

There are several ways to undo the changes you apply in the Color Variations dialog box. You can click Undo to undo the most recent Variations adjustment. You can click Reset Image to revert the image to its original state before you opened the dialog box. You can also click an Increase or Decrease button to undo a previous Decrease or Increase command, respectively.

Did You Know? ☀

The Color Variations dialog box is one way to remove a color cast, for example, a yellowish color that can permeate some old photo prints. Another way to remove a color cast is with the Color Cast command. For more information on the Color Cast command, see task #65.

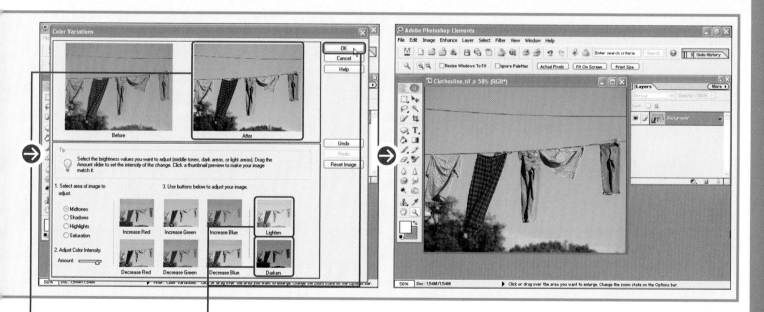

○— The result of the adjustment shows up in the After thumbnail.

○ To increase the effect, you can click the Increase or Decrease thumbnail again.

○— You can increase the brightness of the image by clicking Lighten.

○— You can decrease the brightness by clicking Darken.

⑦ Click OK.

○ Elements makes the color adjustments to the image.

REMOVE COLOR
in an image selectively

Selectively removing color in an image is an effective way to lessen the prominence of certain objects in your image. You can quickly and easily get rid of the color in an area of your image by first selecting the area with a selection tool. Then you can either apply the Remove Color command or decrease the Saturation value of the selection to the minimum. The *Saturation* value of an image describes the image's color intensity. Both the Remove Color and Saturation commands achieve

the same results; they remove all color by converting the colors in the selection to shades of gray.

You can remove all the color in an image by converting the image to Grayscale. This type of conversion, which involves changing the mode of the image, is covered in task #69.

After you have removed color from part of your image, you can selectively restore it using the Brush tool. For more information, see task #66.

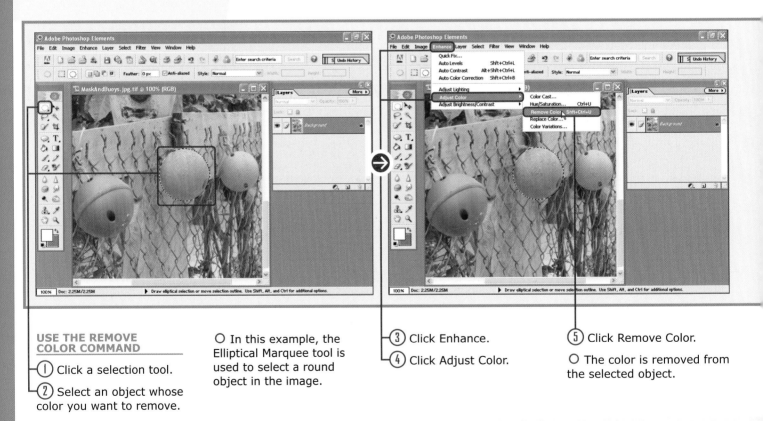

USE THE REMOVE COLOR COMMAND

① Click a selection tool.

② Select an object whose color you want to remove.

○ In this example, the Elliptical Marquee tool is used to select a round object in the image.

③ Click Enhance.

④ Click Adjust Color.

⑤ Click Remove Color.

○ The color is removed from the selected object.

Did You Know? ☀

You can lessen the intensity
of colors in your image
without removing them entirely
by adjusting the Saturation by a value
of −1 to -99. Conversely, increasing the
Saturation from +1 to +100 boosts the
intensity of the colors in your image.

Did You Know? ☀

If you have an image with multiple layers,
the Remove Color command only affects the
currently selected layer. However, converting
the mode of an image to Grayscale removes
the color in all the layers. For more information
on converting the mode of an image to Grayscale,
see task #68.

DIFFICULTY LEVEL

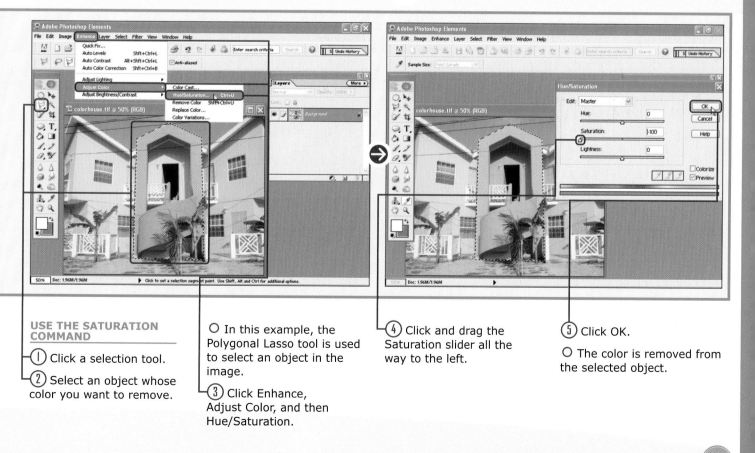

**USE THE SATURATION
COMMAND**

① Click a selection tool.

② Select an object whose
color you want to remove.

○ In this example, the
Polygonal Lasso tool is used
to select an object in the
image.

③ Click Enhance,
Adjust Color, and then
Hue/Saturation.

④ Click and drag the
Saturation slider all the
way to the left.

⑤ Click OK.

○ The color is removed from
the selected object.

Selectively
ADJUST COLOR
in an image

You can quickly and easily adjust the color of an object in an image by selecting the object and then changing the settings in the Hue/Saturation dialog box. This offers an effective way to intensify elements of a washed-out photograph, or tone down parts of an image that are overly bright. You may want to adjust colors in an image that was digitized using a poorly calibrated scanner.

Changing the *hue* of the selected object enables you to shift the color of the object to another color in the spectrum; adjusting the *saturation* allows you to

increase or decrease the color intensity of the selected object. Adjusting color using the hue and saturation settings keeps the lighting and contrast of the object intact. There is no loss in detail, which means your object remains crisp and clear.

You can also get rid of the color of an object entirely by adjusting the saturation. See task #62 for more information about selectively removing color.

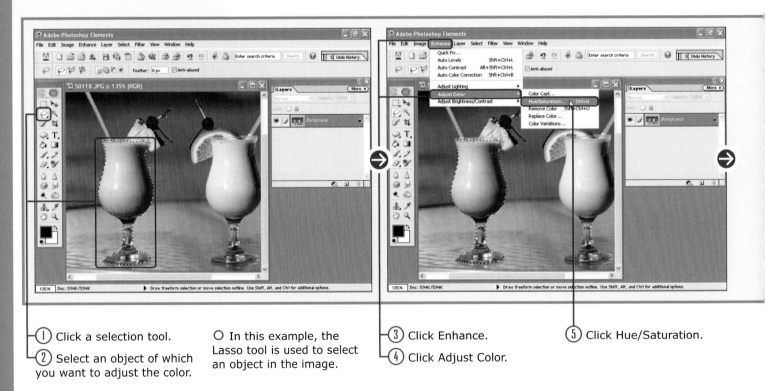

① Click a selection tool.

② Select an object of which you want to adjust the color.

○ In this example, the Lasso tool is used to select an object in the image.

③ Click Enhance.

④ Click Adjust Color.

⑤ Click Hue/Saturation.

#63

Did You Know? ☀

As you drag the Hue slider, colors in your image change according to their position in the color spectrum. With dragging the slider to the right, red changes to orange, yellow, green, blue, and then purple.

Customize It! ☀

The Colorize check box in the Hue/Saturation dialog box allows you to use the feature as a fancy painting tool. Checking the Colorize box turns your current selection into a single solid color. You can then change the color using the Hue slider, and adjust the intensity of the color using the Saturation slider. For an example see task #54.

Did You Know? ☀

If you have a multilayered image, your color adjustments only affect the layer that is currently selected. To affect multiple layers at once, apply an adjustment layer. For information about adjustment layers, see task #69.

DIFFICULTY LEVEL

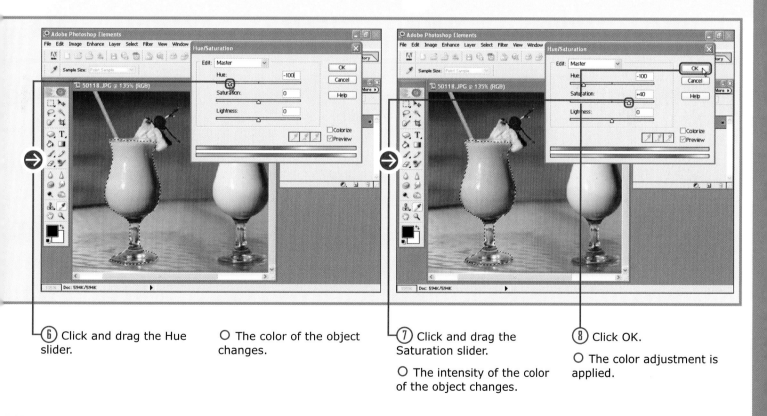

⑥ Click and drag the Hue slider.

○ The color of the object changes.

⑦ Click and drag the Saturation slider.

○ The intensity of the color of the object changes.

⑧ Click OK.

○ The color adjustment is applied.

REPLACE A COLOR
in an image

You can use the Replace Color command to select one or more colors in your image and change them using hue, saturation, and lightness settings. This is useful if you have an image with a number of solid-colored objects and want to change the colors of those objects quickly. The Replace Color command lets you do this without having to select the colored objects one at a time. You just click a sample of the color you want to change. Elements selects all the similar colors in your image automatically.

You select the colors that you want to replace with the help of a black-and-white Selection box. Clicking inside your image selects the corresponding area in the Selection box, as well as any similarly colored areas in the image. Selected pixels turn white in the Selection box. You can then use the sliders in the dialog box to change the selected colors in the image.

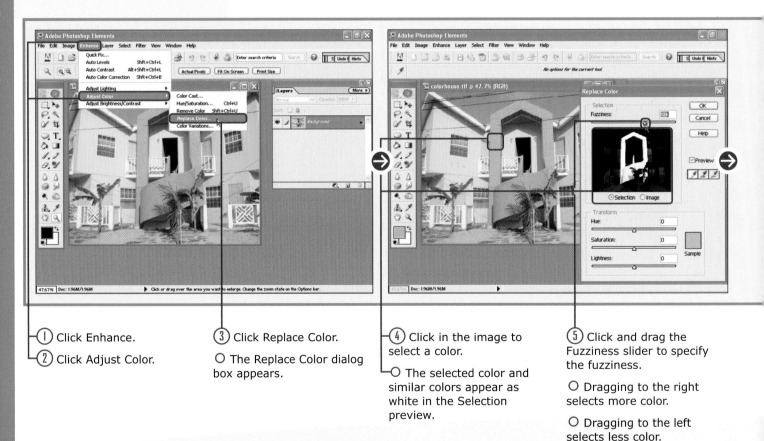

① Click Enhance.

② Click Adjust Color.

③ Click Replace Color.

○ The Replace Color dialog box appears.

④ Click in the image to select a color.

○ The selected color and similar colors appear as white in the Selection preview.

⑤ Click and drag the Fuzziness slider to specify the fuzziness.

○ Dragging to the right selects more color.

○ Dragging to the left selects less color.

Did You Know? ☀

To add more colors to your selection, you can select the Dropper Plus tool (☒) in the Replace Color dialog box and then click inside your image. To subtract colors from your selection, you can select the Dropper Minus tool (☒) and click inside your image.

Customize It! ☀

Clicking the Image radio button in the Replace Color dialog box changes the Selection box from the black-and-white representation of the selected pixels to a miniature color version of your image. You may find it useful to switch back and forth between the Image and Selection options as you select colors to replace or adjust the fuzziness slider.

#64

DIFFICULTY LEVEL

⑥ Click and drag the Transform sliders to change the colors inside the selected area.

Note: For more about Hue and Saturation adjustments, see task #63.

⑦ Click OK.

○ Elements replaces the selected color.

Access
COLOR SWATCHES

The Color Swatches palette gives you a convenient way to access a wide variety of colors as you work on your Photoshop Elements projects. You can access the colors by clicking colored squares in the palette and then put them to work in tasks that use the Brush, Paintbucket, and other painting tools. You can also use the Color Swatches palette to determine the color of the text you create when using the Type tool.

Accessing the Color Swatches palette is convenient if you are building graphics for a Web site and want easy access to the set of *Web-safe colors*. Web-safe colors are a library of 216 colors that display accurately on all Web browsers, no matter what type of computer or color monitor a viewer is using. Building your graphics in Photoshop Elements by using Web-safe colors helps ensure that your Web pages will look their best to everyone.

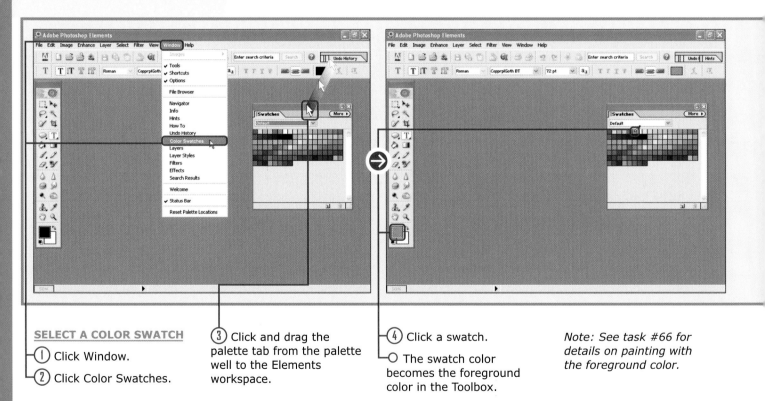

<u>**SELECT A COLOR SWATCH**</u>

① Click Window.

② Click Color Swatches.

③ Click and drag the palette tab from the palette well to the Elements workspace.

④ Click a swatch.

○ The swatch color becomes the foreground color in the Toolbox.

Note: See task #66 for details on painting with the foreground color.

DIFFICULTY LEVEL

Did You Know? ※

Clicking a swatch in the Color Swatches palette sets the foreground color to that swatch. To set the background color, press and hold the Ctrl key while you click a swatch.

Customize It! ※

You can add custom colors from your images to the Color Swatches palette. First, select the Eyedropper tool (🖊) and click a color in your image to store it as the foreground color. Then click in the empty area at the bottom of the Swatches palette. A dialog box appears allowing you to name the new swatch. After you click OK to close the dialog box, the new color swatch appears at the end of the set of swatches.

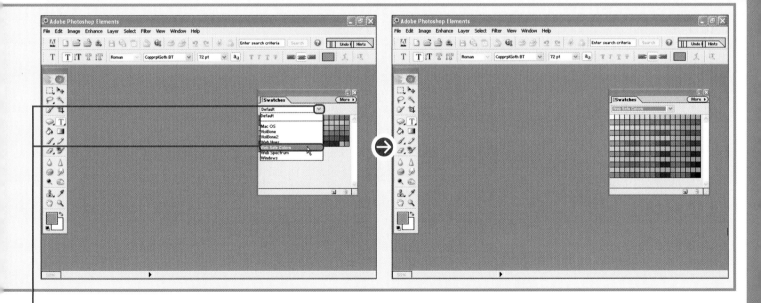

SELECT A CUSTOM SWATCH LIBRARY

(1) Click here and select a swatch library.

O The swatches from that library are displayed.

PAINT A
black-and-white
PHOTO

You can paint color onto a black-and-white photo using the Brush tool. This is a great way to draw attention to interesting objects in an otherwise colorless scene. When applied, the Brush tool adds the current foreground color to your image.

To effectively apply your colors, there are a couple ways to customize your brush. A menu on the Options bar lets you select from several preset Brush sizes with either hard or soft edges. Choose your size based on the size of the objects you will paint. You can place the Brush cursor over the photo to

compare. Brushes with hard edges are useful for objects with hard edges; soft edges can give you flexibility when painting objects with fuzzy silhouettes.

You can also customize your Brush tool by selecting its mode. The mode determines how the color added by the brush blends with the existing colors in your photo. In Normal mode, the Brush tool applies an opaque layer of color to your image, which covers up existing details. To maintain the details in your image, select the Color mode.

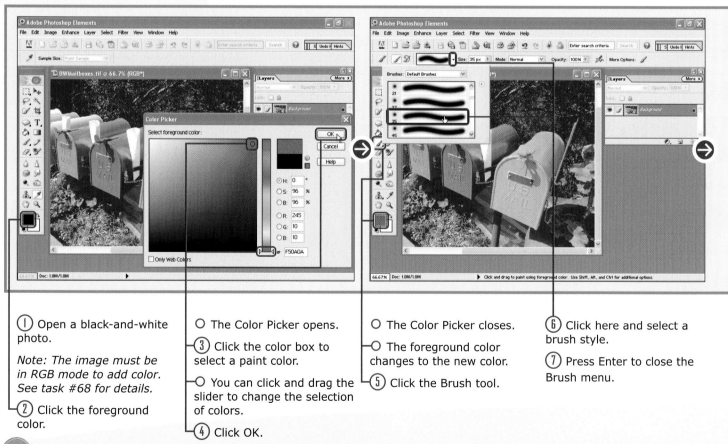

① Open a black-and-white photo.

Note: The image must be in RGB mode to add color. See task #68 for details.

② Click the foreground color.

○ The Color Picker opens.

③ Click the color box to select a paint color.

○ You can click and drag the slider to change the selection of colors.

④ Click OK.

○ The Color Picker closes.

○ The foreground color changes to the new color.

⑤ Click the Brush tool.

⑥ Click here and select a brush style.

⑦ Press Enter to close the Brush menu.

Did You Know? ☀

You can constrain where the Brush tool applies color by making a selection before you start painting. You will only be able to paint the area inside your selection. This can help protect areas in your image that you want to leave black and white.

Did You Know? ☀

You can use the Paint Bucket tool (🪣) to quickly color all the pixels inside a selection. The tool applies color to the area where you click, plus any surrounding pixels that are of similar color.

Customize It! ☀

You can decrease the amount of color added with your Paint Brush by decreasing its opacity to less than 100 percent in the options bar. This can be useful if you want to apply a semitransparent layer of color to your image.

⑧ Click here and select Color.

○ Painting in Color mode allows you to apply color without losing detail.

⑨ Click and drag inside the image to paint.

○ The Brush tool adds color to the image.

Remove a
COLOR CAST

#67

DIFFICULTY LEVEL

The Color Cast command removes the unwanted tint that can sometimes permeate a digital photograph. Removing a color cast can reveal the original color tones of a photo.

A color cast can arise from a variety of factors. An outdoor scene under clear skies may have a naturally occurring blue cast; an indoor scene may have a cast due to light coming through tinted windows; or, if you are dealing with a scanned photo, the cast may be the result of a poorly developed print.

The tool is easy to apply. Click the Color Cast eyedropper on an area of the photo that should be devoid of color — namely, an area that should be white, gray, or black. Elements will adjust the overall color based on the tint of the clicked pixel. You may have to click several different places in your photo before you find a result that is suitable.

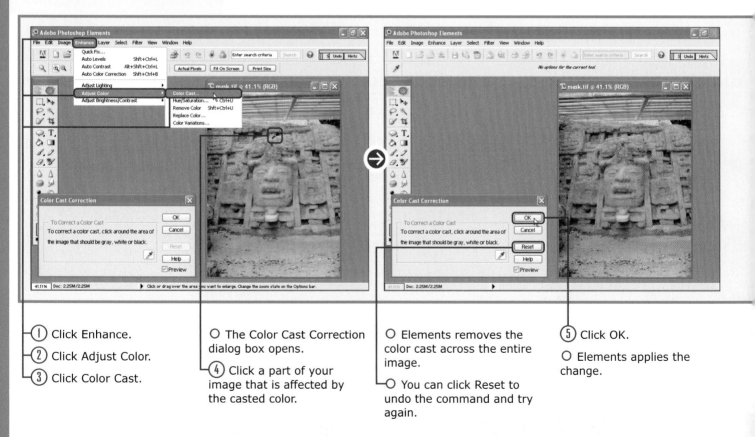

① Click Enhance.

② Click Adjust Color.

③ Click Color Cast.

○ The Color Cast Correction dialog box opens.

④ Click a part of your image that is affected by the casted color.

○ Elements removes the color cast across the entire image.

○ You can click Reset to undo the command and try again.

⑤ Click OK.

○ Elements applies the change.

CHANGE THE MODE
of an image

68

DIFFICULTY LEVEL

Photoshop Elements allows you to switch between several different image modes. You can change the mode to increase or decrease the number of colors available while working on your image. For almost all projects, you will want to work in RGB mode.

RGB Color is the most commonly used mode, has the fewest restrictions of all the modes, and allows you to work with all types of colors. Some Elements commands only work with RGB color images.

Bitmap mode allows only two colors in your image: black and white. You may want to consider using Bitmap if you are working with solid black line art.

Grayscale mode allows you to have black, white, and different shades of gray in your image, but no other colors. Converting a color image to Grayscale can give the image an old-fashioned look.

Indexed Color mode can include all different types of colors, but can only include maximum of 256 in an image. If you open an image saved in the GIF format, it will open in Indexed Color mode.

① Click Image.

② Click Mode.

③ Click an image mode.

○ An Adobe Photoshop Elements dialog box prompts you about discarding color information.

④ Click OK.

○ Elements converts the image to the new mode.

Note: Perform this task on a copy or remember to save as a new name.

Fine-tune color with an
ADJUSTMENT LAYER

You can apply complex color and tonal changes to your image by creating adjustment layers. Adjustment layers are organized in the Layers palette along with the other types of layers in your image. By using adjustment layers, you have the flexibility to fine-tune or remove your changes later. Such layers contain information about changes in hue, brightness, and other image characteristics.

The settings associated with an adjustment layer affect the layers that are below the layer in the Layers palette. This means that a single color or

tonal adjustment is able to affect multiple layers in an image. This is unlike standard color adjustments performed via menu commands, which only affect the currently selected layer.

You can control the intensity of an adjustment layer using the opacity slider in the Layers palette. For example, if you want to lower the color or tonal change of an adjustment layer by half, you can simply decrease its opacity to 50 percent.

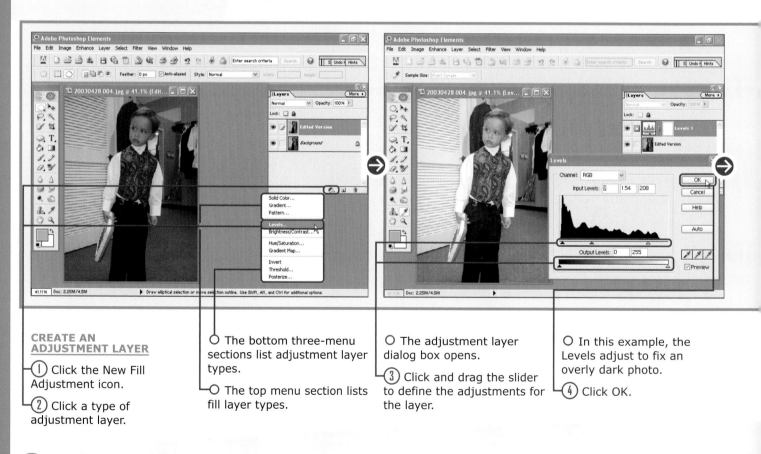

CREATE AN ADJUSTMENT LAYER

① Click the New Fill Adjustment icon.

② Click a type of adjustment layer.

○ The bottom three-menu sections list adjustment layer types.

○ The top menu section lists fill layer types.

○ The adjustment layer dialog box opens.

③ Click and drag the slider to define the adjustments for the layer.

○ In this example, the Levels adjust to fix an overly dark photo.

④ Click OK.

#69

Did You Know? ※

You can click Eye icon (👁) in the Layers palette to hide an adjustment layer and temporarily remove the layer's effect. You can delete an adjustment layer to remove the effect permanently.

Customize It! ※

If you want to create an adjustment layer that affects only part of your image, make a selection before creating your adjustment layer. Elements will add a mask to your adjustment layer so that it affects only the selected portion of the image.

Did You Know? ※

You can apply an Invert adjustment layer to invert the colors in your image, turning the image into a photonegative of it self.

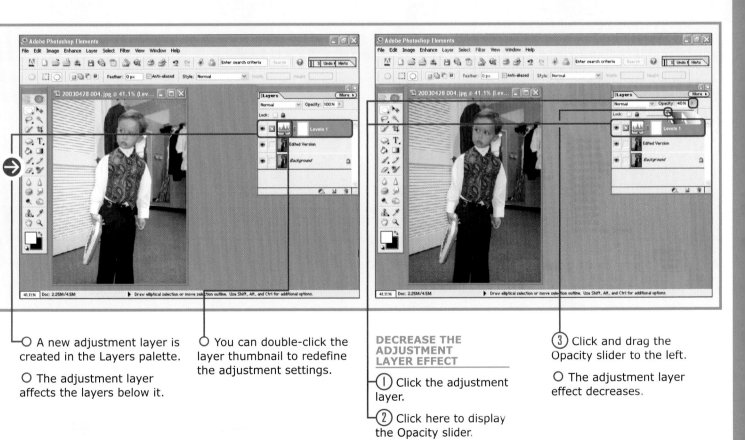

○ A new adjustment layer is created in the Layers palette.

○ The adjustment layer affects the layers below it.

○ You can double-click the layer thumbnail to redefine the adjustment settings.

DECREASE THE ADJUSTMENT LAYER EFFECT

① Click the adjustment layer.

② Click here to display the Opacity slider.

③ Click and drag the Opacity slider to the left.

○ The adjustment layer effect decreases.

Apply color with a
FILL LAYER

You can quickly add colors, patterns, and gradients to an image by applying them as fill layers. Because they store their information in layer form instead of permanently to your image, fill layers give you the flexibility to adjust your fills after you apply them. Fill layers are organized in the Layers palette along with the other types of layers in your image.

You can control how a fill layer is applied using the Opacity slider in the Layers palette. For example, you can make a color or pattern fill semitransparent by decreasing the opacity of the layer to less than 100 percent.

How you customize your fill layer depends on the type of layer you are applying. When adding a color fill, you specify a color from the Color Picker that you want to add to your image as a solid layer. When adding a pattern or gradient fill, you can choose from a number of preset pattern or gradient styles.

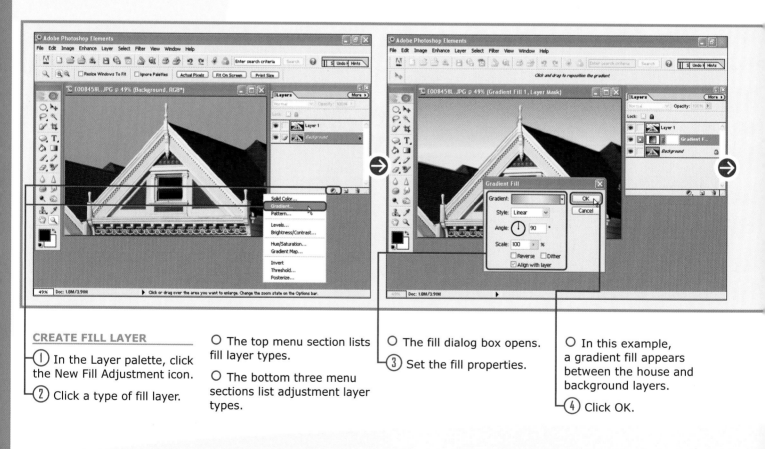

CREATE FILL LAYER

① In the Layer palette, click the New Fill Adjustment icon.

② Click a type of fill layer.

○ The top menu section lists fill layer types.

○ The bottom three menu sections list adjustment layer types.

○ The fill dialog box opens.

③ Set the fill properties.

○ In this example, a gradient fill appears between the house and background layers.

④ Click OK.

Did You Know? ※

In addition to the preset
styles, Elements also allows
you to create custom patterns and
gradients to use as your fill layers.
You can create patterns from scenery
copied from your images. You can create
gradients by specifying sequences of colors.
See the Help documentation for details.

Customize It! ※

You can easily switch the type of fill layer or change a
fill layer to an adjustment layer. Just click Layer, Change
Layer Content, and then a new layer type.

id You Know? ※

You can arrange different fill layers on top of one another
to create interesting effects. For example, you can add a
semitransparent solid-color fill atop a pattern fill to give the
pattern some extra color. You can also adjust how your fill layers
interact with one another by selecting different modes using the
Mode menu in the Layers palette.

DIFFICULTY LEVEL

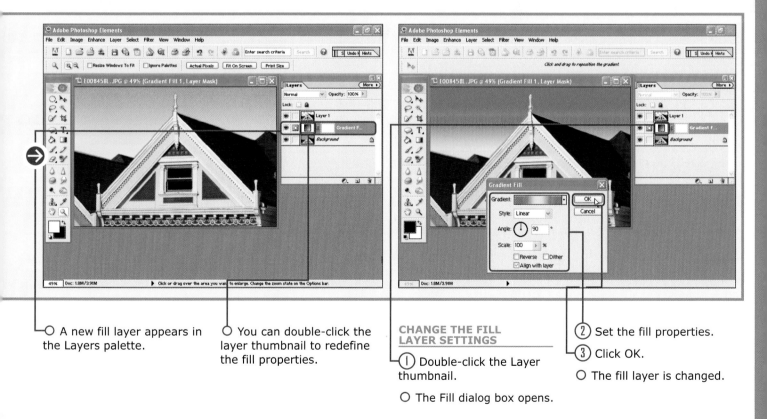

─○ A new fill layer appears in
the Layers palette.

○ You can double-click the
layer thumbnail to redefine
the fill properties.

**CHANGE THE FILL
LAYER SETTINGS**

─① Double-click the Layer
thumbnail.

○ The Fill dialog box opens.

② Set the fill properties.

③ Click OK.

○ The fill layer is changed.

CHAPTER 8

Preparing Images for Printing and the Web

Typically, the final step in a Photoshop Elements project is printing the finished work out on paper. Alternatively, if you are interested in online publishing, it is putting it into a form that you can use on a Web site. Elements includes a number of features that makes printing photographs and other compositions a snap. It also provides tools for creating good-looking images that you can upload straight to the Web.

The Print Preview feature in Elements is something you should always take advantage of before you send your image to the printer. It shows how your image will display on the printed page, and gives you interactive tools to fine-tune the orientation of the image before it is printed.

Elements also offers automated tools that create contact sheets and picture packages. *Contact sheets* consist of many miniature versions of your images that you can print out in order to keep a hard-copy reference for your records. A *picture package* consists of several copies of an image displayed at commonly used sizes, all arranged on a single page for printing.

The Save for Web dialog box is a powerful feature for creating images in the GIF and JPEG formats, the two standard formats for displaying images on the Web. If you want to put a collection of photos online, Elements can even build an online photo gallery for you. All you have to do is upload the Web pages.

TOP 100

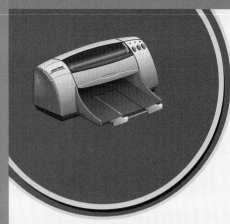

PREVIEW AN IMAGE
for printing

You can preview your image to see how it will print out on paper in the Print Preview dialog box. The dialog box gives you useful information such as the orientation of the image and how big the margins are between the image and the edges of the page. How the image displays on the page depends on its size as measured in pixels, its resolution, as well as the settings for your printer.

In the dialog box, you can adjust the layout of the image by interactively clicking and dragging handles on the corners of the image, or by changing the

distance from the top and left side of the paper. Making these changes in the Print Preview dialog box can be more convenient than using the Resize Image command, which is covered in task #74.

Note that the changes you make in the Print Preview dialog box only affect how the image prints, not the actual size of the image as measured in pixels.

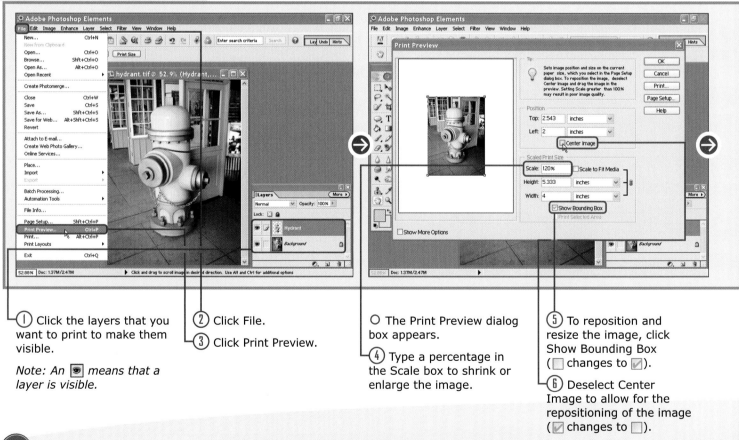

① Click the layers that you want to print to make them visible.

Note: An 👁 *means that a layer is visible.*

② Click File.

③ Click Print Preview.

O The Print Preview dialog box appears.

④ Type a percentage in the Scale box to shrink or enlarge the image.

⑤ To reposition and resize the image, click Show Bounding Box (☐ changes to ☑).

⑥ Deselect Center Image to allow for the repositioning of the image (☑ changes to ☐).

Customize It! ☀

You can maximize the size of
your image when it prints by
clicking the Scale to Fit Media check
box. This will stretch the image so that it
meets the edge of the printed page. The
height and width of the image are kept
proportional to one another.

Customize It! ☀

You can automatically add a caption to your printed
image by clicking the Show More Options check box
and then clicking the Caption check box. Elements
inserts any caption information that you have entered
in the File Info dialog box below your image. For
more information about the file, see task #80.

71

DIFFICULTY LEVEL

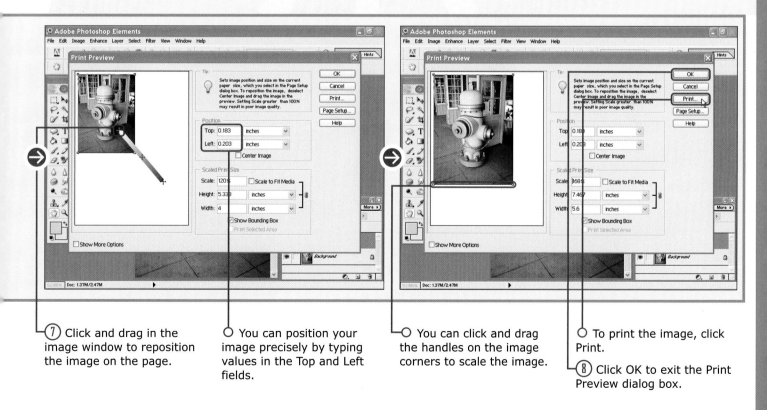

⑦ Click and drag in the
image window to reposition
the image on the page.

○ You can position your
image precisely by typing
values in the Top and Left
fields.

○ You can click and drag
the handles on the image
corners to scale the image.

○ To print the image, click
Print.

⑧ Click OK to exit the Print
Preview dialog box.

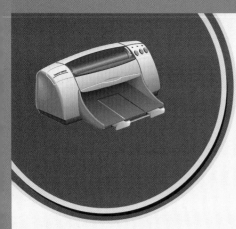

Create a
CONTACT SHEET

You can use Photoshop Elements to automatically create a digital version of a photographer's contact sheet. *Contact sheets* consist of miniature versions of your images that you can print out in order to keep a hard-copy reference for your records. This can be useful if you have a large number of digital photos to keep track of, and want an alternative to printing them all out at full size.

The Contact Sheet dialog box lets you specify the number of rows and columns of images displayed on the contact sheet. It also allows you to add the filename as a caption for each image, which can be helpful for matching up each miniature photo on the sheet with a file on your computer. For information on previewing how the contact sheet will print on a page, see task #71.

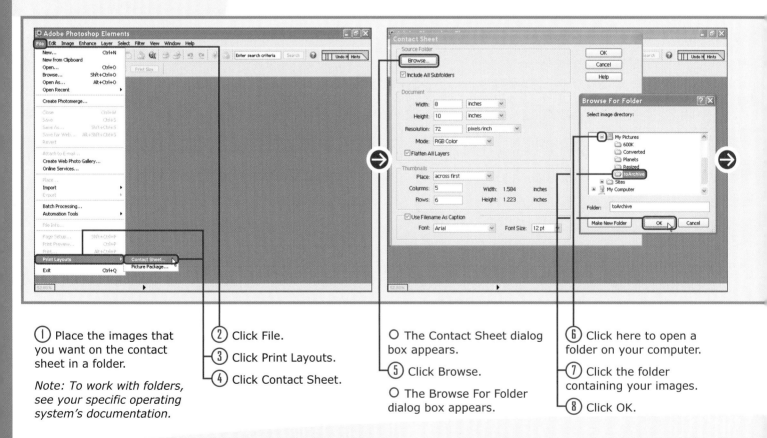

① Place the images that you want on the contact sheet in a folder.

Note: To work with folders, see your specific operating system's documentation.

② Click File.

③ Click Print Layouts.

④ Click Contact Sheet.

○ The Contact Sheet dialog box appears.

⑤ Click Browse.

○ The Browse For Folder dialog box appears.

⑥ Click here to open a folder on your computer.

⑦ Click the folder containing your images.

⑧ Click OK.

#72

Did You Know? ※

You can make the thumbnail images of your contact sheet larger or smaller by adjusting the number of rows and columns. Elements determines the final size of the thumbnails on the contact sheet based on the number of rows and columns as well as the paper size.

Did You Know? ※

After Elements creates the contact sheet, you can continue to edit it in its image window. You may want to use the Type tool to insert additional information on the page, such as the date the images were originally shot or edited, or a general description of their content. For more information about adding type, see task #41.

DIFFICULTY LEVEL

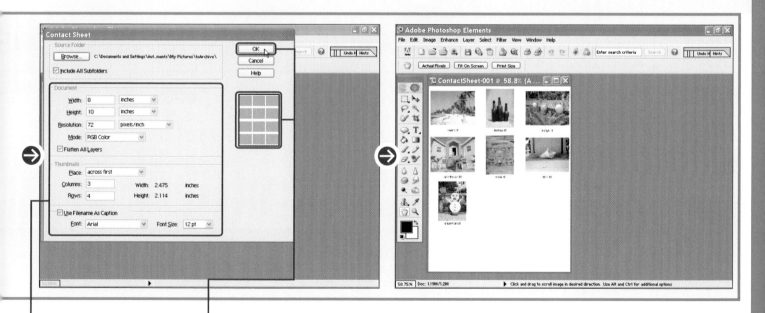

⑨ Set the contact sheet properties by typing values or by clicking and selecting settings.

○ You can set contact sheet size and resolution, the order and number of columns and rows, and the caption font and font size.

○ Elements displays a preview of the layout.

⑩ Click OK.

○ Elements creates and displays your contact sheet.

○ If there are more images than can fit on a single page, Elements creates multiple contact sheets.

Create a
PICTURE
PACKAGE

You can automatically create a one-page layout with a selected image displayed at various sizes using the Picture Package command. You may find this useful when you want to print out copies of a special photo taken with a digital camera for friends, family, or associates. Picture sizes range from wallet size to 10x13, depending on the paper size on which you choose to print.

The Picture Package dialog box allows you to preview the arrangement of the layout as well as

specify the page size, resolution, and mode. You can create a black-and-white picture package by setting the mode to Grayscale.

The quality of the resulting printout depends on the quality of the original image as well as the picture package settings. Starting with an image that is large and increasing the resolution of the picture package are two ways to help make sure the resulting printout looks as sharp as possible.

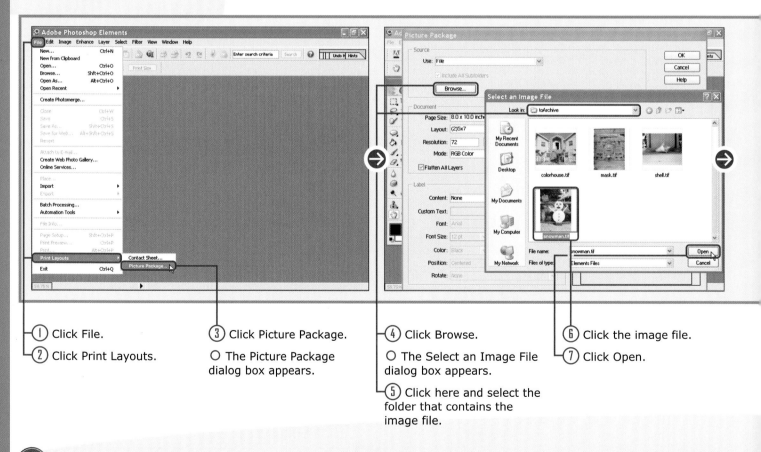

① Click File.

② Click Print Layouts.

③ Click Picture Package.

O The Picture Package dialog box appears.

④ Click Browse.

O The Select an Image File dialog box appears.

⑤ Click here and select the folder that contains the image file.

⑥ Click the image file.

⑦ Click Open.

Customize It! ※

The Picture Package dialog box allows you to add a custom label to each image in the picture package. The labels are placed across the center of each image. This can be useful if you want to prominently display caption or copyright information associated with the image. To specify caption and copyright information for your image, see task 80.

#73

DIFFICULTY LEVEL

Did You Know? ※

You can create multiple picture packages by specifying a folder in the Use menu in the Picture Package dialog box. Elements will take each image in the folder and create a separate picture package image for it.

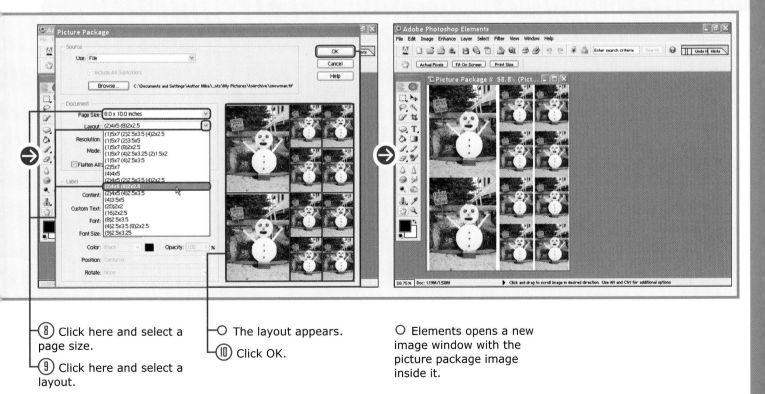

⑧ Click here and select a page size.

⑨ Click here and select a layout.

─○ The layout appears.

⑩ Click OK.

○ Elements opens a new image window with the picture package image inside it.

SCALE
AN IMAGE

You can scale an image to change its size relative to your computer monitor or to the printing paper. This can be useful if you want to fit the image in with other elements on a Web page, or if you want your image to print out at a common photo size.

Resizing for the Web involves changing the pixel dimensions of an image. *Pixels* are the tiny, solid-color squares that make up every image in Photoshop Elements. Decreasing the number of

pixels in an image decreases its size and scales it down on a Web page. Increasing the number of pixels makes an image larger.

The size at which an image prints, also called the document size, depends on the number of pixels as well as the print resolution. When you change the document size in the Image Size dialog box, Elements adjusts the number of pixels in the image so that it prints with the specified dimensions.

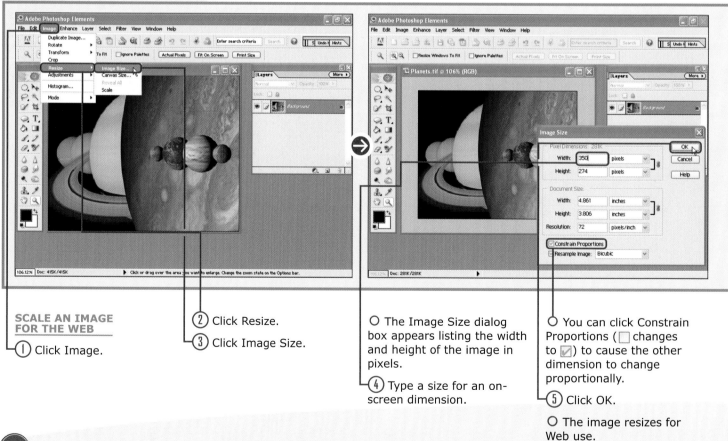

**SCALE AN IMAGE
FOR THE WEB**

① Click Image.

② Click Resize.

③ Click Image Size.

○ The Image Size dialog box appears listing the width and height of the image in pixels.

④ Type a size for an on-screen dimension.

○ You can click Constrain Proportions (☐ changes to ☑) to cause the other dimension to change proportionally.

⑤ Click OK.

○ The image resizes for Web use.

74

Did You Know? ※

Scaling an image by changing
the number of pixels can add
blur to an image. You can offset this
blurring by applying one of the program's
sharpen filters. Click Filter and then Sharpen
to access them.

Customize It! ※

You can change the resolution of your image in the
Image Size dialog box. Changing the resolution does
not affect the number of pixels in the image, so it does
not affect the size of the image on the computer screen or
on a Web page. It does affect how the image prints out.
Increasing the resolution shrinks the image on the page;
decreasing the resolution enlarges it.

DIFFICULTY LEVEL

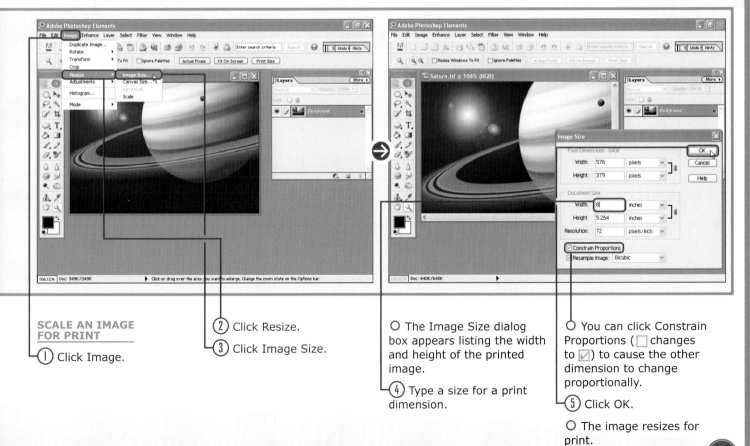

**SCALE AN IMAGE
FOR PRINT**

① Click Image.

② Click Resize.

③ Click Image Size.

O The Image Size dialog
box appears listing the width
and height of the printed
image.

④ Type a size for a print
dimension.

O You can click Constrain
Proportions (☐ changes
to ☑) to cause the other
dimension to change
proportionally.

⑤ Click OK.

O The image resizes for
print.

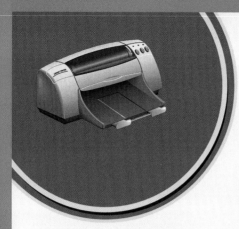

Create an online
PHOTO GALLERY

You can have Elements create a photo gallery Web site that displays your digital images. Elements not only sizes and optimizes your image files for the site, but it also creates the Web pages that display the images and links those pages together.

In the photo gallery Web site, a miniature image known as a thumbnail Elements creates for each gallery image. You click the thumbnail to view the image at its regular size. There are also buttons that allow you to navigate between the different pages that display the thumbnails.

The photo gallery feature is useful if you want a quick and easy way to build a Web site for your digital photos, but do not want to create the HTML pages by hand.

After you create your photo gallery, you can use a Web publishing program such as Macromedia Dreamweaver or Adobe GoLive to upload all the image and HTML files to a Web server. You can also use an FTP program to upload the files.

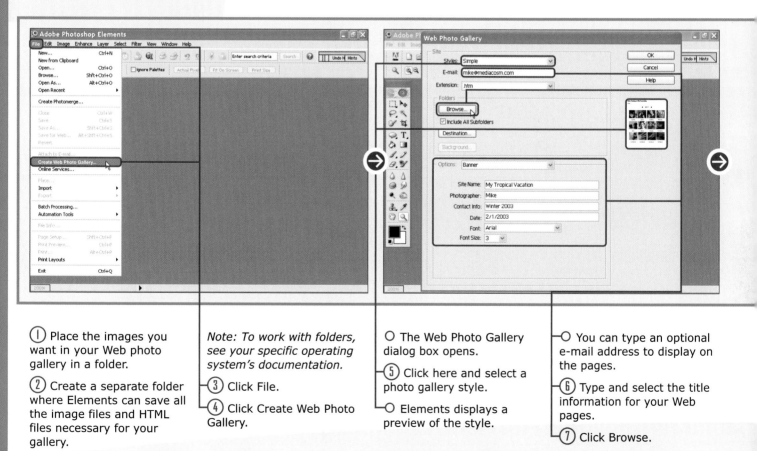

① Place the images you want in your Web photo gallery in a folder.

② Create a separate folder where Elements can save all the image files and HTML files necessary for your gallery.

Note: To work with folders, see your specific operating system's documentation.

③ Click File.

④ Click Create Web Photo Gallery.

○ The Web Photo Gallery dialog box opens.

⑤ Click here and select a photo gallery style.

○ Elements displays a preview of the style.

○ You can type an optional e-mail address to display on the pages.

⑥ Type and select the title information for your Web pages.

⑦ Click Browse.

Customize It! ※

You can customize your photo
gallery pages by selecting
different gallery styles. You do this in
the Styles menu at the top of the Web
Photo Gallery dialog box. The different styles
can add themes to your gallery and display the
images in different arrangements. Some of the
themes include office, outer space, and theater. You
can also select different settings from the Options list
to customize image sizes and link colors for the gallery.

#75

DIFFICULTY LEVEL

Did You Know? ※

You can further customize your photo gallery pages
by opening and editing the HTML pages with a Web
publishing program or HTML editor. This enables you
to change titles, text styles, colors, and other elements
on the pages.

O The Browse For Folder
dialog box appears.

⑧ Select the folder
containing your images.

⑨ Click OK.

⑩ Click Destination and
repeat steps **8** and **9** to
specify the folder in which
to save your gallery.

⑪ Click OK in the Web
Photo Gallery dialog box.

O Elements opens each
image in the specified folder,
creates versions for the
photo gallery, and generates
the necessary HTML code.

O After the processing is
complete, Elements opens
the default Web browser and
displays the home page of
the gallery.

O You can click a thumbnail
to see a larger version of the
image.

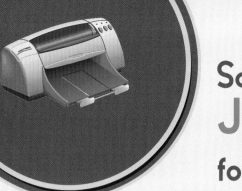

Save a
JPEG IMAGE
for the Web

You can save an image file in the *JPEG,* Joint Photographic Experts Group, format and publish it on the Web. Because the format supports millions of colors in a single image, the JPEG format is especially suitable for photographs and other images with continuous tones. Along with the GIF format, JPEG is a format supported by practically all Web browsers. For more information on the GIF format, see task 77.

When you save an image in the JPEG format, you specify a quality setting for the resulting JPEG image. The higher the quality you specify, the

greater the file size of the resulting image. This tradeoff allows you to balance the need for images that look good with the need for images that are of small file size and download quickly.

The JPEG format is especially good at compressing photographic image information to create files that are compact. A typical one-megabyte TIFF image will usually measure less than 100K when saved in the JPEG format.

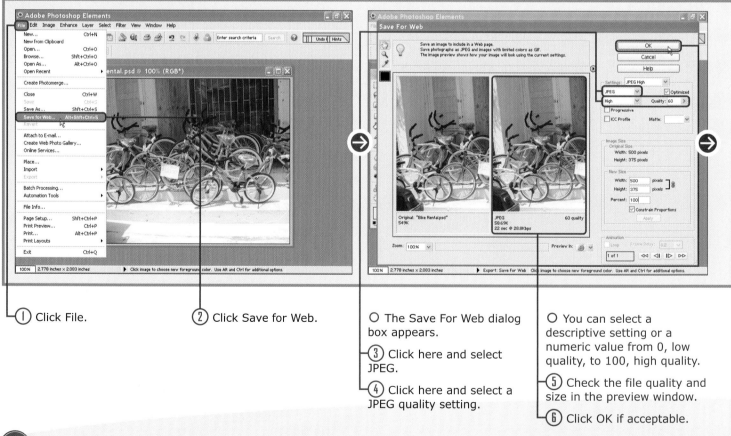

① Click File.

② Click Save for Web.

○ The Save For Web dialog box appears.

③ Click here and select JPEG.

④ Click here and select a JPEG quality setting.

○ You can select a descriptive setting or a numeric value from 0, low quality, to 100, high quality.

⑤ Check the file quality and size in the preview window.

⑥ Click OK if acceptable.

Did You Know? ※

JPEG is known as a *lossy* file
format because there is a loss of
some image information when an
image is saved in the JPEG format. How
much information depends on the quality
setting you choose — the lower the quality, the
greater the information loss. This information loss
can show up as blurriness in the final JPEG image.

76

DIFFICULTY LEVEL

Customize It! ※

You can click the Progressive check box to create a
JPEG file that downloads incrementally onto a Web
page. A progressive JPEG file shows up blurry at first,
and then gets progressively clearer as the file downloads.
Note that some older Web browsers do not support
progressive JPEGs.

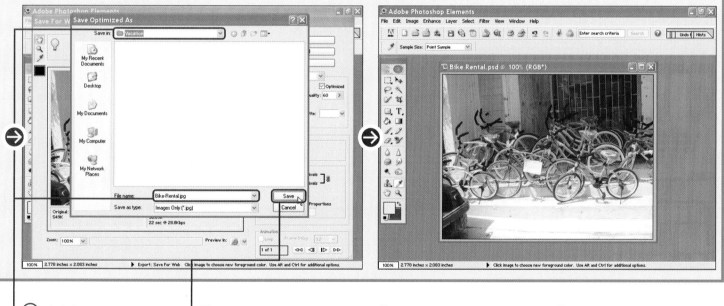

⑦ Click here and select a
folder in which to save the
file.

⑧ Type a filename.

○ Elements automatically
assigns a JPG extension.

⑨ Click Save.

○ Elements saves the JPEG
file in the specified folder.

○ You can open the folder
to access the file.

○ The original image file
remains open in Elements.

Create a
GIF IMAGE
for the Web

You can save an image file in the GIF format and publish it on the Web. *GIF* stands for Graphics Interchange Format. Because the format supports only up to 256 colors in a single image, the GIF format is more suitable for solid-color illustrations or photographs with a limited number of colors.

When you save an image in the GIF format, you specify the number of colors to include in the image. The greater the number of colors in your GIF file, the greater the quality of the image, but also the

greater the file size. This tradeoff allows you to balance the need for images that look good with the need for images that are of small file size and download quickly.

The GIF format also allows you to store multiple image frames in a single GIF image and rotate those frames when the GIF is loaded. This lets you create animations with the GIF file format. For more information, see task 78.

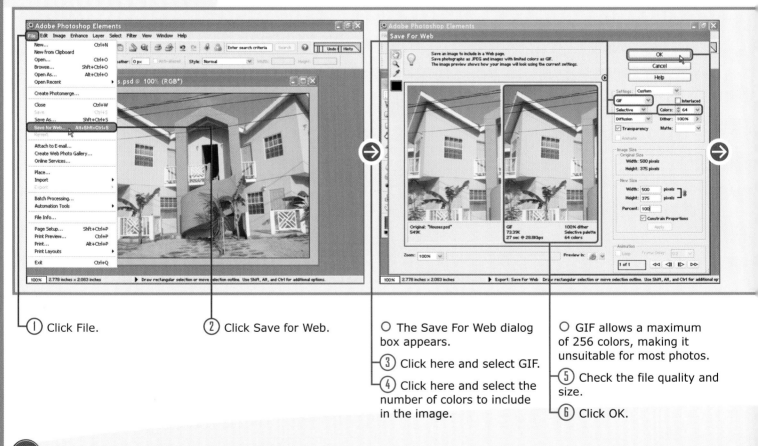

① Click File.

② Click Save for Web.

○ The Save For Web dialog box appears.

③ Click here and select GIF.

④ Click here and select the number of colors to include in the image.

○ GIF allows a maximum of 256 colors, making it unsuitable for most photos.

⑤ Check the file quality and size.

⑥ Click OK.

77

Did You Know? ☀

When deciding on the number of colors to use in your GIF image, it is usually a good idea to start at a low number, such as 32, and work higher. This way, you can gauge at what point adding additional colors no longer improves the look of the image. At this number, you will get the highest quality GIF image at the minimum file size.

Did You Know? ☀

If your Elements image has transparent areas in it, you can select the Transparency check box to keep those areas transparent in the saved GIF file. Unlike JPEG, the GIF format supports transparency. Note that the GIF format does not support semitransparency. Any semitransparent pixels, such as those on the curved edge of objects, will convert to a solid color in a saved GIF file.

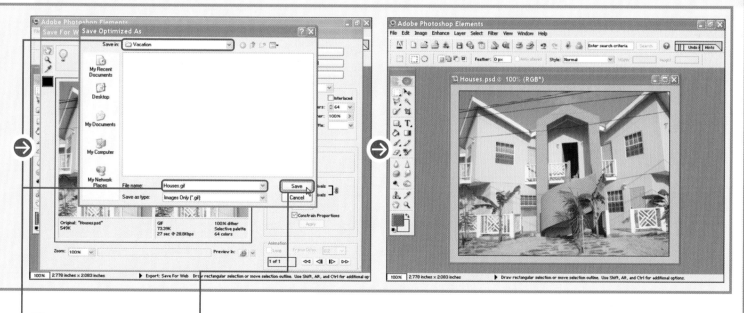

⑦ Click here and select a folder in which to save the file.

⑧ Type a filename.

○ Elements automatically assigns a .gif extension.

⑨ Click Save.

○ Elements saves the GIF file in the specified folder.

○ You can open the folder to access the file.

○ The original image file remains open in Elements.

Create a
GIF ANIMATION

You can create a multilayered image file in Elements and save it as an animated GIF image. Each layer in the image serves as a frame in the animation. *Frames* are snapshots that show an animated object in different positions, like pages in a flip book.

A GIF animation is an effective way to add motion to your Web pages. It is an easy-to-use alternative to more advanced animation techniques such as Flash and Java. Practically all Web browsers can display GIF animations, so you can be sure that most of your Web audience will be able to see them.

Just like a regular GIF image, a GIF animation can only include 256 colors in all its frames. For this reason, GIF animations are best created using flat-color art rather than photographs.

Elements enables you to specify the time that each frame is displayed in the animation and whether the animation automatically starts over after finishing. Adjusting the frame rate helps you ensure that your animation plays smoothly.

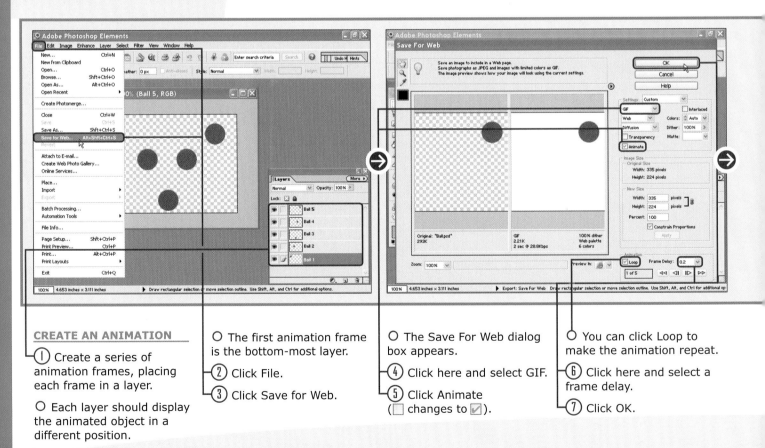

CREATE AN ANIMATION

① Create a series of animation frames, placing each frame in a layer.

O Each layer should display the animated object in a different position.

O The first animation frame is the bottom-most layer.

② Click File.

③ Click Save for Web.

O The Save For Web dialog box appears.

④ Click here and select GIF.

⑤ Click Animate (☐ changes to ☑).

O You can click Loop to make the animation repeat.

⑥ Click here and select a frame delay.

⑦ Click OK.

Did You Know? ※

Because GIF animations involve multiple image frames, they can often result in large file sizes. It is important to check the preview pane in the Save For Web dialog box to make sure the file size does not get too large. You can lower the file size by lowering the number of colors used in the GIF, or by reducing the number of frames in the animation.

DIFFICULTY LEVEL

Did You Know? ※

Sometimes frame speeds can vary across different computer systems. If possible, it is a good idea to test your finished animations on a variety of platforms and browsers.

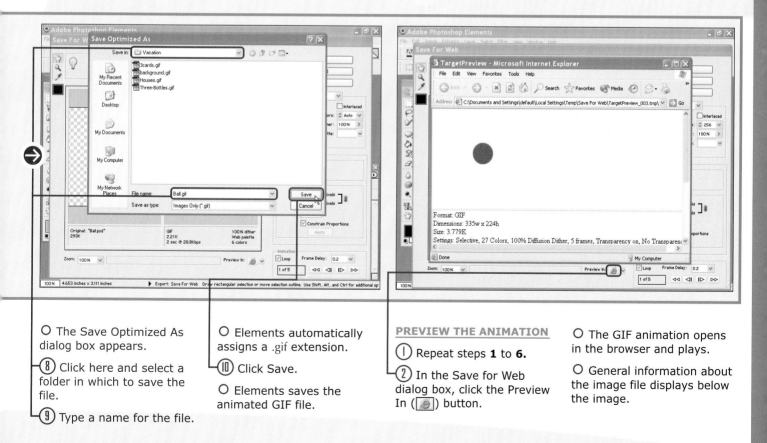

○ The Save Optimized As dialog box appears.

⑧ Click here and select a folder in which to save the file.

⑨ Type a name for the file.

○ Elements automatically assigns a .gif extension.

⑩ Click Save.

○ Elements saves the animated GIF file.

PREVIEW THE ANIMATION

① Repeat steps **1** to **6.**

② In the Save for Web dialog box, click the Preview In (🐾) button.

○ The GIF animation opens in the browser and plays.

○ General information about the image file displays below the image.

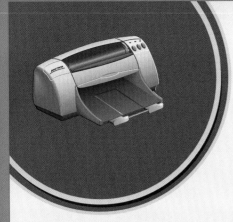

PREVIEW AN IMAGE
in a **Web** browser

DIFFICULTY LEVEL

You can preview your Elements image in a Web browser to see how it will appear to viewers on the Web. This can help you double-check the quality of your JPEG or GIF image, and allow you to check the size of your image relative to the confines of a Web browser.

In addition to displaying the image itself, previewing your image also displays general information about the image such as the dimensions, file size, and compression settings.

It also displays HTML code that you can cut and paste into a Web editor in order to display the image by itself on a Web page.

Did You Know? ※

You can specify that Elements preview the image in a browser other than the default browser by selecting the Other option in the Preview In menu. This enables you to open your image in a browser such as Netscape Navigator if your default browser is Internet Explorer.

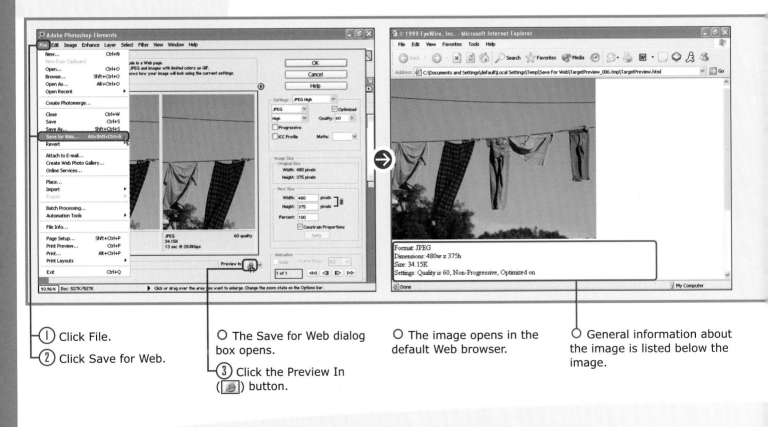

① Click File.

② Click Save for Web.

○ The Save for Web dialog box opens.

③ Click the Preview In (🖼) button.

○ The image opens in the default Web browser.

○ General information about the image is listed below the image.

Add CAPTION AND COPYRIGHT information

You can store caption and copyright information with your Photoshop Elements image. You may find this useful if you plan to sell or license your images, and want the files to retain information about authorship.

Adding caption information is convenient if you are planning to use some of the other features in Photoshop Elements. For example, you can automatically add caption information to your printouts via the Print Preview dialog box. See task 71 for details.

You can also label your images with your caption when creating a picture package. See task 73 for more information.

DIFFICULTY LEVEL

Did You Know? ※

You can view extra information added to photos taken with a digital camera by selecting EXIF in the Section menu in the File Info dialog box. This information includes the make and model of the camera as well as the date and time the photo was shot.

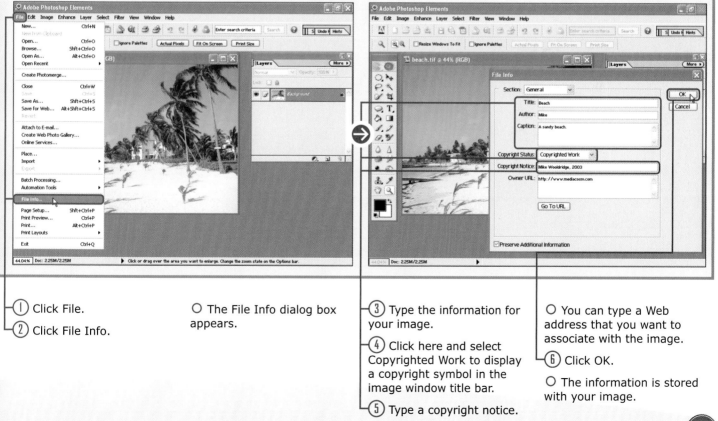

① Click File.

② Click File Info.

○ The File Info dialog box appears.

③ Type the information for your image.

④ Click here and select Copyrighted Work to display a copyright symbol in the image window title bar.

⑤ Type a copyright notice.

○ You can type a Web address that you want to associate with the image.

⑥ Click OK.

○ The information is stored with your image.

CHAPTER 9

Speed Things Up

Keeping things on time and moving smoothly is very important in any workflow or project. People are constantly looking for tools and ways to make things work faster and better. If Photoshop Elements is your tool of trade or pleasure, then you can use the wide set of tips and tricks that help speed up the workflow, improve the performance of your system, and optimize your results.

Using your system can cause your system and software to become sluggish and cumbersome. For example, unused data on a clipboard and fragmented hard drives can cause a computer to run much slower because of the limited resources and jumbled storage space that Elements

has available to use. Cluttered screens and disorganized filing can slow down the user, who must work longer and slower because of the additional steps needed to navigate around the program and images.

You can use the tasks in this chapter to ensure that your processes will go faster and your machine will work smoother. Some of these tricks take place within Elements and some take place in your operating system, but they all help your work performance. Even simple tricks like arranging your files can help speed up the creative process. The whole point is to customize your computer and Elements setup to maximize how you do your personal workflow.

TOP 100

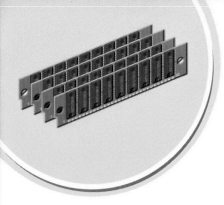

INCREASE RAM

for Elements 2

You can improve the speed and performance of Elements dramatically by customizing the amount of available RAM for use by Elements and by adjusting the use of cache memory. RAM memory is perhaps the single most important performance enhancer for Elements 2.

You can specify a percentage amount of available RAM for use within Elements. By default, 50 percent of your computer's available RAM is assigned to Elements. You can also adjust the amount of cache memory to reduce or increase the amount of RAM used to store thumbnails and other software files for quick retrieval later.

If you find that your system is running slow, but you have plenty of memory assigned, Elements has ways of freeing up that RAM for use. By purging your History States, clipboard, and cache memory, you can immediately re-utilize your computer's assigned memory. Be wary of doing this, though, because purging is irreversible, and any information used there will be lost. Be especially aware of the History States, because they are a great benefit when working on difficult projects.

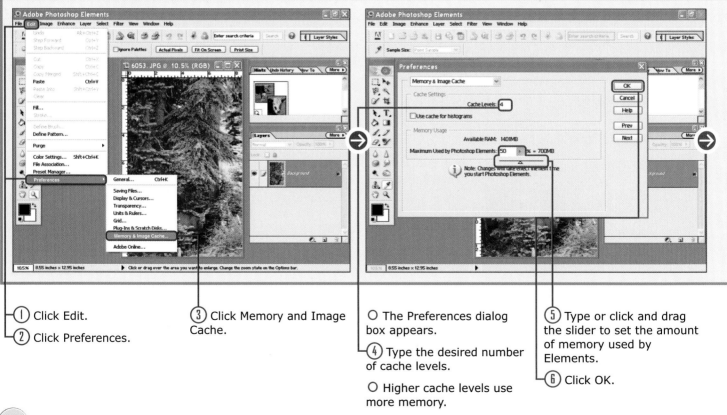

─① Click Edit.

─② Click Preferences.

③ Click Memory and Image Cache.

○ The Preferences dialog box appears.

─④ Type the desired number of cache levels.

○ Higher cache levels use more memory.

⑤ Type or click and drag the slider to set the amount of memory used by Elements.

─⑥ Click OK.

81

Did You Know? ※

Ideally, you should have no
less than 128MB of RAM available
on your computer for Elements to
run. However, you can assign up to 2GB
of RAM to Elements. If you are running with
too little RAM, have additional RAM installed.

Did You Know? ※

Every program running, including your operating
system, uses RAM. If your machine has limited
RAM, running other programs with Elements may
reduce your RAM memory to dangerously low
amounts and cause your machine to lock up or
run extremely slow. If you have limited RAM, be
sure to run Elements by itself whenever possible
to speed up its processing power.

DIFFICULTY LEVEL

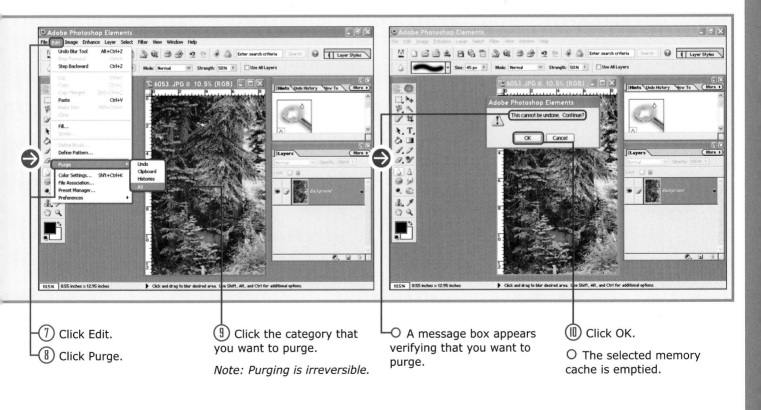

─⑦ Click Edit.

─⑧ Click Purge.

⑨ Click the category that
you want to purge.

Note: Purging is irreversible.

─○ A message box appears
verifying that you want to
purge.

⑩ Click OK.

○ The selected memory
cache is emptied.

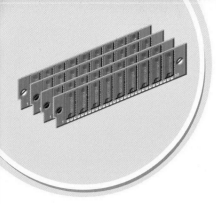

Improve performance with
SCRATCH DISKS

Scratch disks are hard drives or storage units that Elements uses as temporary memory when all available RAM is used up. When Elements treats the hard drive as a memory cache to work with, then Elements can utilize much more space for working with large files or complex filters, speeding up performance. A scratch disk is almost as important as RAM memory for smooth performance.

You can easily set up your scratch disk. By default in Windows, the scratch disk is set to the C: drive when you install Elements. You can edit this setting

and assign a different hard drive if you so choose. Make the scratch disk a different drive, so that when Elements is working on processing a filter on an image on one drive, it can utilize the second drive for other functions and not interfere or have to wait on the other drive to stop processing.

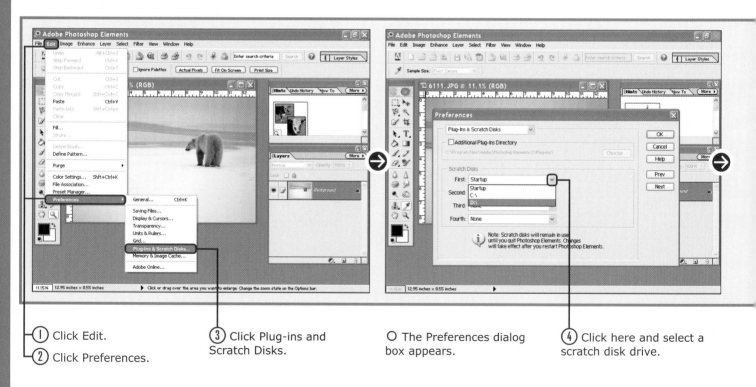

① Click Edit.

② Click Preferences.

③ Click Plug-ins and Scratch Disks.

○ The Preferences dialog box appears.

④ Click here and select a scratch disk drive.

82

Did You Know? ※

Elements can handle up to four
different scratch disk drives.
Should the first scratch disk become
full or unusable, Elements will begin using
the other assigned scratch disks.

Customize It! ※

You can have one hard drive available on your
computer system, and Elements defaults to it.
However, there is a process called *partitioning* that
involves splitting off a section of the hard drive and
transforming it into a recognizable second drive that
you can assign as a scratch disk.

Caution! ※

Any kind of formatting on a hard drive is risky, if you are
inexperienced in this process. Please read your operating
ystem's instructions on partitioning before attempting to
partition your drive, or contact a professional computer
technician. Making a mistake could destroy all files and programs on
you computer.

DIFFICULTY LEVEL

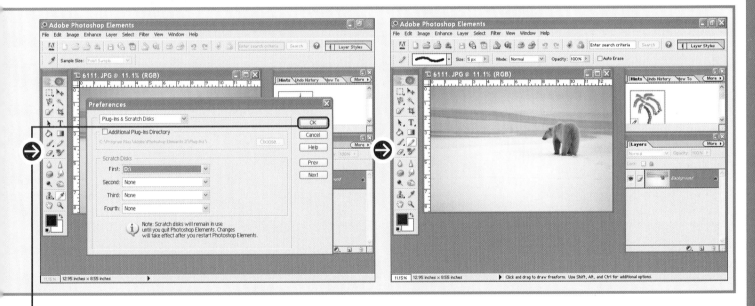

⑤ Click OK.

○ Elements automatically
reassigns the scratch disk.

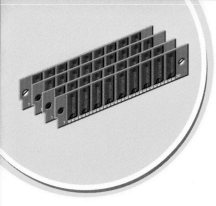

DEFRAGMENT
to speed up your computer

You can improve the performance of Elements if you are using Windows by using a standard Windows tool, the Disk Defragmenter. Defragmenting helps the computer access data for Elements more quickly.

Defragmenting is important because when you save an image to a hard drive, you are placing the information on little spaces called *bits*, and those bits may not rest next to each other on the drive. Sometimes, if there is not enough adjacent space, Windows places some of the file information in one spot and the rest somewhere else.

While your computer knows where all of the information is and in what order the information is supposed to be, having to search in multiple locations for file parts to put together and run can slow a computer down greatly. In Elements, you can easily work with files that reach 20 to 40MB in size, maybe more, depending on your project. When the hard drive gets a file that big, and has to break it up into little pieces to scatter across the drive, it slows down even more.

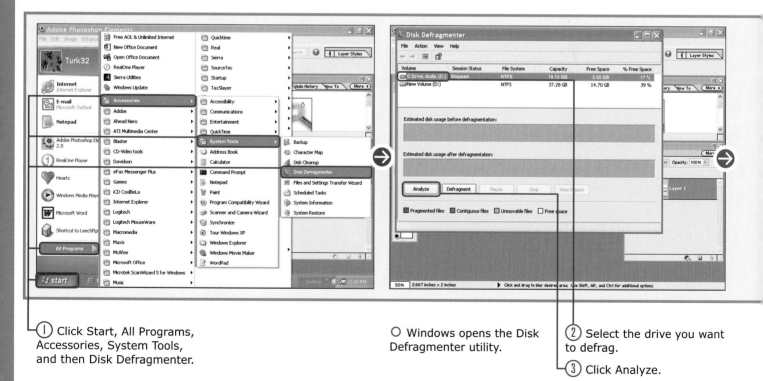

① Click Start, All Programs, Accessories, System Tools, and then Disk Defragmenter.

○ Windows opens the Disk Defragmenter utility.

② Select the drive you want to defrag.

③ Click Analyze.

Did You Know? ※

Removing unused programs is a good way of keeping your system operating faster. If you have numerous unused files, whenever you install new ones, the chance of fragmenting your drive increases, slowing performance. Defragment your system regularly to keep the drive more compact. There is also commercial software available, such as Norton's Windoc from Symantec and DiskWarrior from Alsoft, which does excellent digital housekeeping.

Try it! ※

Use permanent storage means whenever possible. The cost of a CD has dropped to where burning disks is no longer cost-prohibitive, and the introduction of DVD-R media allows for tremendous sized storage. If you have a large number of files, consider burning them to disk. If data is irreplaceable, burn two copies and store them separately.

DIFFICULTY LEVEL

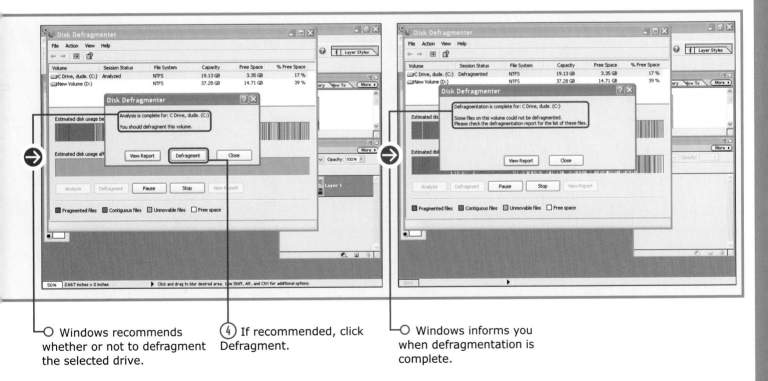

─○ Windows recommends whether or not to defragment the selected drive.

④ If recommended, click Defragment.

─○ Windows informs you when defragmentation is complete.

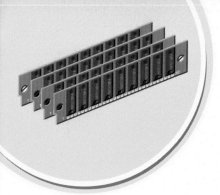

CALIBRATE
your monitor

When working with graphics projects, you want to ensure that your colors are accurate and consistent with your desired results. You can do this in Elements by using the Adobe Gamma Correction tool to calibrate your monitor to the correct ICC (International Color Consortium) color profile to ensure that the color profile you are using is suitable for your monitor. This calibration keeps your monitor showing the colors in the truest manner.

The Gamma Correction tool has control panel and wizard-based methods for you to adjust and create your ICC color profile. Calibrating your monitor

involves such things as adjusting for brightness, contrast, and gamma colors, as well as selecting the *white point*, the point where your monitor recognizes the total absence of color, or white. Many of the wizard screens recognize hardware preferences and default settings, but you can make minor to complete changes to your monitor setup and save the final color result under a custom name.

Be sure to calibrate your monitor using the light conditions in which you normally work. The light in your working environment can dramatically influence how color is displayed on your monitor.

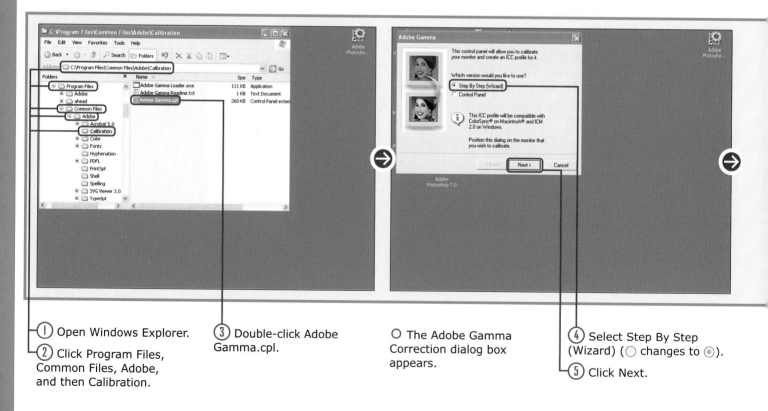

① Open Windows Explorer.

② Click Program Files, Common Files, Adobe, and then Calibration.

③ Double-click Adobe Gamma.cpl.

○ The Adobe Gamma Correction dialog box appears.

④ Select Step By Step (Wizard) (○ changes to ⦿).

⑤ Click Next.

Customize It!

You can find more color files
for custom monitor calibration.
There are numerous files in the Color
folder where you found the Adobe
Gamma Calibration folder. You can create
your own or load a saved one. Businesses
sometimes have a specific ICC color profile
designed for their own brand recognition and
company colors. If you do print work, some printers
may require you to supply your own color file for print to
guarantee color equality.

84

DIFFICULTY LEVEL

Did You Know?

You can access additional color profiles on your monitor's install
disks. Browse through the disks to locate additional profiles you
can load through Adobe Gamma. You can also find additional color
profiles at your monitor manufacturer's Web site. Check your
monitor's manuals for Web site or additional information.

○ Adobe Gamma begins the wizard walk-through.

⑥ Work through the steps and click Continue until completed.

⑦ Toggle between Before and After to compare your previous color settings to your new color settings (○ changes to ◉).

⑧ Click Finish to save your settings.

○ The Save As dialog box appears.

⑨ Click here and navigate to the folder where you want to save the profile.

⑩ Type a filename for the profile.

⑪ Click Save.

○ Elements saves your new color profile and assigns it to your monitor.

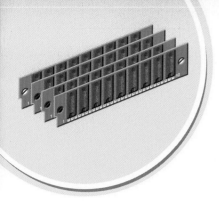

MAXIMIZE
your workspace

Even if you have a very large, flat-screen monitor, you can still only fit so much information or graphics on-screen, and graphics work always leaves you wishing you had more. You can work with the flexibility that Elements allows in placing toolbars and palettes to make the most out of the limited available screen space.

You can maximize your Elements workspace several ways. If you have a couple of favorite palettes on-screen, you can merge the two together under one title bar. Elements creates separate tabs for each

merged palette so that you can easily switch between them. Any number of palettes can be joined like this, but avoid merging too many or the tabs will be difficult to read clearly. You can also adjust the size of on-screen palettes. Although Elements has set minimums for width, you can adjust height very short.

Regardless of how you arrange your workspace, find a style that works for you and stick with it. Familiarity with a setup is the greatest factor in increasing your productivity.

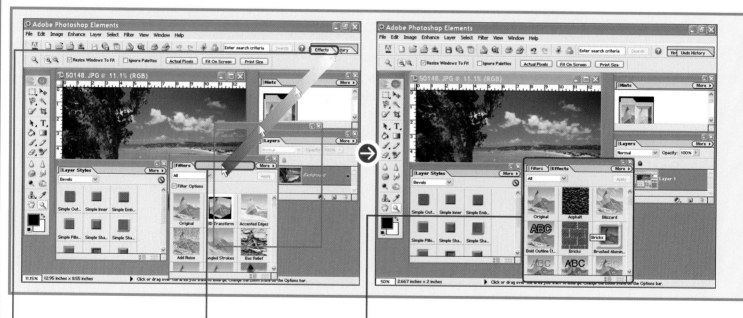

MERGE PALETTES

① Position the mouse cursor over the tab of the palette you want to merge into another palette.

② Click and drag the tab next to the tab of the target palette and release the mouse button.

○ Elements merges the two palettes with tabs visible for both. You can merge as many palettes as you like, but keep palette legibility in mind.

Customize It! ☀

You can use several other
simple tricks that can help you
maximize your Elements workspace.
Just rearranging your palettes or turning
off unused palettes greatly helps with space.
If you press the Tab key, Elements removes all
undocked palettes and toolbars from the screen;
press the Tab key again to restore the elements.
Similarly, pressing Shift and Tab simultaneously
removes all undocked palettes but leaves the basic
toolbar visible.

Apply It! ☀

If you want to keep more than one palette open but still have
screen space issues, you can merge similar palettes. For
example, if you like to work with graphical text and Web buttons,
consider merging the Filters, Effects, and Styles palettes. The
resulting grouping saves space while giving you quick and easy
access to your most frequently used palettes.

DIFFICULTY LEVEL

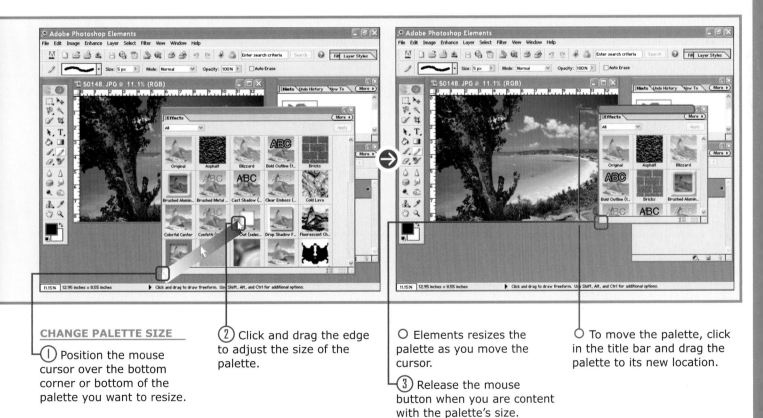

CHANGE PALETTE SIZE

① Position the mouse
cursor over the bottom
corner or bottom of the
palette you want to resize.

② Click and drag the edge
to adjust the size of the
palette.

○ Elements resizes the
palette as you move the
cursor.

③ Release the mouse
button when you are content
with the palette's size.

○ To move the palette, click
in the title bar and drag the
palette to its new location.

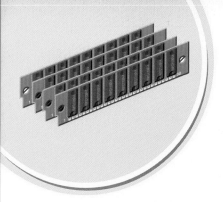

Work with
MULTIPLE MONITORS

You never seem to have enough workspace in Elements. If you shrink the viewable size of the image to fit on-screen, you lose detail; if you enlarge the image to see more detail, it spills outside the viewable area and you cannot see the whole image. To resolve these issues, you can use multiple monitors to increase your available screen space.

Using multiple monitors essentially expands your computer's desktop to a second monitor. When you move your cursor off the right edge of the left

monitor's screen, the cursor appears to float to the other monitor's window. The practical implication of this is that you can move essential Elements tools around, allowing you to work more efficiently with more room in which to create.

You can use multiple monitors many ways. The screens below demonstrate two common multiple-monitor arrangements, putting all of the palettes on the second monitor, and using the second monitor to work on another image.

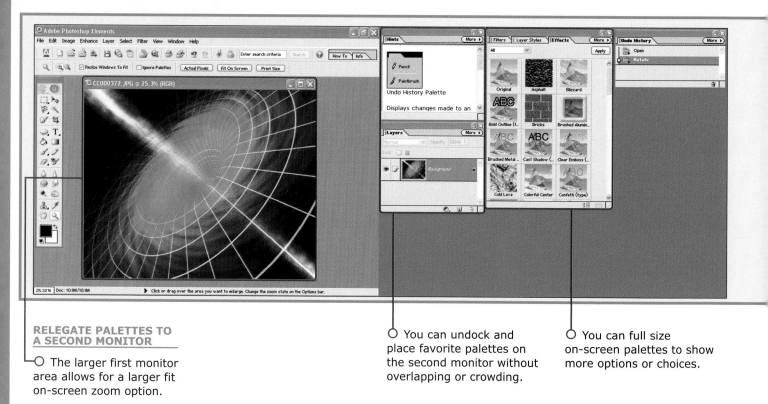

RELEGATE PALETTES TO A SECOND MONITOR

O The larger first monitor area allows for a larger fit on-screen zoom option.

O You can undock and place favorite palettes on the second monitor without overlapping or crowding.

O You can full size on-screen palettes to show more options or choices.

Customize It!

When using dual monitors, pick your favorite and most commonly used palettes and place them full screen towards the center of the workspace, and place any open images on either side.

Apply It!

If you work with more than one program at a time, dual monitors are almost essential. Try using Elements full-screen on one monitor with the tool palettes on the second monitor. With your second program, put the main screen on the second monitor and any palettes or toolbars on the first monitor. This will make it easier visually to distinguish between the two when you click between programs, and will give you maximized workspace for both.

DIFFICULTY LEVEL

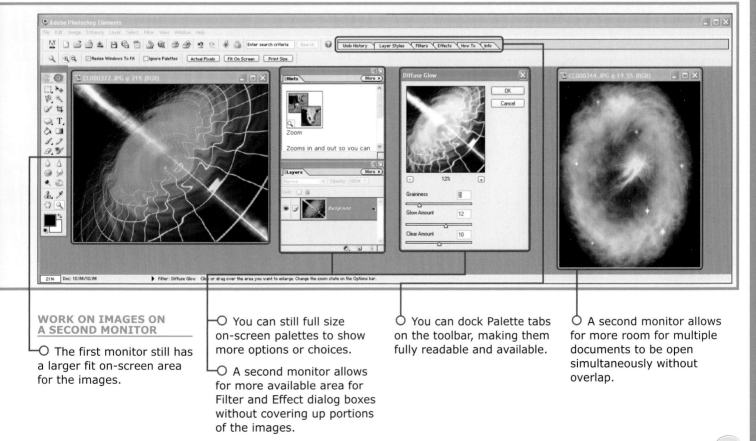

WORK ON IMAGES ON A SECOND MONITOR

O The first monitor still has a larger fit on-screen area for the images.

O You can still full size on-screen palettes to show more options or choices.

O A second monitor allows for more available area for Filter and Effect dialog boxes without covering up portions of the images.

O You can dock Palette tabs on the toolbar, making them fully readable and available.

O A second monitor allows for more room for multiple documents to be open simultaneously without overlap.

USE RECIPES
to speed up common tasks

You can speed up some everyday tasks with Recipes in the How To palette. The How To palette contains a group of instructional tutorials that teach or remind you how to do certain tasks. You can choose from a wide variety of topics from Web page design to color correction on an image.

Each recipe is laid out in a step-by-step format that you can follow through the entire task. The How To menu explains options that are available, and provides links to other recipes that are related in some manner to the recipe on which you are working.

You can also speed up your recipes with the How To palette's automatic completion feature. Many steps within the recipes have a Play icon next to the text *Do this step for me.* You can click the Play icon, and Elements will either complete the step automatically or open the appropriate dialog box for you to customize the step yourself. This feature is a very handy time saver when using this palette.

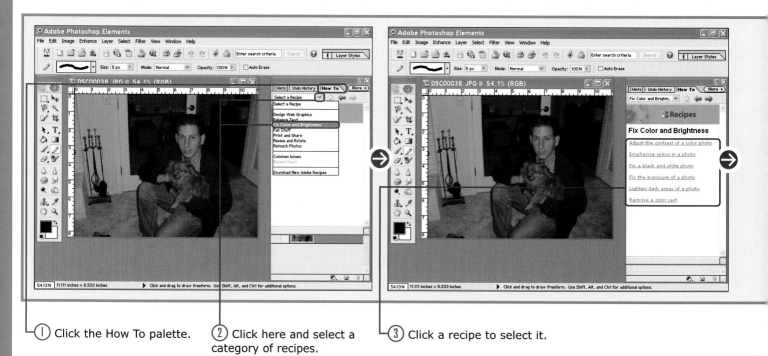

① Click the How To palette.

② Click here and select a category of recipes.

③ Click a recipe to select it.

#87

Did You Know? ※

You can also download more recipes to use in Photoshop Elements 2 directly from Adobe. Elements provides access to these recipes in the How To palette's drop-down menu. You can select from Adobe's recipes or any available third-party recipe that Adobe suggests.

Did You Know? ※

You can use the Common Issues selection in the How To drop-down menu to view the recipes that apply to the most common issues for Elements users.

Did You Know? ※

The How To palette has navigational buttons across the top of the palette that allows you to move back and forth between recipe pages and menus that you have already visited in the palette. This is useful in retracing your steps if you used multiple recipes or if you want to review a process you looked at earlier.

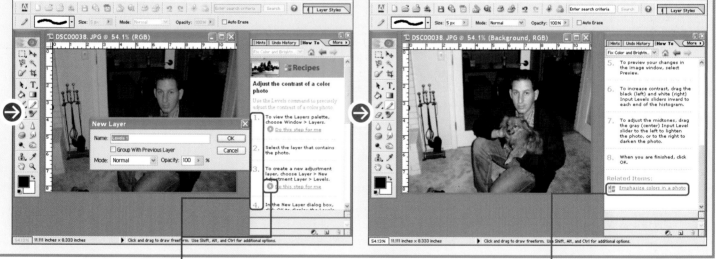

○ The recipe appears in the How To palette.

○ The New Layer dialog box may appear prompting you to name a new layer. You may click Cancel.

④ Follow the steps through completion.

○ Play buttons can automatically complete some steps for you.

○ Your image implements the recipe's task completed result.

○ Elements suggests related recipes for use.

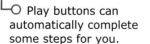

AUTOMATE
file conversions

Some projects, such as downloading images from a digital camera, involve having to change a number of images from one file type to another. Going from TIF format to JPG format is very common with today's digital photographer. From family photos to serious events, a digital camera commonly holds from 40 to 150 images, and having to convert them one by one is tedious. You can use the Batch Processing utility to turn that task from a chore into a quick and easy process.

The Batch Processing tool takes all images from a user's chosen folder, applies the conversion to every acceptable image format in that folder, and saves the images in a destination folder in the new format. You should set up your source and destination folders in advance to keep things running smoothly. After you establish the settings for the file conversion, Elements does all the legwork for you, and in a lot less time than going through every image individually.

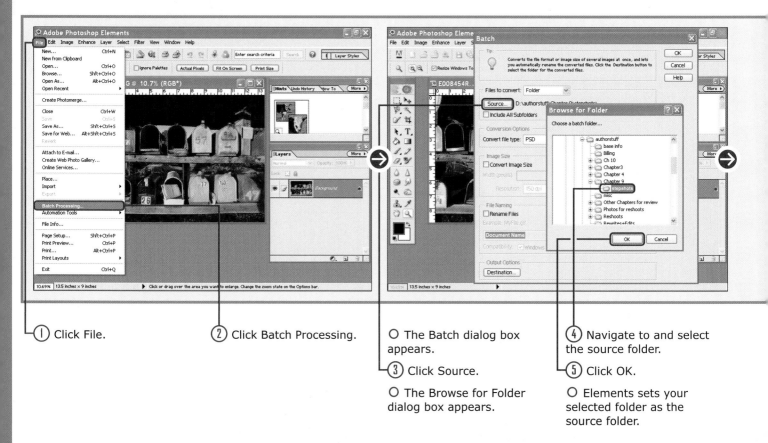

① Click File.

② Click Batch Processing.

○ The Batch dialog box appears.

③ Click Source.

○ The Browse for Folder dialog box appears.

④ Navigate to and select the source folder.

⑤ Click OK.

○ Elements sets your selected folder as the source folder.

#88

Caution! ✳

One thing to remember with
the Batch Processing tool is that it
converts every file it finds within the
designated source to the specified
format, and sometimes not every file
requires it. Be careful to have the source
location only contain those files you want to alter.
By doing this, you ensure that unnecessary work
and duplicate files are avoided.

DIFFICULTY LEVEL

Customize It! ✳

Batch processing is a great way to format photos for an
online photo album or Web site. If your digital camera has 140
TIF photos that you want to save as more compact JPG photos
for a Web site, when you hook up the camera to the computer,
directly denote the camera as your source folder

⑥ Click here and select the files to convert option.

⑦ Click here and select a file type format to which to convert.

⑧ Click Destination.

○ The Browse for Folder dialog box appears.

⑨ Navigate to and select the destination folder.

○ If needed, you can create a new destination folder.

⑩ Click OK to close the Browse for Folder dialog box.

⑪ Click OK to close the Batch dialog box.

○ Elements quickly converts your file formats.

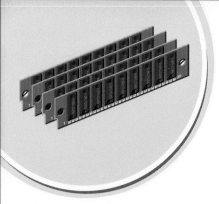

AUTOMATE
other details in batches

You can use the Batch dialog box to automate more than just file conversions. For example, you may have 140 JPEG images on a digital camera that do not require converting to a different format, but the images are just a bit too big. Or, perhaps you need thumbnails for a Web site or layout, and have 200 images to resize to a specific set of measurements. You can enter the height and width you want the images to end up as, and even specify the image resolution in case the conversion is for print, and the Batch dialog box does the rest.

In addition, you can rename files using the Batch dialog box. The dialog box allows you to make minor changes to a filename as you apply other changes to the image, as a means of differentiating between two similar files. Common extensions are listed in a drop-down menu and shows examples of how the file works when you select an extension format. Elements offers plenty of different styles and choices for your extensions.

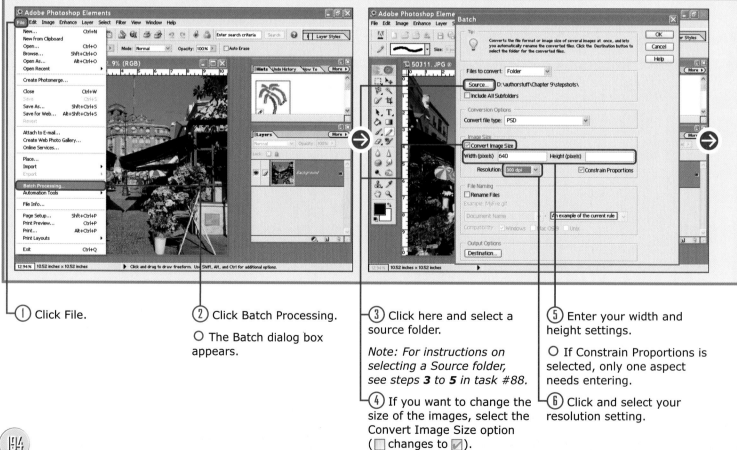

① Click File.

② Click Batch Processing.

○ The Batch dialog box appears.

③ Click here and select a source folder.

Note: For instructions on selecting a Source folder, see steps 3 to 5 in task #88.

④ If you want to change the size of the images, select the Convert Image Size option (☐ changes to ☑).

⑤ Enter your width and height settings.

○ If Constrain Proportions is selected, only one aspect needs entering.

⑥ Click and select your resolution setting.

Caution!

When performing file
conversions, remember that
several file formats, especially, JPEG,
are considered *lossy* formats, meaning
that each save loses a little detail due to the
compression technique. If resolution is a factor,
such as with print, use TIF. It is a more inflated,
but lossless, file type, and keeps the clarity.

Apply It!

When renaming files, be as descriptive as possible. File
organization begins with filenames, and poorly chosen
formats, like numeric filenames with date extensions, makes
it difficult to differentiate between files. Keep the original
filenames descriptive so that when you run a batch process on
the files you have more flexibility should you need to add a
code-like numeric extension.

DIFFICULTY LEVEL

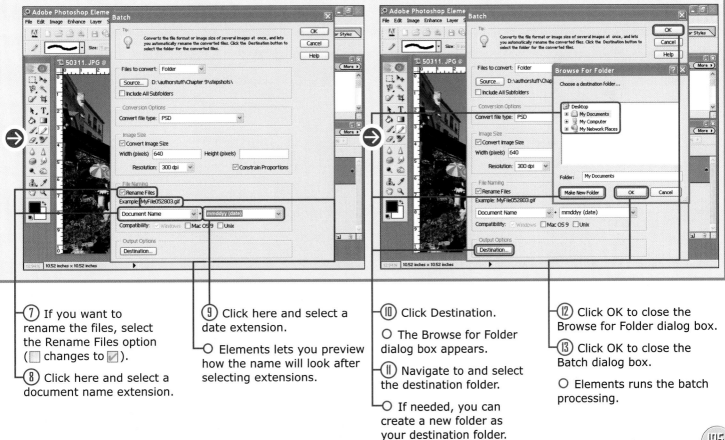

⑦ If you want to
rename the files, select
the Rename Files option
(☐ changes to ☑).

⑧ Click here and select a
document name extension.

⑨ Click here and select a
date extension.

○ Elements lets you preview
how the name will look after
selecting extensions.

⑩ Click Destination.

○ The Browse for Folder
dialog box appears.

⑪ Navigate to and select
the destination folder.

○ If needed, you can
create a new folder as
your destination folder.

⑫ Click OK to close the
Browse for Folder dialog box.

⑬ Click OK to close the
Batch dialog box.

○ Elements runs the batch
processing.

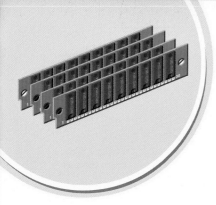

ORGANIZE
your files

If you have worked with images for any length of time, you know how time-consuming using the Open method on the File menu can be when trying to locate an image. Similarly, not having critical information about an image handy can slow you down. Fortunately, Elements has two built-in features that can help you embed information in an image and quickly find images.

The File Info menu option allows you to input certain information into the file itself. You can enter your personal information, descriptions, copyright information, even Web site URL information. If you enter copyright information, the copyright symbol

appears in the title bar when viewing the image. By entering image information, any program that recognizes embedded information will allow you to view this information.

The File Browser option allows you to navigate through your files while still in Elements. The File Browser window has multiple features that can let you browse to, preview, and read information about a particular image. The File Browser window also has available tools that allow batch renaming and folder creation, to help you save additional time.

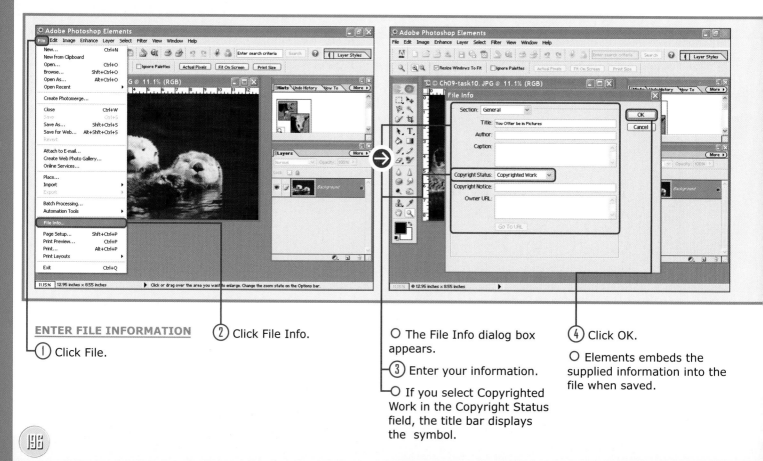

ENTER FILE INFORMATION

① Click File.

② Click File Info.

O The File Info dialog box appears.

③ Enter your information.

O If you select Copyrighted Work in the Copyright Status field, the title bar displays the symbol.

④ Click OK.

O Elements embeds the supplied information into the file when saved.

90

Did You Know? ☀

By clicking the More button in the File Browser window, you can access additional tools and utilities, including Batch Rename and Create New Folder. You also have the option to resize the thumbnails to view more images per screen or larger views. You can also access option buttons to expand the thumbnail view, sort the files by different criteria, and adjust the thumbnail size.

Did You Know? ☀

You can simultaneously remove all undocked palettes but leave the basic toolbar visible by clicking Shift+Tab. This shortcut comes in very handy when working in the File Browser window. The File Browser window hides behind other palettes, similar to an image, which can make viewing information difficult. By clicking Shift+Tab, you eliminate all of the other palettes, and you can then resize the browser window for maximum viewing.

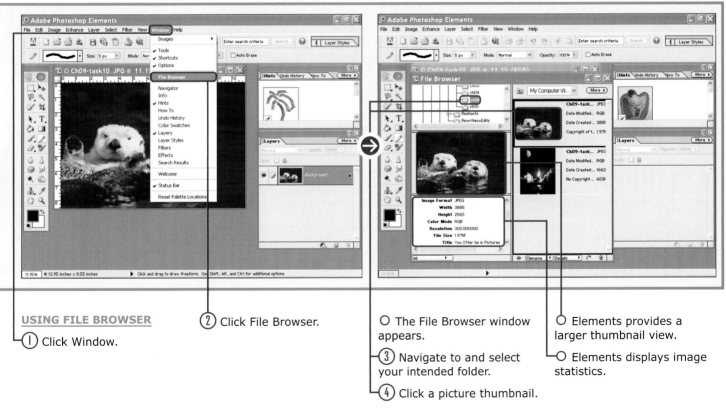

USING FILE BROWSER

① Click Window.

② Click File Browser.

○ The File Browser window appears.

③ Navigate to and select your intended folder.

④ Click a picture thumbnail.

○ Elements provides a larger thumbnail view.

○ Elements displays image statistics.

CHAPTER 10

Working with Other Elements Tools

You can occasionally achieve the same effect in Photoshop Elements 2 in different ways. Sometimes a class of tools or filters can have items within its own group that overlap each other in uses. Most tools are defined by usage, such as selecting, inserting content, and pixel manipulation. There are also many tools and utilities that are not categorized with the other tools. These unique items are included in this chapter because they are important enough to mention but do not quite fit within the other categories. You can create and utilize these tools to do all sorts of useful tasks and results.

You can work with new items such as the Elements 2 PDF Slideshow and learn ways on how to manage

third party plug-ins. Scanning images, and Presets and Patterns, are covered here. You can take advantage of little tricks like using the Information palette as a measuring tool, or sketching from a scanned image. The ability to convert a PDF file into something usable by Elements, and saving it again into PDF, also add depth to this program. These are all very useful tools in Elements that are not part of a collection of related items, such as the blurs or artistic brushes. Each of the tools and tricks in this chapter are unique and carry their own benefits to your work. You can easily see that Elements is a powerful tool, offering valuable abilities for everyone from the professional to the hobbyist.

TOP 100

Create a
GRAPHICAL PATTERN

You can use Elements to create graphical patterns to use in your projects. You often see patterns in advertisements, art, Web designs, and graphics designs. You can use Elements to utilize available patterns, incorporating them into your layers or selections. You can apply a pattern to an entire image or a simple selection within the image, such as text or a shape. Elements has a nice package of pre-made patterns useful for all sorts of projects.

In addition, you can define custom patterns with almost any graphic, and then use them to create

with. Patterns are used often for effect in Web site backgrounds and digital graphics. In digital photography, they can be used for cartography, geographical layouts, sectionalizing a photo, or countless other things. After you apply a pattern to an image, the results are as changeable as any simplified graphic.

You can quickly and easily define a pattern, and using them in your graphics is simple as well. Although patterns are easy to create, they are enormously useful.

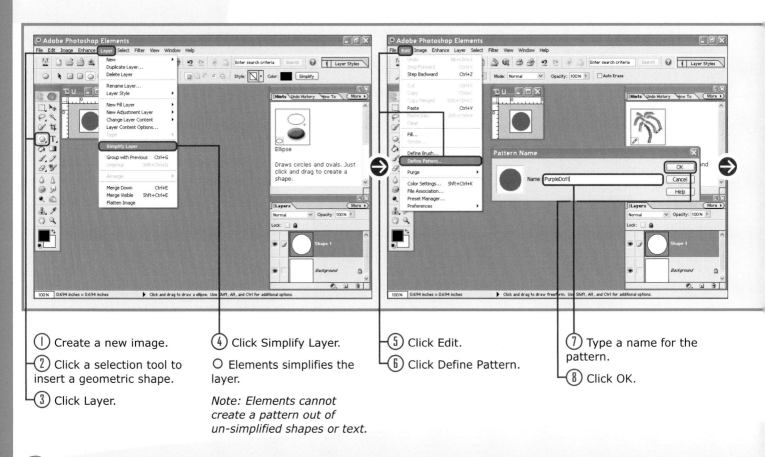

① Create a new image.

② Click a selection tool to insert a geometric shape.

③ Click Layer.

④ Click Simplify Layer.

○ Elements simplifies the layer.

Note: Elements cannot create a pattern out of un-simplified shapes or text.

⑤ Click Edit.

⑥ Click Define Pattern.

⑦ Type a name for the pattern.

⑧ Click OK.

Apply It! ※

You can easily create a grid.
Start by making a small, square
document. Click the Line tool and
draw a one to three pixel vertical line,
and then one horizontal line. Now you can
click Edit, then Define Pattern to set your
image as a pattern. When you use the Fill
command to fill a document or selection with this
pattern, this pattern will generate a grid.

#91

DIFFICULTY LEVEL

Did You Know? ※

You can scale up the size of a pattern, but it
could result in graininess of the pattern.
Instead, create your pattern in a larger size.
Then, click Image and then Duplicate Image. You
can now resize this duplicate to smaller scale and
define it as a pattern. Repeat these steps until you
have a useful range of sizes of your pattern.

⑨ Create a new image.

O This image should be
significantly larger than the
pattern image.

⑩ Click Edit.

⑪ Click Fill.

O The Fill dialog box
appears.

⑫ Click here and select
Pattern.

⑬ Click here and select a
new pattern.

⑭ Click OK.

O Elements automatically
patterns the new image with
our new pattern.

Manage THIRD-PARTY PLUG-INS

You can use Element's dozens of filters and effects to create amazing results. However, there are other software packages intended for use with Elements, such as third-party plug-ins. Third-party plug-ins can expand on or create new effects in your graphics. There are quite a few plug-ins available, and with that many, they can quickly become disorganized.

Separating the plug-ins from the program is the key to good organization. By default, plug-ins are stored in your Adobe/Elements 2/Plug-ins folder. To keep

better track of your plug-ins, you may want to store them outside of Elements. You can designate a second plug-ins folder to be loaded during startup, so you can expand your plug-ins outside of Elements and remain organized. This is very helpful to back up your plug-ins and troubleshoot with conflicting plug-ins. If you ever need to reload Elements, you would only have to redefine the secondary plug-ins folder, and not worry about installing all of your plug-ins again.

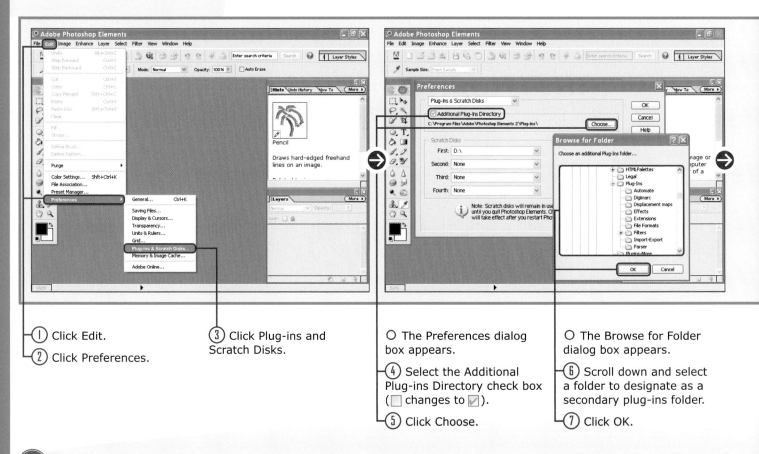

① Click Edit.

② Click Preferences.

③ Click Plug-ins and Scratch Disks.

○ The Preferences dialog box appears.

④ Select the Additional Plug-ins Directory check box (☐ changes to ☑).

⑤ Click Choose.

○ The Browse for Folder dialog box appears.

⑥ Scroll down and select a folder to designate as a secondary plug-ins folder.

⑦ Click OK.

\#92

DIFFICULTY LEVEL

Did You Know? ※

One very good reason for keeping plug-ins external is safety. If you need to reinstall Elements, all your default folders would be reset, and you would have to reinstall the plug-ins. Filing separately will save you a good amount of time.

Did You Know? ※

After installing plug-ins, you must restart Elements to access your plug-ins. When Elements reads a plug-in, the program places it in the Filters menu, but if the menu becomes too full, Elements places it in the Filters, Other submenu.

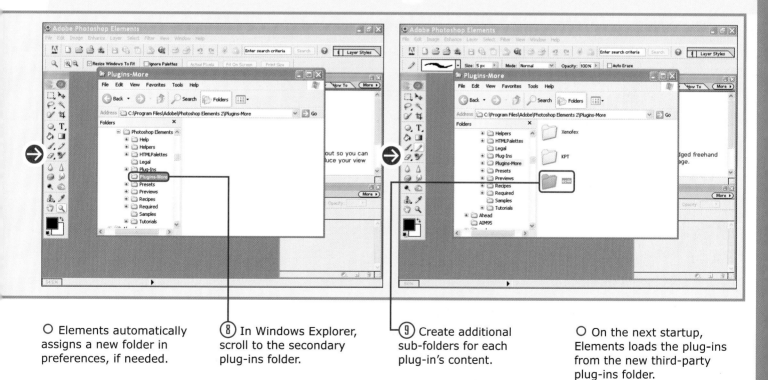

○ Elements automatically assigns a new folder in preferences, if needed.

⑧ In Windows Explorer, scroll to the secondary plug-ins folder.

⑨ Create additional sub-folders for each plug-in's content.

○ On the next startup, Elements loads the plug-ins from the new third-party plug-ins folder.

Manage your
TOOL PRESETS

When you open tools in Elements, you will see dozens of optional variations from which you may choose. Many tools, such as gradients, brushes, and shapes, have numerous variations. You can also add more variations to some of these tools, or if needed, delete some tools. You can make many changes in these palettes and tools. Elements makes it easy to track, edit, and reset these preset groups of tool options.

With the Preset Manager, you can manage your tool presets. The Preset Manager is located in the Edit

menu. When you click the Edit menu, it opens a dialog box that gives you options for brushes, color swatches, gradients, and patterns. You can use these menus to change the available tool variations for each tool as well as import more tools. For example, you can change the current brush set to a different group of brushes. Other options include changing patterns, gradients and color swatches.

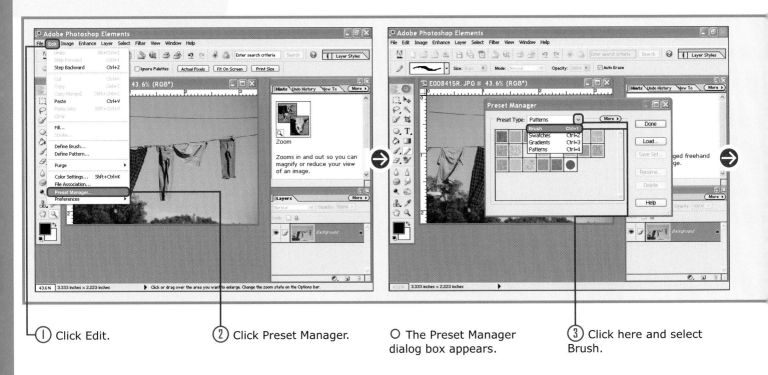

① Click Edit.

② Click Preset Manager.

○ The Preset Manager dialog box appears.

③ Click here and select Brush.

Customize It! ※

You can make numerous changes to your Preset sets when using the Preset Manager. Options to Delete, Rename, Save Set, and Load are available so you can customize your own sets. You can design a set of your favorite brushes by deleting and defining new brushes. You can then save the set as a custom brush file. Now you can load your favorite brush set whenever needed. Do not save over the default sets or you will lose the original set.

Did You Know? ※

You can import brush sets from outside of Elements. Simply download the ABR format brushes file from its source into the Adobe/ Elements 2/ Presets/ Brushes folder. Load the brush sets in the Preset Manager to use them.

93

DIFFICULTY LEVEL

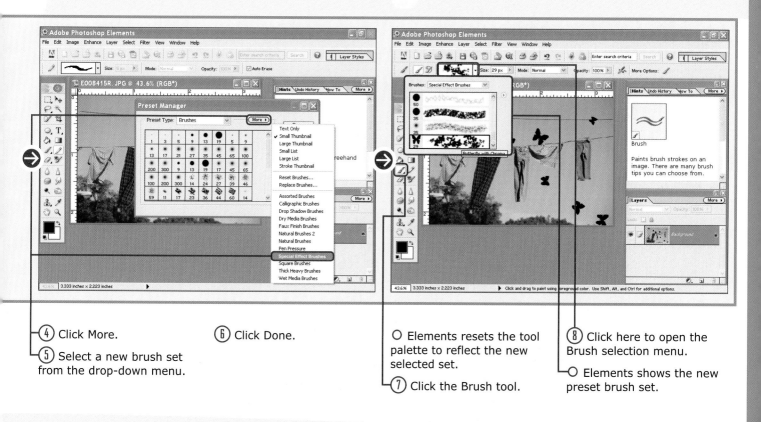

④ Click More.

⑤ Select a new brush set from the drop-down menu.

⑥ Click Done.

○ Elements resets the tool palette to reflect the new selected set.

⑦ Click the Brush tool.

⑧ Click here to open the Brush selection menu.

○ Elements shows the new preset brush set.

Work with the
TRANSFORM TOOL

You can transform and distort your images for different uses in your projects. You can manipulate your layer objects in a similar fashion. Elements' Free Transform tool allows you to manipulate the shape and scale of your images with your mouse. You can add perspective, distort the basic shape, and resize your graphics. This tool is useful to scale an object to fit into a larger or smaller space.

You can find the Free Transform tool in the Image menu. Click the object you want to transform, and it becomes surrounded by a square-bounding box. You can click and drag any of the square intersection points

to scale it. If you press and hold the Ctrl key while you drag, you can skew and distort your object. When you are finished, you can click the Commit button, or double-click the object within the bounding box. Transforming can be a lot of fun, and is very useful for custom designing shapes and photo collages.

You can transform vector graphics, such as un-simplified text and shapes, without ruining the clarity of the edges. You can transform simplified graphics, such as photographs, but excessive transformation may cause loss of clarity and pixelization.

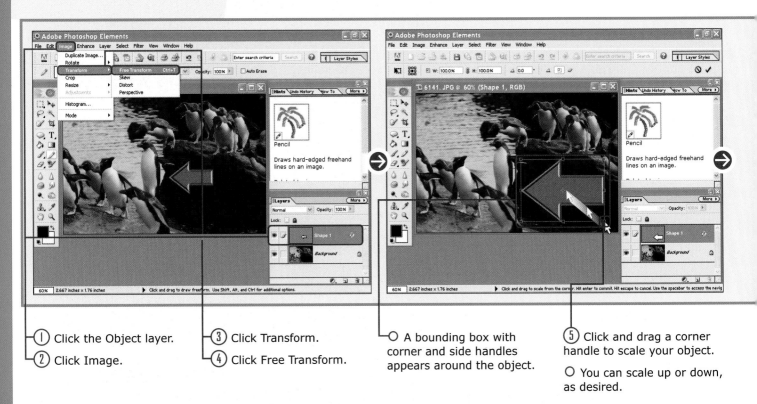

① Click the Object layer.

② Click Image.

③ Click Transform.

④ Click Free Transform.

○ A bounding box with corner and side handles appears around the object.

⑤ Click and drag a corner handle to scale your object.

○ You can scale up or down, as desired.

Did You Know? ※

You can apply transformations equally horizontally or vertically from your object midpoint. If you press and hold the Shift key while scaling, it will constrain proportions to remain equal, so your image stays proportional to the original size.

Did You Know? ※

You can free transform any object or layer, except backgrounds. If you try to change a background, a prompt will appear asking you to change the background to a layer.

Did You Know? ※

While you can also scale image selections and simplified images, you should exercise caution when doing so. Scaling a JPG, BMP, or other bit-mapped formats can result in pixelization and loss of clarity.

DIFFICULTY LEVEL

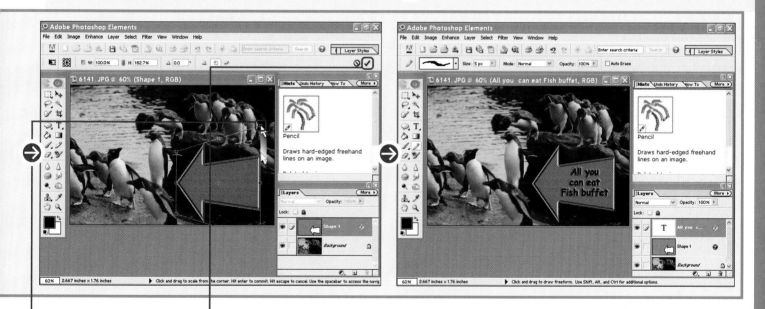

○ To distort your object, press and hold the Ctrl+ Shift+Alt keys and drag a corner handle.

○ To distort your object in perspective, press and hold the Ctrl+Shift+Alt keys and drag a handle.

○ To distort only one handle, just click and drag.

⑥ Click here to accept transformations.

○ Elements applies transformations.

○ You can now use the object.

Convert a PDF
to a PSE2 file

You can import PDF files directly into Elements for editing as a graphic. PDF files are gaining huge popularity these days, because of their amazingly compact sizes, compatibility, and their ability to maintain graphic integrity. Because of their popularity, having a tool you can work on them with is very handy. Fortunately, Elements is very compatible with the PDF format.

There are two methods for importing a PDF. The first is opening the PDF just like any image, such as a TIF or JPG. When you import a PDF by using the

Place method, it imports similarly to a vector graphic, and can be manipulated and scaled to some extent prior to being accepted, and as a result, simplified.

You can use the Place method to position the PDF file, scale it, and transform it without damaging the clarity of the file. When you use the Open method with the PDF file, you lose those advantages because the image is automatically simplified, and the image is once again a simple JPG or TIF file.

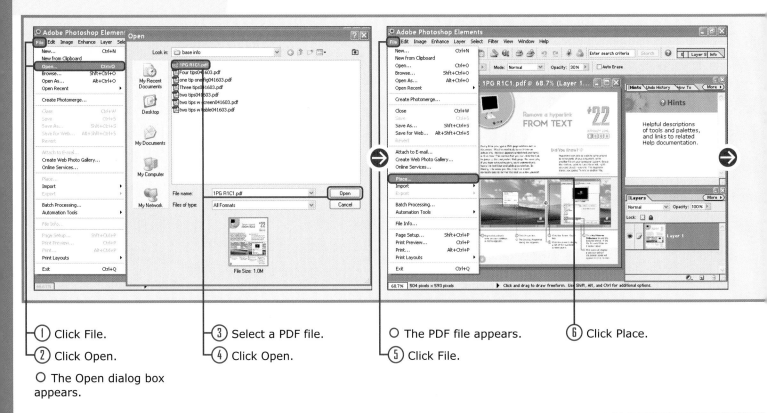

① Click File.

② Click Open.

○ The Open dialog box appears.

③ Select a PDF file.

④ Click Open.

○ The PDF file appears.

⑤ Click File.

⑥ Click Place.

#95

DIFFICULTY LEVEL

Did You Know? ※

You can also use the Import command to bring a PDF file into Elements. Click File, Import, and then PDF Image. Browse to your PDF and click Open. However, this acts like the regular Open command, in that it opens a new document and the PDF is already rasterized.

Did You Know? ※

You can use the Place command to bring a PDF into Elements. You can do the same steps to bring in Adobe Illustrator (.ai), EPS, and PDP files as well. Each of these file formats are considered vector graphics and are scalable with no discernable loss immediately after placing the image.

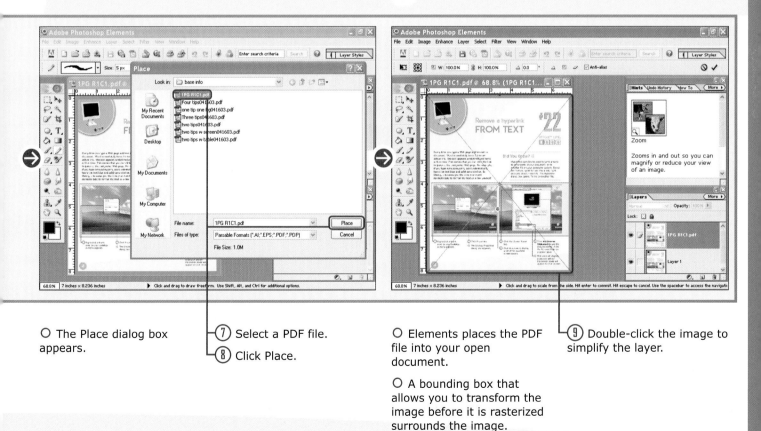

O The Place dialog box appears.

—⑦ Select a PDF file.

—⑧ Click Place.

O Elements places the PDF file into your open document.

O A bounding box that allows you to transform the image before it is rasterized surrounds the image.

—⑨ Double-click the image to simplify the layer.

Create a
PDF SLIDESHOW

You can finally do something with all your digital pictures that is both useful and fun. Elements has a great tool available to help you organize and share your images. You can take your pictures and place them in a PDF Slideshow, a new tool in Elements 2.

You can now import a good number of photos and Elements will compile them into a PDF format slideshow. This utility imports files from a location that you specify, and lays them out as rotating slides, saved in a PDF format. You can choose the images, and Elements does all the legwork.

Elements also gives you transition timers and special effects options to make it even more exciting. The process is quick and simple.

This is very useful for storing and sharing your photos. The PDF format is widely accepted, and the Adobe Acrobat Reader is free for download, so you can send family members the slideshows they always avoid when they come to visit, or business partners a set of layouts. This is a great new addition to Elements.

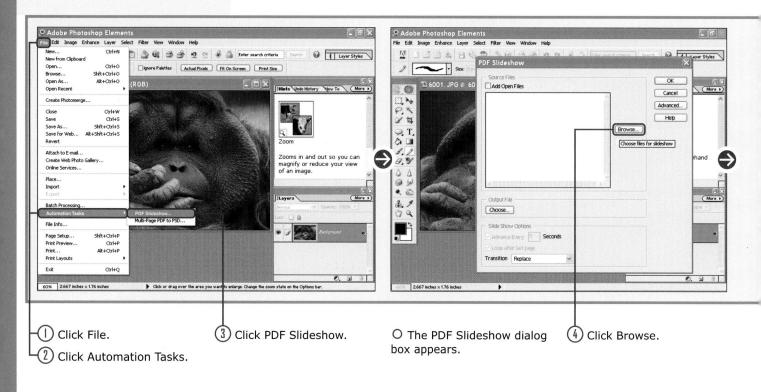

—① Click File.

—② Click Automation Tasks.

③ Click PDF Slideshow.

○ The PDF Slideshow dialog box appears.

④ Click Browse.

Customize It! ※

The Slideshow Options radio buttons control three important optional elements for your slideshow. The first is Advance every X seconds, where you specify the length of delay between changes in the slides. The second is Loop, where you determine if the slideshow goes through only once, or if it loops around and repeats the slideshow until intentionally stopped. Third, you can select from several styles of transitions between slides. Experiment with each to see what each transition effect does.

Customize It! ※

You can choose images from more than one source folder by selecting from one folder, and then clicking Choose again to select from other folders. You also have the option to delete files contained within the slideshow before you save it by highlighting the image you want to delete and then clicking Remove.

#96

DIFFICULTY LEVEL

CONTINUED ▶

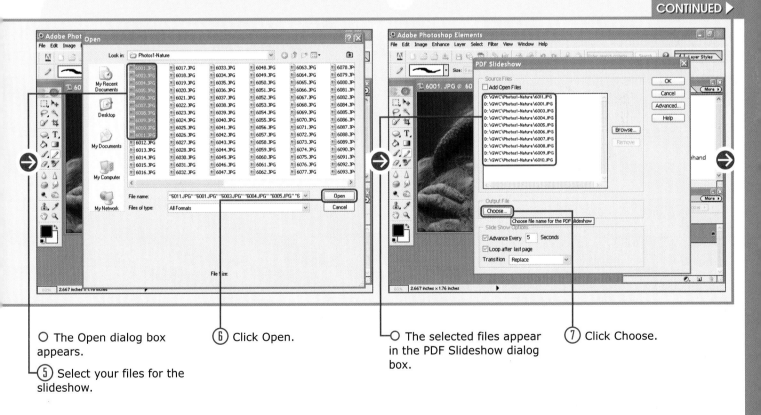

○ The Open dialog box appears.

⑤ Select your files for the slideshow.

⑥ Click Open.

○ The selected files appear in the PDF Slideshow dialog box.

⑦ Click Choose.

Create a
PDF SLIDESHOW

You can set the available slideshow options in a variety of ways. How you set these options can make a difference in your slideshow's character. With all of the options, you can enjoy using a large number of combinations to create a variety of different styles of slideshows. This added flexibility makes this a great tool.

You can affect the speed in which the slides rotate with the Advance Every X Seconds option. Works of art would benefit from longer pauses, whereas very similar and repetitive slides could benefit from a shorter pause.

You can select the Loop After Last Page to have the slides roll continuously through the sequences. If you leave the Loop unchecked, the slideshow progresses once and stops on the last image. A running presentation for a tradeshow would use Looping.

There is also a wide variety of transition selections available to make your slideshow stand, such as Split Vertical out and Dissolve. Transitions enable you to move smoothly from slide to slide.

CONTINUED ▶

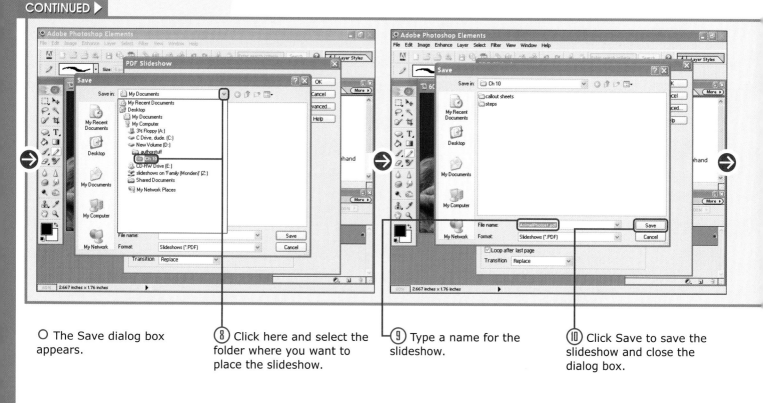

○ The Save dialog box appears.

⑧ Click here and select the folder where you want to place the slideshow.

⑨ Type a name for the slideshow.

⑩ Click Save to save the slideshow and close the dialog box.

Did You Know? ※

You can rearrange the order of your slides as you create the slideshow. You can click and drag a file from one position to another for a smoother transitional order. In addition, you have the option to delete a slide if it does not belong in the show.

Caution! ※

You can quickly make slideshows that are extremely large in size. Each image you place inside the PDF slideshow adds to the total size of the end results, and the file size of those images should be watched. If you have a large number of images you want to insert, you may consider saving them as JPEG images with a lower quality setting to reduce file size. You can have high quality images in there as well, but it is recommended that you keep the total image count low. By limiting file size or count, you can create a great slideshow without making it enormous in file size.

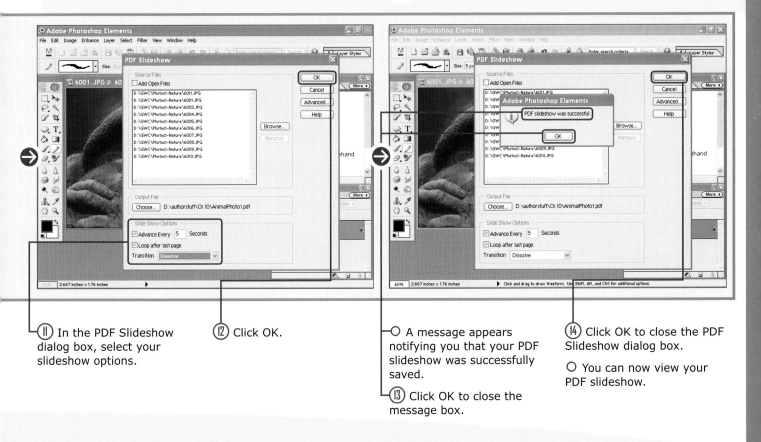

⑪ In the PDF Slideshow dialog box, select your slideshow options.

⑫ Click OK.

○ A message appears notifying you that your PDF slideshow was successfully saved.

⑬ Click OK to close the message box.

⑭ Click OK to close the PDF Slideshow dialog box.

○ You can now view your PDF slideshow.

Select with the
INFO PALETTE

You can use the Information palette as a handy precision tool for drawing and selecting in Elements. The Info palette tells you where your cursor is located and information such as HSB color data, RGB color data, and selection width and height. This tool is an excellent source for checking spot colors and area sampling. Select your Eyedropper tool and move your mouse over any area in the image, and it tells you the color values. However, the Info palette is also a great source for selection information. You can use any of the Marquee Selection tools, and as

you drag your selection out, the Info palette gives you height and width size data for that selection.

This a very useful tool for cutting out and cropping images. If you are creating a Picture Package layout set up for four 5x7 images, but one of your chosen images is 10x8, you can use the Info palette to guide you to scale a 5x7 selection for cropping. You can also use this great tool for eliminating extra space around a subject, while maintaining a certain image size.

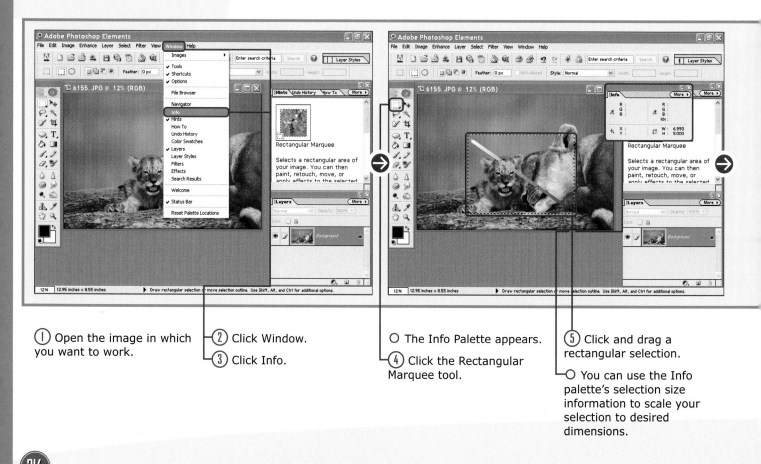

① Open the image in which you want to work.

② Click Window.

③ Click Info.

○ The Info Palette appears.

④ Click the Rectangular Marquee tool.

⑤ Click and drag a rectangular selection.

○ You can use the Info palette's selection size information to scale your selection to desired dimensions.

Did You Know? ※

The Info palette has an Options palette that allows a user to adjust several viewing options, including color modes and the ruler units for the palette. Because you can view the size of the marquee in several different formats, including pixels, centimeters, and percents, among others, this is very useful. You can have different styles of image processing based on your projects. For example, Web designers use the pixel measurement more frequently, while print designers use inches or picas.

DIFFICULTY LEVEL

⑥ Click Image.

⑦ Click Crop.

○ The image appears cropped based on its selection size.

SCAN in a PHOTO

You can use your scanner to import all of those old photographs into your computer for cleanup, cropping, and reproduction. Scanners are probably the best tools to come around for the home photographer. It seems that everyone has a hundred boxes of photos and never shows them unless you visit. Now you can use your scanner to put your photos into digital format on a computer and use them for the Web, slideshow, or e-mail distribution. Scanners also do wonders for reproducing old or

damaged photos, allowing you to repair the scrapes, fades, and torn edges, and finally reprint onto high quality photo paper. This is a wonderful way of keeping old photos alive and well.

Scanners vary from brand to brand, but the basic functions are similar, even though the import software may vary. Scanning is easy, and is a great tool for digitally preserving your photographs.

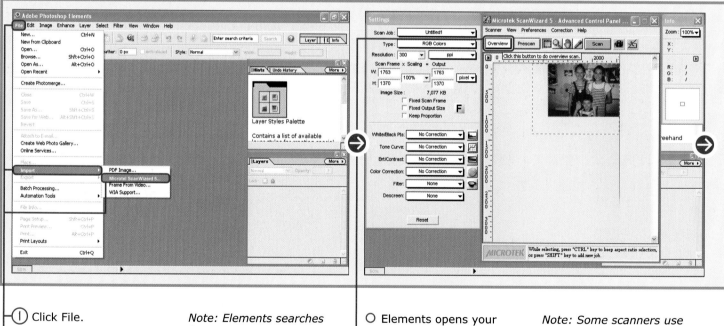

-① Click File.

-② Click Import.

-③ Select a scanner from the submenu.

Note: Elements searches for scanners at startup. If your scanner is not listed, restart Elements or check installation of scanner.

○ Elements opens your scanner software.

-④ Click the Overview option.

Note: Some scanners use Preview instead of Overview.

Did You Know? ※

Most scanner software has image adjustment options available that you can use before you scan the image. Be cautious using these adjustments, after you scan, the changes are permanent. You can do many more adjustments in Elements with the added bonus Undo History tool for error correction.

#98

DIFFICULTY LEVEL

Put It Together! ※

You can save a lot of time by scanning more than one image at once. You can place multiple photos on the scanner, and scan them all at the same time. Use your selection tools to select an image. Click Layer, New, and then Layer via cut, placing the selected image on its own layer. Copy and Paste the image layer into its own file to save.

(5) Click and drag to adjust the selection box to your desired size and position.

(6) Click Scan.

O Scanner software scans the image, and returns scan to Elements.

O You may have to close the scanner software, depending on the brand.

O Your image returns as a new document.

SCAN SKETCHES
as templates

You can use scanners for much more than importing pictures. You can use scanners to reduce production time on original artwork and reproductions. Many artists, regardless of mediums, create a sketch or storyboard of the art they are about to create to help them with the final creation. You can do the same with scanners when working in Elements. Simply create a sketch or obtain a copy of an image you want to reproduce. Scan it in with the Import function in Elements. Then by using this scan as a base image, you can paint or draw on a new layer,

and use the scan as a guide or template for your work.

This works wonderfully for reproducing images. Items such as logos, characters, and custom shapes are excellent candidates for scanning copies for a guide. Usually, you can more accurately reproduce an image in Elements by tracing than by freehand. When you are finished tracing the sketch, you have a fully editable image in Elements you can use on future projects as well.

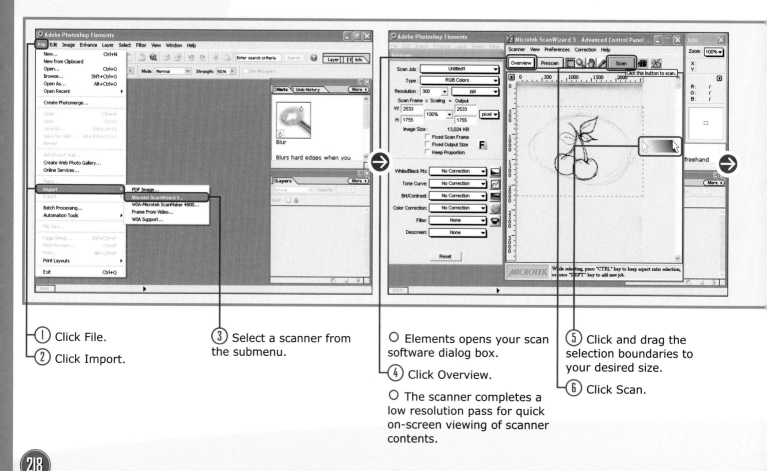

① Click File.

② Click Import.

③ Select a scanner from the submenu.

○ Elements opens your scan software dialog box.

④ Click Overview.

○ The scanner completes a low resolution pass for quick on-screen viewing of scanner contents.

⑤ Click and drag the selection boundaries to your desired size.

⑥ Click Scan.

Did You Know? ※

You can have better scan results if you keep your sketches simple, with no shading. If you are using a hand-drawn sketch, be sure to create it on unlined, blank white paper with a dark blue or black ink or dark pencil. This will prevent the scanned sketch from distracting you from your reproduction.

Did You Know? ※

You can lower the opacity on the scan to clarify your Elements artwork. Select the scan layer, and click Layer, New, and then Layer from Background. Next, click Layer, New, and then Layer. With this new layer selected, click Layer, New, and then Background from layer. This creates a new solid background, and you can lower your scanned image's opacity without having the transparency grid showing to distract you from your reproduction work.

#99

DIFFICULTY LEVEL

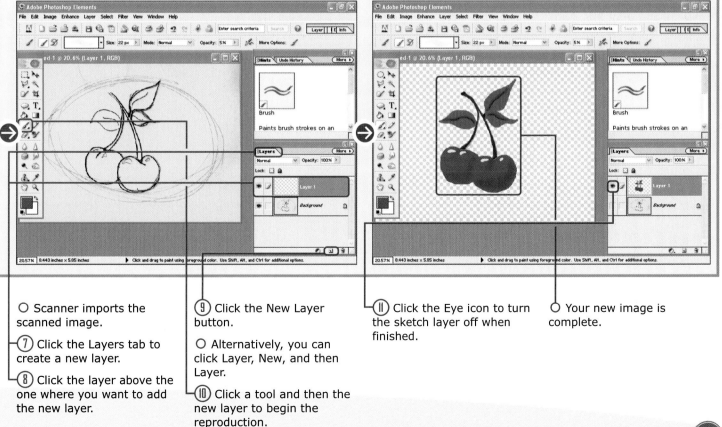

○ Scanner imports the scanned image.

⑦ Click the Layers tab to create a new layer.

⑧ Click the layer above the one where you want to add the new layer.

⑨ Click the New Layer button.

○ Alternatively, you can click Layer, New, and then Layer.

⑩ Click a tool and then the new layer to begin the reproduction.

⑪ Click the Eye icon to turn the sketch layer off when finished.

○ Your new image is complete.

Locate
ONLINE RESOURCES
for Elements 2

You can do so much with all of the Photoshop Elements tricks and tips you learned in this book. You have learned to do new and exciting things with your graphics and photos that you probably cannot wait to get started using. However, if you want to learn more, you should avail yourself of all the good stuff on the Internet. You can find plenty of Adobe resources, many of which cater to Photoshop Elements directly.

You can never learn too many tricks or tutorials. There will always be some new way to do an old

trick, or a brand new effect that you can learn and apply to your own work. You can take advantage of any tutorials and tips you find to continue to grow in skills with Elements.

One thing you can do is visit some wonderful sites set up online that show additional tutorials and secrets to helping you develop skills using Photoshop Elements.

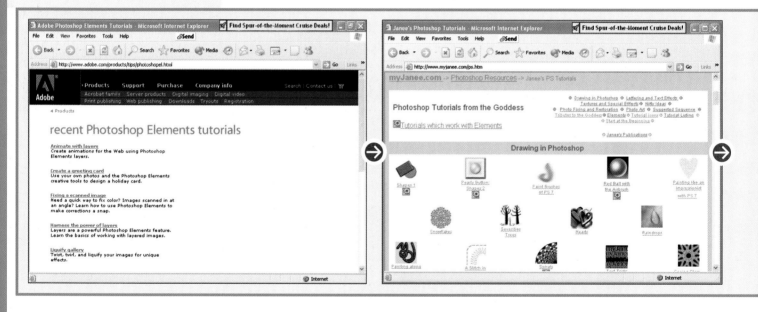

① Open your Web browser and type **www.adobe.com/ products/tips/photoshopel. html** in the address field.

○ The Adobe Web page appears.

② Open your Web browser and type **www.myjanee.com**.

○ The MyJanee Web page appears.

#100

DIFFICULTY LEVEL

Did You Know? ☀

You can find other Photoshop Elements resources on the Internet. There are plenty of sites that dedicate themselves to graphics, including Elements. Try doing a search for Photoshop Elements Tips on your favorite Browser search engine, and you will find many resources available for research and education.

Did You Know? ☀

You can translate Photoshop tutorials into Photoshop Elements tutorials. Many of the steps and filters allow the tutorials to cross over from Photoshop to Elements. Just follow the steps of a tutorial as they appear, and most often, you can reproduce the effect, even if it is not specific to Elements.

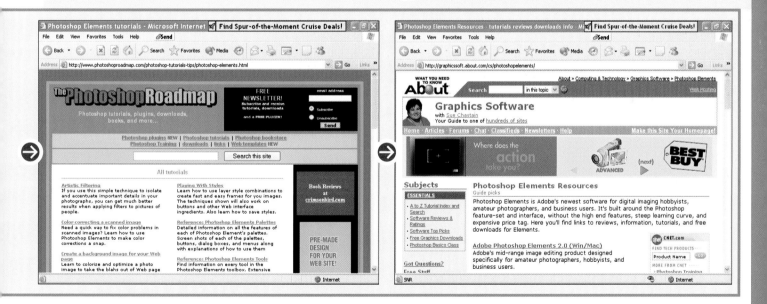

③ Open your Web browser and type **www.photoshoproadmap. com/photoshop-tutorials-tips/photoshop-elements.html**.

○ The Photoshop Roadmap Web page appears.

④ Open your Web browser and type **http://graphicssoft. about.com/cs/pselements tools/**.

○ The Graphics Software from About.com Web page appears.

INDEX

INDEX